TEAM SPORTS
FOR GIRLS
AND WOMEN

4TH EDITION

MARGARET H. MEYER, Ph.D.
MADISON PUBLIC SCHOOLS, MADISON, WISCONSIN

MARGUERITE M. SCHWARZ, Ph.D.
AMERICAN MEDICAL ASSOCIATION, WASHINGTON OFFICE,
WASHINGTON, D.C.

ILLUSTRATED BY RUTH ALLCOTT AND GAIL CAVALIER

W. B. SAUNDERS COMPANY · PHILADELPHIA · LONDON · 1965

Team Sports for Girls and Women

To BLANCHE M. TRILLING

PREFACE

This book originally was written to provide teachers, coaches, officials, students and players with concise information on the individual technics and team tactics that are essential to the six most popular team sports for girls and women. Beginning with the first edition, methods and formations for organizing squad practices for groups of various size and attainment have been an important feature of this book.

The basic purpose of the book has been unchanged through three editions. The text and diagrams now have been revised and rewritten to conform to the current, official rules of the six sports included. The official rules are revised and republished at regular intervals by the Division for Girls and Women's Sports, a section of the American Association for Health, Physical Education and Recreation.

The several sports guides of the DGWS are an essential supplement to this book. The official rules for girls and women are changed in minor details from time to time by DGWS. Only those rules that are essential to the fundamental skills and tactics described in this book are summarized in it.

The text of the fourth edition of this book again has been presented in the brief outline form in which it originally appeared. In addition to the revisions to bring the book up to date, it has been redesigned to make it possible for the users to find material more readily and to apply the information more effectively. The diagrams have been renumbered for easier use and quicker reference. The chapters on basketball and volleyball have been completely rewritten because of major changes in rules since the previous edition. Also, illustrations of technics have been increased and material added for more advanced play.

The authors wish to express their appreciation to Dr. Christine Meyer, Dr. Joan Waterland, Miss Barrett A. Morf, and Mr. Daniel V. Smith for their advice and assistance with portions of the text.

MARGARET H. MEYER, PH.D.
MARGUERITE M. SCHWARZ, PH.D.

CONTENTS

THE VALUE OF TEAM SPORTS 1

Concentration on individual and dual sports because of their greater "carry-over" value (and preoccupation with the dangers of team competition) generally characterize the programs of physical education and recreation for girls and women. Little emphasis has been placed upon the mastery of team skills, and few opportunities are provided for wholesome competition between teams. As a result, the immeasurable values of and interest in team sports for girls and women are all but lost in the early teens.

Formal programs that largely ignore team sports or fail to bring players to high standards of team skills lack balance. The development of the individual and the group can, with adequate practice and training, be greatly furthered through team sports.

It is fair to assume that those who succeed in playing together on teams are better equipped to work together as the demands for getting along with others increase. Teachers of physical education need to be better prepared to teach team skills and to recognize the opportunities of guiding social adjustment that underlie team activities.

The opportunities lost by the teacher or coach usually outnumber those found. Much more study needs to be done on the possibilities for social learning through team sports, their "carry-over" values in these categories, as well as the methods of training for greater improvement in skills.

Broadly stated, the common goals of any program of sports or dance for students in any age group are quite similar:

1. To increase the efficiency and strength of the body.

2. To improve and maintain the more important but less tangible elements of personal fitness, the emotional and spiritual health of the individual and her group.

Team sports add to these objectives the improvement of social behavior through practice and discipline in group strategy and teamwork.

The terms "group strategy" and "teamwork" imply the full application and, at the same time, the subordination of individual prominence

2   to the efficiency of a group having the same goals. The teacher or coach of a team sport has a matchless opportunity to guide both individual and group relationships in an atmosphere of fun and satisfaction that is conducive to learning, if she uses it.

No fixed rules guarantee acceptable social behavior in sports or games. It is part of the training and the merit of the program. The conduct of a player or spectator at a sports contest is as likely to be barbaric as it is to be socially mature and responsible. The teacher or coach in team sports should encourage the students to draw up and practice under a code of conduct designed by them, defining in some detail what the teacher or coach can expect of the players and the behavior that the players can expect of themselves and each other.

A few suggestions for a list or code which the players themselves may expand and develop to good advantage are given here.

Individual Behavior.   The player herself, in her own attitudes toward her own play:

1. Is persistent and willing to practice with others.
2. Is aggressive without being annoying to others.
3. Shows willingness to learn new skills for her own improvement.
4. Takes criticism without being hurt or offended.

Team Cooperation.   The group as a whole, with respect to each other:

1. Is considerate of the safety of others on the team.
2. Recognizes the importance of individual assignments to the success of the team, including both offensive and defensive play of the team.
3. Accepts responsibility for leadership or follows directions in squad drills, team management, or any practice periods whether given by an authorized member of the group or by the coach or teacher.
4. Recognizes that the development of the skills and behavior of the entire squad is essential to the success of the team.

Personal and Cooperative Behavior in Competition.   The individual and the team as a whole with respect to opponents:

1. Show friendship to opponents. They are challengers in a game of skills and intelligence, not enemies.
2. Play the best possible game within the spirit as well as the letter of the rules. In other words, play fairly.
3. Accept decisions of officials without arguments or complaint.
5. Try to prevent injuries to an opponent.

Many girls and women are not as well coordinated and as strong as they might be to meet the normal cycles of work and play that are required throughout life itself. Team sports, in the main, are big-muscle activities that demand endurance as well as such basic skills as running, jumping, throwing, batting and catching. There is much to be learned and done well before real satisfaction comes to the players in team sports and much that can be retained for future use.

One of the major handicaps to a successful program of team sports, or to any part of the physical education schedule, for that matter, is the

CHAPTER 1.   THE VALUE OF TEAM SPORTS

haste required of students in changing costumes and reappearing at another class in some semblance of tidy grooming. More investigation is needed to determine how much actual time is spent in physical activity and what can be done about relieving the stress of getting to and from the average class in physical education with dignity.

One approach to this ever-present annoyance is to provide for double periods or laboratory hours even though resulting classes may be larger. By careful organization of classes into squads, the drills and contests to practice the skills required in the team sports can be used regularly and frequently. Student leaders can be of great assistance in organizing and training the squads as well as officiating. Such leadership opportunities should be developed to the fullest both in small as well as in large groups in sports.

2   BASIC DRILLS FOR SQUAD PRACTICE IN ALL TEAM SPORTS

It is an accepted principle of teaching that learning is accelerated if the experience is satisfying. The acquisition of skills is further aided by repeated practice sessions and by an understanding on the part of the student of the objectives to be achieved.

The beginner in team sports should be placed in a game situation with a minimum of preliminary discussion and practice. Drill periods should grow from the players' recognition of the need for more proficiency and therefore more practice in the individual skills which they must have to play a better game.

From the many skills needed for team sports, the program for beginners should be carefully selected in terms of the ages and capacities of the group. Obviously, the speed of development will vary with different groups, even though they may be of the same age level.

One efficient method of teaching motor skills is by the use of squad drills. If the drills are properly motivated by encouragement and achievement, players will respond quickly. Several general suggestions in the use of drills follow.

GENERAL SUGGESTIONS

Use variety; repetition of the same drill leads to monotony and loss of interest unless a specific play is being practiced.

Use a drill that resembles a game situation as players progress in understanding and skill.

Advance the complexity of drills as the players' skills improve.

Add competition between squads as early as possible, no matter how simple the drill.

Keep individual and squad records of achievement.

SIMPLE DRILLS

The following drills may serve a twofold purpose: to present elementary or new skills and to serve as warm-up drills for players of any skill level. These drills are adaptable to practically all team sports in one form or another. They may be turned into contests by establishing restraining lines, setting the number of circuits and determining which squad finishes first or maintains the highest achievement.

The more intricate drills for each sport are incorporated into the specific chapter on the sport.

Relay or Single Column (Fig. 2–1). Players stand one behind the other facing in the same direction. Beginning with X^1, each player takes her turn and goes to the end of the column. The distance to the turning line depends upon the activity to be practiced.

Relays with Leader (Figs. 2–2 and 2–3). The formation is as shown in Figures 2–2 and 2–3, with the leader stationed at a designated distance from the squad. The leader faces the squad and gives each player her turn at the pass or throw.* Players may return to the end of the column as in Figure 2–2, or each may follow her pass to a position behind the leader as in Figure 2–3.

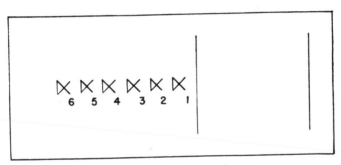

FIG. 2–1. Relay or single column.

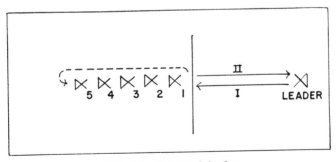

FIG. 2–2. Relay with leader.

*In this section, the term "pass" is used to indicate any method by which the ball is moved from one player to another. "Heading," "lifting ball to partner," "volleying" and other similar technics are not listed as such but are included in the term "pass."

CHAPTER 2. BASIC DRILLS FOR SQUAD PRACTICE IN ALL TEAM SPORTS

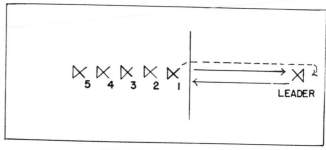

FIG. 2-3. Relay with leader.

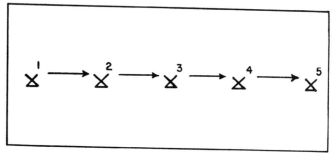

FIG. 2-4. Single line.

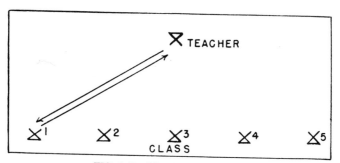

FIG. 2-5. "Teacher and class."

Single Line (Fig. 2-4.) Players stand side by side. The object is started with X^1 and is passed from player to player. The drill may finish when the object reaches X^5 or when it has been returned again to X^1.

"Teacher and Class" (Fig. 2-5). The "class" stands in single line or semicircle, while the "teacher" stands in front of and facing her "class." The "teacher" serves as leader until each player has had her turn, then the "teacher" may be changed.

Shuttle (Figs. 2-6 and 2-7). Each squad is divided in half. Each half forms a single column facing the other half. In Figure 2-6, X^1 passes to X^2 and goes to the end of her own column. X^2 passes to X^3 and returns to the end of her column, etc. In Figure 2-7, players follow the pass and

CHAPTER 2. BASIC DRILLS FOR SQUAD PRACTICE IN ALL TEAM SPORTS

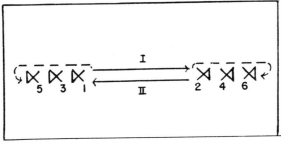

FIG. 2-6. Shuttle.

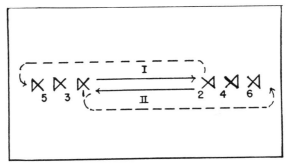

FIG. 2-7. Shuttle.

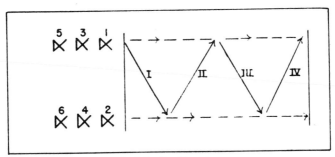

FIG. 2-8. Double column.

go to the end of the opposite column. The drill may continue until all have returned to original positions.

Double Column (Fig. 2-8). Players stand in double columns. X^1 passes diagonally forward to X^2, X^2 returns pass to X^1 and they continue for 3 or 4 passes. X^1 and X^2 may carry the object to a line opposite the starting line, followed by X^3 and X^4, etc., or X^1 and X^2 may carry the object back to X^3 and X^4 at the starting line after having covered a designated distance.

Double Lines (Figs. 2-9 and 2-10). Players stand in two lines facing each other directly as in Figure 2-9, or they may be spaced in zigzag formation as shown in Figure 2-10. The object is started with X^1 and

CHAPTER 2.   BASIC DRILLS FOR SQUAD PRACTICE IN ALL TEAM SPORTS

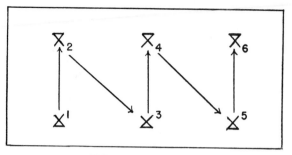

FIG. 2–9. Double lines.

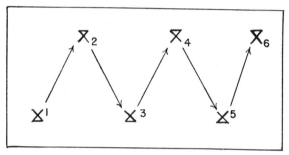

FIG. 2–10. Double lines.

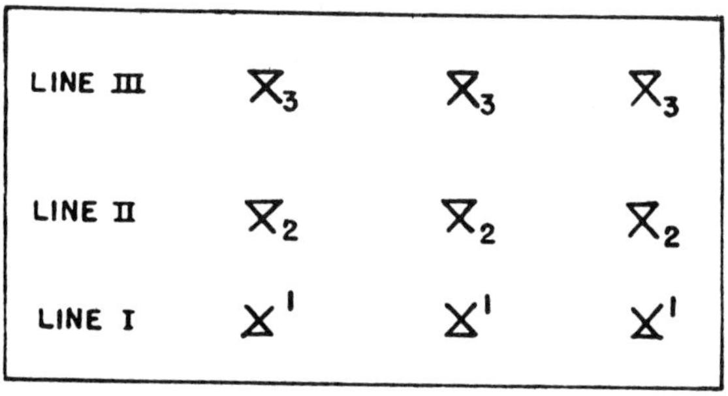

LINE III	X_3	X_3	X_3
LINE II	X_2	X_2	X_2
LINE I	X^1	X^1	X^1

FIG. 2–11. Three lines.

passed to each player in turn. The drill may end when the object reaches X^6 or when a designated number of circuits have been completed.

Three Lines (Fig. 2–11). Players in Line I face those in Lines II and III. X^1 attempts to pass over or around X^2 to X^3. X^2 attempts to tackle or intercept as the sport requires. Shift players to different lines.

Or X^1 may pass to X^2 who then passes to X^3. X^3 returns the pass to X^2, and X^2 returns to X^1. (This is especially good when space is limited.)

Square (Fig. 2–12). Four or more players form the square. The object is passed around or diagonally across the square.

Circle (Figs. 2–13, 2–14, and 2–15). Players stand in a circle facing inward as in Figure 2–13. The object may be passed across the circle,

CHAPTER 2. BASIC DRILLS FOR SQUAD PRACTICE IN ALL TEAM SPORTS

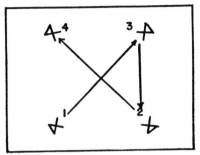

FIG. 2–12. Square.

or from one to the next, or X[1] may carry the object around the circle, then pass it to X[2] and so on. Players stand in a circle facing the same direction as in Figure 2–14. The drill may be conducted as a moving formation with the players passing the object as they run around the circle.

A third formation may be used from the circle by placing a leader in the center as in Figure 2–15. The object is passed from the leader to the player, back to the leader and so on.

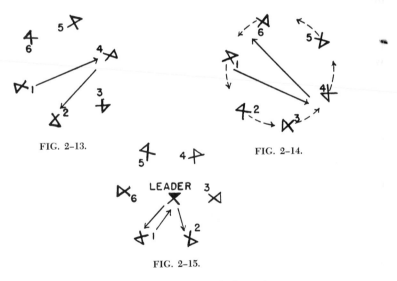

FIG. 2–13.

FIG. 2–14.

FIG. 2–15.

FIGS. 2–13, 2–14, and 2–15. Circle formations.

CHAPTER 2. BASIC DRILLS FOR SQUAD PRACTICE IN ALL TEAM SPORTS

3

FUNDAMENTAL SKILLS OF BODY CONTROL AND FOOTWORK

Skills in any sport depend first upon the ability of the participant to move her body quickly and efficiently. The player on the *offensive* must be able to elude her opponent with cleverly executed starts, stops, changes of pace, turns, pivots and dodges, and to approach her goal at least a step ahead of her opponent. The player on the *defensive* must be able to adjust her position in accordance with the tactics of the player on the offensive.

The technic of starts, speed in running, changes of pace and sudden stops is essentially the same for all sports and is therefore explained in this section. The pivots and turns are described in the basketball section, while throwing, catching and hitting are included under the discussion of each sport using those skills.

STARTS

BODY MECHANICS

Starting Position. The weight should be kept low, by flexing the hip and knee joints, and on the entire sole of the foot for a good push-off.

The knees should be slightly flexed and the feet not too far apart so that the weight can be shifted quickly in any direction.

A gained step away from an opponent is of vital importance. A feint in one direction followed by a quick start in another will often give a step advantage.

COACHING SUGGESTIONS

Keep the weight low.
Make the push-off and first step very quickly.

Keep the sole of the rear foot firmly planted on the push-off to gain
better traction and therefore avoid slipping.

RUNNING FOR SPEED

BODY MECHANICS

Starting Position. Following a vigorous push-off, the rear foot should be lifted quickly but immediately thereafter forced into a short step.

The full stride should not be reached until the third or fourth step.

Feet and legs should move straight ahead toward the objective of the run.

A slight body tilt should be maintained throughout the run while the legs propel the body forward. If the head is thrown backward, the run will be retarded.

In fast running, the arms are a distinct aid to speed, and in sports where it is unnecessary to carry some type of equipment in the hands, the arms should be used vigorously.

The elbows should be flexed and as one arm moves backward the other moves forward.

The hand of the arm moving forward is raised about shoulder height, and the arm moving backward should approximate hip level.

COACHING SUGGESTIONS

Toe straight ahead.
Avoid a high kick in back.
Lift knees high in front.
Keep all body action of arms and legs directly in line.

STOPS

A player on the offensive who has mastered the sudden stops can often cause the defensive player to overrun her. Stops are usually classified as (1) the running stride stop, (2) the jump stop and (3) the skip stop. The jump stop may be done either with the feet in running stride or in the side stride position.

The Running Stride Stop

BODY MECHANICS

Landing Position. The feet should be in the same position as for the running stride.

CHAPTER 3. FUNDAMENTAL SKILLS OF BODY CONTROL AND FOOTWORK

The forward foot should be placed firmly on the ground with the entire sole in contact.

The rear leg should be bent and the weight carried low.

The weight should be on the back leg, but the trunk should be fairly erect, never forward over the knee.

COACHING SUGGESTIONS

Keep the weight low.

Point the toes forward.

Use soles with good suction to avoid slipping on the floor. In the field sports on grass, rubber cleats should fulfill the same purpose.

THE JUMP STOP

BODY MECHANICS

Landing Position. The feet may be placed either in the side stride or the running stride position.

The take-off for the jump to the side stride position may be made from one or both feet, but the landing should be on both feet.

In the side stride position, the feet should be parallel and apart and the knees bent to absorb the jar of landing.

The weight should be evenly divided and low.

In the jump to a running stride stop, the landing position is similar to that of the same stop without the jump.

The jump should be only a few inches off the floor.

COACHING SUGGESTIONS

Let the knees "give" to absorb the jar.

Keep the weight low and back.

Turn the knees out in landing.

THE SKIP STOP

BODY MECHANICS

Landing Position. The foot on which the hop is taken should touch the floor first.

The foot on which the step is taken should be in a forward stride position.

The soles of both feet should be firmly on the floor.

The rear leg should be slightly bent, the weight carried low and over that leg. The front leg should be slightly bent to help absorb the jar in landing.

The trunk should be bent slightly forward.

CHAPTER 3. FUNDAMENTAL SKILLS OF BODY CONTROL AND FOOTWORK

Keep the weight low.
Avoid dragging the rear leg after the step.
Practice run, hop, step, stop.

PRACTICE FOR BODY CONTROL AND FOOTWORK

The most useful drills for the development of body control are those which are developed as a part of other practice drills of the specific sports. Isolated practice drills of these fundamental skills remove the judgment and timing so essential to sport skills.

Some values may accrue from the two drills listed here:

Entire Class in Line. The class forms a line facing the leader. On the first signal run, next signal stop, next signal run and so on. Introduce the element of competition by declaring the winner to be the first player to reach the opposite wall. Eliminate those who fail to stop within two counts of the signal for stopping or those who start ahead of the signal.

"Stop." Line up the players as just described. A leader counts from one to ten and during that interval the players attempt to run as far as possible. Anyone failing to stop promptly on the count of ten or detected moving before the next count of one must start again from the original line. Repeat the counts until a player has reached a finish line. The one who finishes first may become the leader for the next game. The leader should vary the speed of counting to attempt to trap the players who fail to stop promptly on the count of ten.

SECTION I. INTRODUCTION

HISTORY

Basketball is the result of an experiment by Dr. J. A. Naismith to develop an indoor game to fill in the seasons between football and baseball. When originated by Dr. Naismith in 1891-92, peach baskets served as goals and a football was used for the ball.

The most drastic changes in the game came during the first 2 years of its existence. As many as 50 played on one team during this period. The number of players was reduced to nine almost immediately, then seven and, about 1894, to five. The first method of putting the ball in play was a free-for-all in which the ball was tossed down the center of the floor between the teams lined up on either side.

The value of the game for girls was soon recognized, and in 1899 women's rules were formulated. The first *Basketball Guide*, edited by Miss Senda Berenson, was published shortly after the turn of the century. The first rules committee of women recommended a three-division court, eliminated snatching and batting of the ball as too rough, restricted the dribble to three bounces, ruled a foul for holding the ball more than 3 seconds, entered a plea for the elimination of star playing and urged the development of team play.

In 1936, the three-division court was changed to two divisions. The balanced court with three forwards in one half of the court and three guards in the other remained the official game for more than 25 years.

The concept of a team being defensive or offensive was strained as long as the rules permitted only one half of a team to guard the basket and the other half to make the goals. The roving-player scheme was a step toward giving basketball for women some of the opportunities for movement and strategy that were impossible under the many limitations of the older game.

free throw after a foul scores 1 point. The winner is the team with the highest total score in the playing time, or extra time in case of a tie score.

Team. Basketball for girls and women is played by two teams of six players each. The team in possession of the ball is the *offensive* team. The team not in possession of the ball is the *defensive* team. Positions have no formal designations such as forward or guard.

Playing Area. The court is divided into two equal divisions for the roving-player game. Half of the court is the front court of one and the back court of the other. Any four players of a team may be in their front or back court at one time. In other words, a team must have a minimum of two players in one half of the court at all times.

Advancing the Ball. The ball may be passed, batted, bounced, handed or rolled from one player to another. A player may advance while in possession of the ball by certain legal tactics known as the air juggle, bounce and dribble. She may take no more than two steps while holding the ball.

Playing Time. A game is played in quarters of 8 minutes each. Regular rest periods after the first and third quarters are 2 minutes. The intermission after the second quarter is 10 minutes. If the score is tied at the end of playing time, one or more extra periods of 3 minutes each, with an intermission of 2 minutes between each, are played. The game terminates if a team is ahead at the end of any extra period.

BASKETBALL TERMINOLOGY

Air dribble. A play, formerly called the juggle, to advance the ball by throwing or tapping it into the air and regaining possession before it touches the floor or another player.

Back court. The half of the court that contains the opponents' basket.

Blocking. A foul involving personal contact that impedes the progress of a player with or without the ball.

Bounce pass. A pass that is bounced to the floor and rebounded to the receiver.

Charging. A foul involving personal contact by a player with the ball moving her body or the ball into an opponent whose path or position is legal or already established.

Defensive player, defender. Any player on the team not in possession of the ball.

Dribble. A tactic to advance the ball by bouncing it to the floor and back to the hand a number of times in succession without catching it until the last bounce. The *limited dribble* permits the player to give impetus to the ball no more than three times. The ball may be started from one or both hands on the first impact. Subsequent bounces may be made with one hand only.

Foul. An infraction of the rules for which the opponent is awarded one or more free throws. There are individual and team fouls. A player is disqualified from further play when she has committed five fouls. She may be disqualified for a single foul of unsportsmanlike conduct. In general, individual fouls involve personal contact.

Free throw. An unguarded throw for the basket from a line 15 feet from the face of the backboard and within the restraining circle. Multiple free throws may be awarded for a foul against an opponent in the act of shooting if a field goal is missed.

Front court. The half of the court that contains a team's basket.

Goal. A ball that passes through the basket from above, having been legally thrown or tapped by any player within the half court where the goal is made.

Goal tending. A foul involving interference with the ball or basket when the ball is in *downward* flight toward the basket or in passage through the net.

Hand-off. Handing the ball to a teammate.

Jump ball. A jump in a restraining circle to tap a ball tossed between two opponents by an official.

A jump ball is taken in the *center* circle:

1. At the beginning of each quarter and each extra period of a tie game.

2. After the last free throw following a double foul.

A jump ball is taken in the *nearest* restraining circle after:

1. A tie ball.

2. A time-out when no player in bounds had possession of the ball in play when time out was called.

3. Simultaneous contact with the ball by opponents causes it to go out of bounds.

Man-to-man defense. A type of defense in which each player has an assigned opponent with whom to stay.

Offensive team, offensive player. The team or any member of the team in possession of the ball anywhere on the court.

Out-of-bounds award. A throw-in for the opposing team from out of bounds after:

1. Violations.

2. A successful free throw (or after the last, if multiple free throws are awarded).

3. A successful field goal.

Own basket. The basket for which a team is shooting.

Pass. Throwing, batting, handing, bouncing or rolling the ball to a teammate.

Pivot. A legal tactic in which a player holding the ball steps once or more than once in the same direction with the same foot. The other foot, the pivot foot, keeps its initial contact with the floor.

Post. An offensive station around the free-throw lane of a team's front court. The player in the post position, often called the pivot player, usually stands with her back to the basket in the passing attack. A *low* post is a position in the vicinity of the basket. A *high* post is a position near the free-throw line.

A player without the ball may stay no more than 3 seconds in the free-throw lane of her front court when her team has the ball.

Press. A style of defense in which defenders play their opponents closely in all areas of the court.

Roving player. A player who legally crosses the center division line on offense or defense.

Screen. A legal play to prevent or delay an opponent from getting into a desired place or position. A legal screen involves no bodily contact.

Tagging. A foul involving constant or repeated contact with the hand, elbow or body against an opponent.

Tie ball. A tie ball occurs when:

1. Two or more players on opposing teams place hands firmly on the ball simultaneously.

2. A player places one or both hands firmly on the ball already held by an opponent.

Throw-in. Putting the ball in play from out of bounds at the side line or end line.

1. The throw-in is taken by an opponent outside the nearest side line opposite the spot where a violation occurred, except when a player causes the ball to go out of bounds at the end line. In that event, the throw-in is from outside the end line at the point where the ball left the court.

2. The throw-in is taken by an opponent at any point outside the end line when a goal has been scored.

Traveling. Illegal progress in any direction while retaining possession of the ball.

Violation. Infraction of the rules for which an out-of-bounds award is given the opposing team.

Zone defense. A type of defense in which players are responsible for guarding areas of the court rather than individual opponents.

SAFEGUARDS IN THE TEACHING OF BASKETBALL

Basketball skills should be developed in the early elementary grades through various games involving running, jumping, dodging, quick starting and stopping, ball handling and guarding.

With adequate skills and regular conditioning exercises and drills, basketball can be enjoyed by a variety of age groups with little danger to themselves or others.

The most common injuries in basketball are sprains of the ankles, knees and fingers.

All too frequently, girls are reluctant to practice to improve their basic skills in basketball or any other sport. The game would be more fun and safer if they did.

There is no positive answer to the question of whether or not girls

FIG. 4–2. Key to basketball diagrams.

and women should play basketball during the menstrual period. Medical opinions vary. No hard and fast exclusion from play, or demand to play, should be enforced against any player. For any who have known menstrual problems, the decision should rest with that individual's family doctor rather than the coach.

Coaches should be aware of the standards for basketball competition established by the Division for Girls and Women's Sports of the American Association for Health, Physical Education and Recreation.

SECTION II. INDIVIDUAL SKILLS AND TACTICS

Ball handling is the essential skill of basketball. The team that controls the ball can get it to the basket.

Much more is involved in ball handling than catching, passing and shooting for the basket. Basketball is a game of variety of movement. A player must learn to run to meet the ball, to stop and turn when she has it, to move with it and to fake and dodge to elude an opponent. Weight control, balance and clever footwork are part of any offensive or defensive play.

Practice in one or more of the fundamental skills described in Chapter 3 should be an integral part of all teaching or coaching sessions.

The drills and contests that have been suggested for teaching the individual skills and tactics are elementary. As players progress, practice sessions should include drills that involve several skills in one. Rarely should drills begin with the player standing to receive the ball. Drills should be varied and should keep the players in action.

CATCHING

BODY MECHANICS

The fingers should be curved, spread and relaxed until the instant of contact with the ball. For balls above the waist, the fingers should point diagonally upward with the thumbs 4 or 5 inches apart. For balls below the waist, the fingers should point diagonally downward, palms turned slightly outward and little fingers 4 to 5 inches apart.

The hands should be parallel and cupped with wrists bent back. First contact in catching the ball is with the tips of the thumbs and fingers. After contact with the ball, the heel of the hand should grip firmly, followed immediately by the fingers. The hands should be on the sides and to the back of the ball.

The arms should be relaxed and extended forward as the ball approaches the body, but the elbows should be somewhat flexed.

As the arms "give" with the catch, the ball should be drawn into position for the next pass.

COACHING SUGGESTIONS

Watch the ball.

Curve and relax the fingers. Catch with the fingers, thumb and heel of the thumb.

Point the fingers upward or downward (depending upon height of the ball) but never at the ball.

Pull the ball in toward the body. A common error is to push the hands at the ball as contact is made. Hands and ball should be moving in the same direction at impact – toward the body.

Advance to meet the ball. Catch on the run. Avoid standing to wait for the ball.

FIG. 4–3. Catching the ball.

CHAPTER 4.   BASKETBALL

"Hot Potato" Circle Formation (see Fig. 2–13). Toss the ball around the circle as quickly as possible. The catch and pass should be in one motion. For competitive purposes have each squad count the number of passes caught in a given time. If the ball is dropped, a pass will not be counted, or the count must start again at one.

Circle Formation (see Fig. 2–13). Start the ball with player 1, who tosses it sideward to player 2, and so on. When the ball gets to the last player, the whole team should turn, face in the opposite direction and toss the ball back to player 1. For competition, require a team to make three complete circuits with the circle facing around each time the first and last players get the ball. Everyone must handle the ball on each circuit. No player may be skipped.

PASSING

Numerous ways of passing the ball may be taught, but for developing team passing, only a few are really essential. However, the aptitude of the players should be considered, and if certain individuals are successful in using other passes, they should be encouraged. Mastery of a few basic passes is better than a variety poorly delivered.

Because advanced players are capable of a greater variety of skills and may, by preference, choose others, an analysis is given here of more passes than are necessary to any team or player. Successful team play can be accomplished with the following basic passes:

1. Two-hand chest,
2. Two-hand underhand,
3. One-hand underhand,
4. One-hand shoulder,
5. Bounce pass.

In general, passes should be short and sometimes only a hand-off. The speed of the ball should be adjusted to the distance from the receiver. A hard pass at short distance is difficult to hold.

THE TWO-HAND CHEST PASS

The most widely used pass by men and women, and the one easiest for girls to handle, is the two-hand chest pass. It is the basic basketball pass.

BODY MECHANICS

Starting Position. The ball is held directly in front of the chest. The hands should be in somewhat the same position as for catching at chest level.

CHAPTER 4. BASKETBALL

The fingers should be pointed upward and on the sides of the ball
with the thumbs behind it.

The ball should be gripped by fingers and thumbs only.

The elbows should be flexed easily at the sides.

The feet should be in side stride or forward stride position.

The knees should be flexed and easy.

The trunk may be erect, inclined forward for a direct pass forward or to the side for a deceptive pass.

Application of Force. The arms should be pushed forward from the shoulders, and the elbows should be extended as a quick flick is given by the wrists. The arms and shoulders should be relaxed, not tense.

The hands should rotate inward with the pass.

The thumbs add to the pushing movement.

The thumbs should be kept behind the ball rather than drawn under the ball. A pull with the thumbs under the ball will add back spin and make the pass more difficult for the receiver to handle.

A transfer of weight to the forward foot will give additional power, but with some variations of the pass it is not always possible.

Follow Through. The palms face the direction of the pass.

The hands, wrists and arms should be straight at the end of the pass and following the direction of the ball.

For a pass directly forward, the trunk should be inclined forward.

The pass may be executed with the body moving away from the pass. In that case, the follow through of the hands and arms is similar to the pass forward, but the step is away from the direction the ball is taking. The trunk then is inclined away from the direction of the ball.

USES

The chest pass makes an effective short pass because the ball can be easily controlled.

If passing to the right, left and forward is mastered, the chest pass becomes a good deceptive pass.

Because many passes are caught chest high, the chest pass gives the receiver an opportunity to pass with little delay.

COACHING SUGGESTIONS

Keep the elbows close to the sides. If the elbows are out from the sides, the throw is awkward.

Keep the thumbs behind the ball.

Grip the ball with the heel of the thumbs and the fingers, not the palms.

TEACHING PROGRESSION

1. Explain and demonstrate the pass directly forward.

2. Give individual corrections in a stationary practice drill in which the pass is forward.

3. Pass from chest to the right or left.

4. Pass and run.

5. Pass from a moving base, for example, after the dribble or immediately after a pivot.

SQUAD PRACTICE

Circle Formation (Fig. 2–13).   The circle should be not more than 10 feet in diameter. Pass to anyone in the circle. Pass as soon as the ball is received. Stress handling the ball quickly.

Move around the circle in an easy jog. Pass the ball across the circle while running but never run with the ball. Change direction of the run often. Stress passing ahead of receiver.

Advanced Squads: Shuttle Formation (Fig. 2–7).   Groups should be 20 to 30 feet apart. Dribble and follow immediately with a chest pass.

The Two-hand Underhand Pass

BODY MECHANICS

Starting Position.   The ball may be thrown from directly in front of the body or from either side about hip level. The ball can be protected better if the pass is from the right or left side (Fig. 4–4).

The hands should be cupped and spread on the sides of the ball, fingers pointing downward, thumbs to the top of the ball and pointing forward.

FIG. 4–4.   Two-hand underhand pass.

CHAPTER 4.   BASKETBALL

The elbows should be slightly bent, the right elbow turned out to the side if the pass is from the right side.

The feet should be in forward stride or side stride position, with knees flexed. The left foot should be forward for passes from the right side.

The trunk should be inclined forward in the direction of the pass.

Application of Force. The arms should be swung forward and upward with a quick straightening of the elbows. The ball should be released about waist height.

A quick snap of the wrists usually adds sufficient power for the purpose for which this pass is used; the pass is more of a toss or flick than a long pass.

Additional force may be added by a step in the direction of the pass.

Follow Through. The elbows should be straight with the hands following the ball as far as possible.

The ball should travel slightly upward but no higher than the shoulders. The arms should be no higher than the shoulders at the end of the swing.

USES

This is a good short pass, particularly following a pivot or a reverse turn. It is employed most frequently to feed the ball to a player cutting toward the basket.

If the ball has been received waist high or lower, the two-hand underhand is a good pass to use to pass quickly to a teammate in a better offensive position. Because the pass is easily guarded, it is not effective with an opponent directly in front of the passer.

COACHING SUGGESTIONS

Grip the ball with the thumbs and fingers.

For a pass from the right side, keep the right elbow well away from the body.

Control the release. A late release means a high loop pass.

TEACHING PROGRESSION

1. Explain and demonstrate the pass from the right side, the stronger side for right-handed players.
2. Pivot and pass.
3. Pass from the weak side.

SQUAD PRACTICE

Double Lines, 8 to 10 feet apart (see Fig. 2–9). Pass from stationary positions in direction indicated in the figure.

Double Lines, 10 to 15 feet apart (Fig. 4–5). 1. X^1 passes to X^2

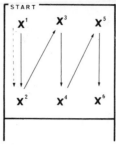

FIG. 4–5.

and runs to X^2's position. X^2 passes to X^3 and runs to X^1's position. Each player runs to the position directly opposite her own. When X^6 receives the ball she passes to X^1 and takes the spot vacated by X^5. Start with short distances between the two lines of players.

2. Receive the ball on the run, make the indicated pass and go to the position on the opposite side. The bounce or dribble may be used prior to passing.

THE ONE-HAND UNDERHAND PASS

This pass resembles the underhand baseball pitch but it is neither a distance nor power pass.

BODY MECHANICS

Starting Position. The ball may be passed from either side at approximately hip level or a little behind the hip.

The fingers should be spread with the ball resting on the upturned fingers and against the forearm. The other hand may be placed on top of the ball to steady it.

The elbow should be bent.

The feet may be in side stride or forward stride position.

Application of Force. The force comes from the forward swing of the arm and the straightening of the elbow. The swing should be parallel with the body. The ball should be released from straight fingers at approximately waist height.

The weight should be transferred to the forward foot, or if the feet are in side stride position, a step may be taken in the direction of the pass.

The trunk should rotate forward and to the opposite side with the arm swing.

Follow Through. The ball should be directed by the finger tips, and the hand and arm should follow the direction of the pass. The palm should be facing upward after the ball is released.

If a step is taken, it should be in the direction of the pass.

CHAPTER 4. BASKETBALL

This pass is one of the most useful of the one-hand passes. With a fake it may often be used when guarded.

The one-hand underhand may be a short, easy pass or simply a hand-off to an offensive player cutting toward the basket.

COACHING SUGGESTIONS

A forward step may help to flatten the arc of the arm swing and improve the accuracy of the pass.

For beginners, the left foot should be forward to pass from the right side. Advanced players can learn to pass with either foot forward.

If the pass goes too high, it is probably due to failure to straighten the fingers on the release at waist height.

TEACHING PROGRESSION

1. Explain and demonstrate the pass from the strong side of the body.
2. Put free hand on top of ball to steady it.
3. Use one hand only.
4. Pass from either side, using the left hand when passing from the left side and the right hand to steady the ball.

SQUAD PRACTICE

"Teacher and Class" (see Fig. 2–5). "Teacher" stands 10 feet from the "class."

1. Teacher passes to each player who passes back to the teacher. When last player has ball, the teacher goes to the end of the line and the first player takes her place. All take a turn as teacher.
2. Use as a relay. In the relay, all distances should be fixed. Chalk marks should be used to establish the distance of the pass. Game is not finished until all have acted as teacher.

Number Passes, Double Lines (see Fig. 2–10). Using any passes learned so far, pass the ball zigzag to complete as many passes as possible in a given time. Each player says aloud the number of the pass as she receives it. A fumbled pass does not count. Squads may compete on the basis of reaching a set number, or for the highest number in a given time. If a pass is fumbled, a squad may be penalized by beginning the count at one after each fumble.

THE BOUNCE PASS

This pass may be made from a variety of positions and from one or both hands. It is frequently made from the same position as the two-hand chest pass.

CHAPTER 4.   BASKETBALL

At certain times it may be useful to put some spin on the ball to achieve a rebound to one side or another or closer to the receiver than a normal rebound would be.

Side spin is easier to achieve with one hand than two. If no spin is to be given, the ball may be thrown with one or both hands.

ONE-HAND BOUNCE PASS

Without Spin. The ball should be held between chest and waist height with the throwing hand behind and toward the top of the ball, fingers pointing upward. The ball should be supported on the other hand.

The elbow should be bent and close to the side.

Force is applied by straightening the elbow and wrist and pushing the ball to the floor.

With Spin. By pulling the hand to the outside with the palm facing in, the ball will rotate away from the passer. The rebound will then be at an angle away from the flight of the ball.

TWO-HAND BOUNCE PASS

Without Spin. The ball should be held waist high, fingers spread and at the sides of the ball, thumbs behind the ball, 4 or 5 inches apart.

The elbows should be in close to the side, wrists bent slightly backward.

Force is applied by quick straightening of the elbows in a forward push. The thumbs should push directly behind the ball.

With Back Spin. The grip is the same as above.

As the elbows are extended, the thumbs should pull sharply under the ball.

Back spin will cause the ball to rebound higher and in a more vertical plane than an ordinary bounce.

With Forward Spin. The grip is the same as the two-hand grip without spin: as the elbows are extended, the fingers and thumbs should be brought over the top of the ball, causing the ball to rotate away from the passer. A longer, lower bounce will result.

USES

The bounce pass should be used sparingly as it is slow, but with an opponent between the passer and the receiver, it is often effective.

It may be used for a short pass in the scoring area, particularly against a zone defense.

Effective out-of-bounds plays may be built around the bounce pass when a defender is close to the boundary line.

COACHING SUGGESTIONS

Coach players to bounce the ball about 12 inches to the side of the opponent's feet.

CHAPTER 4. BASKETBALL

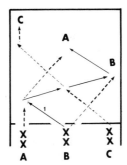

FIG. 4–6.   Bounce passing, squad practice.

The rebound should be about waist high.

The bounce should be 4 or 5 feet in front of the receiver.

The ball will rebound at approximately the same angle at which it strikes the floor; for that reason, the angle must be adjusted according to the distance between passer and receiver.

A feint with hands and ball should precede the bounce to make it deceptive.

Beginners should be taught to use the bounce with two hands and without spin.

TEACHING PROGRESSION

1. Explain and demonstrate the pass and the angles of rebound. Begin with the hands in the same position as the two-hand chest pass.
2. Bounce pass using two hands.
3. Bounce pass using one hand.
4. Bounce pass with someone between passer and receiver.
5. Bounce pass putting various spins on the ball.

SQUAD PRACTICE

Circle Formation (see Fig. 2–13).   1. Bounce pass to anyone in circle. Stress having ball bounce 4 or 5 feet in front of receiver.

2. Bounce pass to elude a player placed in the center of the circle.

Three Columns, Facing Same Direction (Fig. 4–6).   Columns should be 6 or 8 feet apart. B passes to A, who has started to move forward. B moves in opposite direction ahead of column C. A passes to C who moved to the center of column B. The passer should run behind the other crossing player as the passer will not receive a return pass immediately. This drill is useful for teaching passing and receiving on the run. The timing is important and should be carefully practiced. Pivots may also be added after this drill has been learned, also a dribble before passing.

THE ONE-HAND SHOULDER PASS (BASEBALL PASS)

This pass is somewhat like the overhand softball throw.

Starting Position.   The ball should be raised to the right shoulder in the right hand when passing from the right. The left hand is across the body to steady the ball.

The ball should rest on the upturned hand, fingers spread and pointing upward. It should be held just above the shoulder, with the supporting hand in front of the ball.

The elbow of the throwing arm should be bent and out from the side. The supporting hand is withdrawn as the arm is cocked back to throw. The ball should be 4 or 5 inches from the ear as it is carried back.

The trunk should rotate to the throwing side.

The feet may be in forward or side stride position.

Application of Force.   The elbow should extend as the arm swings forward.

The wrist should snap quickly, with the fingers coming behind and under the ball. The ball may be pushed rather than thrown if a short pass is intended.

The trunk should rotate forward, and the weight should shift to the forward foot.

Follow Through.   The hand and arm should follow the ball with the palm facing downward at the completion of the throw.

The arm should finish straight out from the body and pointing in the direction of the throw.

USES

Beginners will find the one-hand shoulder pass the most natural way to throw a fast, hard pass or one at medium range.

While long passes are difficult for the receiver, a team should know one to move the ball quickly toward the front court when the offensive has been regained deep in the back court. The baseball pass can be used in such situations.

COACHING SUGGESTIONS

Teach the pass with the wrist snap for distance and with a push as in the shot put. Keep the elbows up and behind the ball.

Use the free hand to steady the ball.

Let the ball roll off the finger tips.

TEACHING PROGRESSION

1. Explain and demonstrate the pass.
2. Use free hand in front to steady ball.
3. Use no support.
4. Use right or left hand.

CHAPTER 4.   BASKETBALL

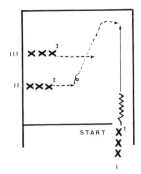

FIG. 4–7. Passing, squad practice, advanced players.

SQUAD PRACTICE

Relay Formation with Leader (see Fig. 2–3). Leader is 12 to 15 feet from line. Leader passes to each player in succession, who then goes to end of line. Rotate position of leader.

Same Formation with Relay Competition. The winner is the team which is back in the original order after all have received the ball from the leader and passed it back to her. The leader must use the same pass as the squad.

Squad Practice, Advanced Players (Fig. 4–7). X^1 in column I has the ball. As she dribbles the ball toward the basket, X^2 and X^3 move toward her, X^3 acting as X^2's opponent. X^2 should check suddenly, pivot and cut behind X^3 toward the basket. X^1 using a one-hand shoulder pass should throw the ball as X^2 reaches the basket. The timing should be so perfected that the pass comes immediately following the dribble. X^1 goes to the end of column II, X^2 to column III, X^3 to end of column I.

The Backward Pass

BODY MECHANICS

Starting Position. The ball may be thrown from the same position as the two-hand underhand pass, with a backward flip, or from the one-hand position as described.

The ball should be gripped with both hands at the sides of the ball, fingers cupped and pointing downward.

If the pass is from the right side, the right elbow should be flexed and turned away from the side, the left should be flexed and close to the body.

As the pass is about to be made, the hands should turn the ball so that the palm of the right hand is facing the direction of the pass. The left acts only as a support until the right hand is in position.

The feet may be in side stride or forward stride position.

The trunk should rotate slightly toward the ball.

CHAPTER 4.   BASKETBALL

Application of Force. Sufficient force can be given by a quick flick of the wrist and a short swing of the right arm. The pass must be easy or it will be fumbled.

Follow Through. For accuracy, there should be a follow through of the arm and fingers of the throwing arm in the direction of the pass.

USES

The backward pass may be used when a teammate is directly behind the player with the ball, as in a screen play.

COACHING SUGGESTIONS

The backward pass requires careful *timing* and must be practiced if it is to be used successfully.

The pass should be thrown with little force, as a teammate is usually moving away from the pass or directly into it.

TEACHING PROGRESSION

    1. Use two-hand underhand grip.
    2. Use one-hand backward throw as described.
    3. Increase range of use by passing to player running behind passer.

SQUAD PRACTICE

Relay Formation (see Fig. 2–1). Players are 5 to 6 feet apart.

When the ball reaches the last player, the whole column turns and faces opposite direction and continues to pass.

Relay Formation with Leader 10 Feet to Side (Fig. 4–8). X¹ does a front pivot, runs behind the leader and receives a backward pass from the leader. X¹ replaces leader, who goes to end of line. X² pivots, runs behind leader, receives a backward pass and replaces her, and so on. Pass should be received on the run.

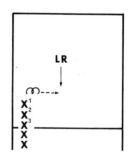

FIG. 4–8. Backward pass, squad practice.

CHAPTER 4. BASKETBALL

BODY MECHANICS

Starting Position. Technically this is not a pass as the ball is not secured in the hands before it is passed. It is merely a deflection of the ball either directly to a teammate, a bounce pass to her, or the first impetus given the ball on a dribble.

The fingers should be spread and cupped slightly, elbows flexed.

The shove is usually made while the passer is in motion.

Application of Force. The hands should be firm and the elbows extended quickly but not completely. The ball should be directed by the fingers.

The action is really a stiff arm push.

Follow Through. Palms and arms should follow through in the direction of the ball.

USES

The shove pass may be effective if players are moving parallel to each other.

This pass can be deceptive to the defensive players as the ball may be deflected in any direction but backward.

A fumble may often be avoided by using the shove pass to gain control of a wild throw.

COACHING SUGGESTIONS

Keep the ball under control by taking it in front of the body.

Use two hands to complete the shove, whenever possible.

Control the ball with either hand after skill with two hands has been acquired.

Direct the ball with the fingers and thumbs rather than the fist or heel of the hand.

TEACHING PROGRESSION

1. Explain and demonstrate ways to deflect the ball to an advantageous position when complete control may not be possible.
2. Use two hands.
3. Use one hand.
4. Pass from moving base, combining with a bounce pass or a dribble.
5. Combine with practice of a lay-up shot, first directing the ball into a dribble.

CHAPTER 4.   BASKETBALL

BODY MECHANICS

Starting Position. The ball may be thrown from directly overhead or from a little behind the head.

The fingers should grip the ball on the sides. The fingers should be spread and the thumbs a little behind the ball.

The elbows should be slightly bent and the arms extended above the head.

The knees should be easy.

The trunk may be extended slightly backward if the throw is from a set position.

Application of Force. The arms should swing forward and slightly downward. Much of the force comes from a snap of the wrists and the forward swing of the arms. The release should come about halfway in the forward swing.

The trunk should be inclined forward as the weight is transferred to the forward foot, or a forward step may be taken.

Follow Through. The arms should finish forward at about shoulder height. The fingers should point in the direction of the pass.

USES

If a high pass is caught, the ball may be thrown immediately from this position.

The two-hand overhead pass is used frequently in modern basketball from the high point of a jump.

COACHING SUGGESTIONS

The merit of the two-hand overhead pass is mainly for tall players. Short players should be encouraged to use it only when not too closely defended except when the pass from a jump is mastered.

If the pass is a high loop, the ball probably has been dropped behind the head and the arms swung forward in an arc. A step with the pass may help to keep the ball down.

Start the ball above the head.

Swing the arms forward in as straight a line as possible.

TEACHING PROGRESSION

1. Explain and demonstrate the pass from a set position and from a high pass.

2. Use mostly when a high pass has been received and the ball is to be passed immediately.

3. Emphasize a *direct pass* — with no loop.

CHAPTER 4.   BASKETBALL

BODY MECHANICS

Starting Position. The pass is made from above the right or left shoulder.

The hands should grip the ball at the sides with the thumbs slightly behind the ball. The fingers and thumbs should point upward and back.

The wrists should be bent backward.

The elbows should be bent and the right in close to the side for passes from the right shoulder.

The left arm is across the front of the body.

The feet may be either in side stride or forward stride position, knees easy.

The trunk should rotate to the throwing side.

The weight should be to the throwing side.

Application of Force. The greatest force comes from a quick straightening of the elbows and a snap of the wrists. There is little throwing action otherwise.

Added power may be given by a forward rotation of the trunk and a step in the direction of the pass.

Follow Through. The arms should extend in a straight line in the direction of the pass.

The fingers should follow the ball as far as possible and finish pointing in the direction of the pass.

The pass may be made in any forward or sideward direction. To insure accuracy, the arms should follow the direction of the pass.

The trunk also may follow the direction of the pass, but for passes to either side, if the trunk moves in the opposite direction, the pass becomes more deceptive.

USES

This pass is fairly easy to do and should be used for short passing when the ball has been received at shoulder height.

The possibilities for deception increase its value.

COACHING SUGGESTIONS

Keep the elbow on the throwing side close to the body.

Snap the wrists. This makes a throw rather than a push.

Beginners tend to send the pass in a high loop. Watch the arm swing to see that it is in a line rather than an upward arc.

Beginners should be able to master a forward pass before other variations are added.

CHAPTER 4.   BASKETBALL

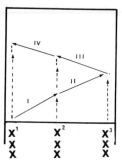

FIG. 4–9. Two-hand shoulder pass, squad practice.

TEACHING PROGRESSION

1. Explain and demonstrate the pass.
2. Practice the pass forward from the right side of the body.
3. Practice the pass from the right side of the body to the right, then to the left.
4. Practice the pass from the left side to the left, then to the right.

SQUAD PRACTICE

Three Relay Columns Facing Same Direction (Fig. 4–9). Lines are about 10 feet apart. X^1 with the ball passes to X^2, X^2 passes to X^3. Players in X^1 and X^3 positions dribble before return pass is made to player in X^2 position. X^1 goes to end of column 2, X^3 goes to end of column 1, and X^2 goes to end of column 3.

Shuttle Formation. (see Figs. 2–6 and 2–7). Place squads about 10 feet apart for this drill. Pass and receive on the run.

THE HOOK PASS

BODY MECHANICS

Starting Position. This is an overhead throw usually taken with a jump and turn.

The pass should start with the ball resting in one hand about waist high. The fingers should be spread and pointing forward and upward. The ball should rest against the forearm.

The trunk should be turned so that the left shoulder is toward the target.

The weight should be back and the back knee flexed.

Application of Force. The ball should be carried back behind the shoulder with a full arm swing.

The arm swing should continue to an overhead arc where the final momentum is given by a wrist snap.

CHAPTER 4. BASKETBALL

The hand should be pulled under the ball as it rolls off the finger
tips.

A jump is usually added to give height to the pass.

Follow Through. The fingers should follow the ball as far as possible in the direction of the pass. The palm should face downward on completion of the pass.

The throwing arm should be curved overhead, the free arm out to the side for balance (Fig. 4–10).

USES

The pass may be used when running toward the side or end line to return the ball to a teammate in court.

The pass may be used against a defender who is pressing closely. The ball may be faked toward an underhand pass and hooked instead.

COACHING SUGGESTIONS

Support the ball against the forearm of the throwing arm.

The pass is difficult for girls to execute because of the comparatively small size of their hands. One of its chief values lies in the fact that it is difficult to defend.

The control overhead and the timing of the release are most difficult to master. A looping pass is usually worthless.

In presenting the pass to a class, it should first be done from a

FIG. 4–10. The hook pass.

CHAPTER 4. BASKETBALL

38   stationary position, with the side to the receiver, then with the jump and finally the jump turn.

Advanced players should be able to use the pass when the back is turned toward the target.

TEACHING PROGRESSION

1. Explain and demonstrate the pass from a set position, left side toward receiver when pass is with the right hand.
2. Stand with back to receiver, jump and pass as the body is turned toward the target.
3. Stand with back to receiver, dribble away from her, then hook pass to her.

SQUAD PRACTICE

Relay Formation with Leader 12 or 15 Feet Away (Fig. 4–11).   Start the ball by a pass from the leader to X¹, who comes toward her on the run. X¹ dribbles to her right and hooks a pass back to X². X¹ becomes the leader; the original leader goes to the end of the column. Return the ball to the leader. The leader might be used as a defensive player who moves toward the direction of the dribbler.

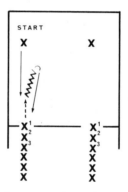

FIG. 4–11.   Hook pass, squad practice, in relay formation.

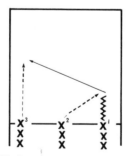

FIG. 4–12.   Hook pass, squad practice, in three lines.

CHAPTER 4.   BASKETBALL

Three Lines (Fig. 4–12). X^1 is in possession of the ball. X^2 stays on the inside as a defensive player. X^1 dribbles toward side lines and hooks a pass to X^3, who has started back on line with X^1. X^3 may then cut diagonally across the floor. This drill may be used in a practice with the lay-up shot. X^3 receives the pass, dribbles and shoots. Players return to the end of a different line from which they started.

THE DRIBBLE

The dribble is an individual play to advance the ball through a series of bounces by the same player. Girls' and women's rules long denied this invaluable offensive tactic, first by limiting it to one bounce, then two, then three.

Every player should be able to dribble with the right or left hand and to dribble when necessary. Overuse of the dribble, which is one of its disadvantages, has been discouraged in the past by limiting the number of impacts that a player may give the ball while dribbling.

Although the dribble can never take the place of a pass-and-run game, it can be used in various ways by the offensive team to their advantage. When taking the offensive after a rebound from the opponents' backboard, the dribbler can move away to the side of the court to pass with less chance of a dangerous interception near the opponents' basket.

A fast-breaking offense often gets underway with a dribble. The dribble into the basket and a lay-up shot often are an unbeatable combination.

The offense must never lose sight of the fact that a dribble is slower than a pass. The defense has more time to adjust to a player dribbling the ball than it has to adjust to quick passing.

The ball may be started from one or both hands but subsequent impacts by the same player must be with one hand only. The ball may not be caught or held between impacts by the same player.

BODY MECHANICS

The weight of the body should be low, knees bent, head up, eyes ahead rather than on the ball. The ball should be in front and to the side of the knee. The fingers and wrist control the ball. The action should be smooth rather than a series of hits.

The right or left hand may be used or the hands may be used alternately. When the dribble is to start with the right hand, the ball should rest on the left hand with the right hand on top. The ball should be held firmly.

The dribble starts from a crouch with the ball kept low (Fig. 4–13). For a dribble with the right hand, the easier starting position is with the right foot forward. When necessary, the player dribbling should keep her body between the ball and a defensive player. The dribbling motion

FIG. 4–13. The dribble.

starts from the elbow but the main action is from the wrist. Fingers complete the pushing or stroking action.

The bounce should be low in an area where the defense is pressing.

In a fast break, or when the defense has been faked out of position, the bounce may be as high as the waist and farther from the dribbler.

Skill and control should be sufficient to dribble with the hand farthest from the opponent. In moving from the left side of the court to the right side, the right hand should be used. The left hand should be used when moving from right to left on the court.

Many of the drills suggested for practicing passing or shooting should soon include the dribble. While the dribble is an essential tactic, players must learn that it should never be used when an effective pass is possible. The pass is faster and more interesting to teammates.

SQUAD PRACTICE USING OTHER SKILLS
WITH PASSING

Dribble and Pass (Fig. 4–14). X^1 dribbles, then passes to X^4, who has started to advance. X^4 dribbles, pivots and passes to X^2, who has

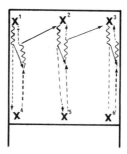

FIG. 4–14. Dribble and pass, squad practice.

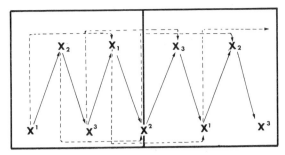

FIG. 4-15. Pass and run, squad practice.

started to advance. Following the dribble the player goes to the opposite side. When the last player has completed her dribble, she should pass to the X^1 position to start the drill again.

Competition might be introduced by counting the completed passes in a given time or by declaring the winner to be the team which passes the longest time without fumbling.

Pass and Run (Fig. 4-15). Three players stand in V formation 8 or 10 feet apart, X^1 with the ball. X^1 passes to X^2, follows immediately, runs behind X^2 and cuts forward slightly to receive the pass now coming from X^3. X^2, upon receiving the first pass, passes immediately to X^3, cuts behind her and moves forward to receive a pass now coming from X^1. Try to achieve timing which makes the passing short and continuous.

Pass with Pivot (Fig. 4-16). Players line up one behind the other. The squad leader stands 15 feet away and to the side. X^1 passes to the leader, runs forward in a straight line and receives a return pass from the leader. On receiving the pass, X^1 pivots and passes to X^2, then goes to the end of the line. X^2 passes to the leader, runs forward and so on. Change the leader after running through the drill several times.

Dribble, Pivot and Pass (Fig. 4-17). Squads are arranged in relay formations with X^1, X^2, X^3 and X^4 forming a square. X^1 dribbles toward the center, pivots and passes to X^2. X^2 dribbles toward the center, pivots and passes to X^3 and so on. Each player follows her pass and goes to the end of the receiver's line.

Passing Game. Choose equally matched teams of four to six players each. Two games may be played simultaneously, using one half of the floor for each game.

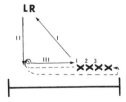

FIG. 4-16. Pass and pivot, squad practice.

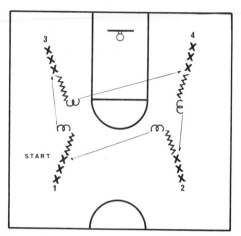

FIG. 4–17. Dribble, pivot and pass, squad practice.

Start with a jump between two players of equal height. The team with the ball passes the ball in an effort to complete 8 passes. If the pass is intercepted, the other team takes the offensive and begins its count. Each player should call out the number of the pass. Rules of running with the ball, holding the ball, out of bounds and defensive play should be followed. Players may not rove across the division line.

GENERAL COACHING SUGGESTIONS FOR PASSING

Short, quick passes will speed the play and decrease the number of interceptions.

The level for pass receiving should be between the shoulders and waist. Low or high passes cause fumbles.

Teach relaxation of the arms and shoulders and of the fingers except when gripping the ball.

Coach players to receive the ball while in motion. Waiting for the ball means that it will probably be intercepted. It is not necessary to move directly into the pass, but it should be met while moving.

The receiver of the pass should watch the ball until it is secure in her hands.

A pass to a teammate running directly toward the ball should be easy.

Players should be skilled in passing from the right or left sides and with either foot forward. Encourage players to develop passing from the right or left hand.

Passes to a teammate moving forward should be to a spot ahead rather than directly to her.

Passes close to the opponents' basket should be to a side line away from the congested area under the basket. An opponent may intercept and score easily.

CHAPTER 4. BASKETBALL

For all passes, the ball should be gripped by the fingers and thumbs **43** rather than "palmed."

Pass immediately after a pivot or dribble to prevent the defense from getting set.

GOAL SHOOTING

All shots for the goal are either *banked* against the backboard or dropped *over the rim*.

Banked shots are aimed at a spot on the backboard and rebounded into the basket. Rim shots are aimed at the near rim and intended to fall through the rim without touching it or the backboard.

While individual differences in skills will always exist, the aim of the shot at the backboard or rim should, in general, depend upon the angle and distance from the basket. Figure 4–18 provides certain guides for shooting.

Angles I and II in Figure 4–18 are approximately 22½°. All others are approximately 45°. The 8-foot radius is the short area, radius of the freethrow line is the medium, and beyond that, the long area.

1. Forty-eight per cent of all successful shots are thrown from the short areas; 43 per cent from the medium areas, and only 8+ per cent from the long areas.

2. The short areas of angles III and IV produce the greatest percentage of successful shots.

3. All areas of angles III, IV and V result in more accurate shots than any areas in angles I and II, showing that the offense is weakest from areas near the end line except for specialists in rim shots.

4. Rim shots have the highest percentage of accuracy from the

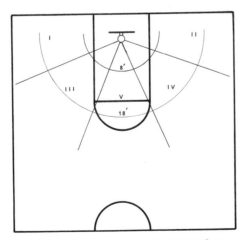

FIG. 4–18.   Areas for banked and rim shots.

short areas of angles III and IV. Banked shots have the highest percentage of accuracy from the short areas of angles I, II and V.

5. In general, long shots should be rim shots. The aim should be at the near curve of the rim.

Rim shots should be somewhat arched. The highest point of the arch should be closer to the basket than to the player. With this type of arch the ball will drop vertically toward the basket. If the ball approaches the basket on its initial flight in a straight line, the chances for the ball entering the rim are lessened. Further, a rebound from a shot without an arch will be in a straight line from the basket, eliminating the possibility of a drop toward the rim.

A ball descending vertically has two chances of success: a clean shot without touching the rim or a rebound downward toward the basket.

Modern basketball has tended to reduce the height of the arch of the shot. However, the general principle of looping the ball when taking a rim shot is best for the majority of players.

Practically all passes may be adapted to goal shooting with some slight variations. Because in shooting it is necessary to add the arch, the application of force and the follow through must be directed upward toward the target. The grip and body positions for both pass and shot otherwise are essentially the same.

THE TWO-HAND CHEST OR SET SHOT

BODY MECHANICS

Starting Position. Similar positions of the body may be used for the pass and the shot. The shot may follow a bounce or dribble or it may be taken from a set or stationary position with the feet together.

The chin should be up, eyes focused on the target.

The feet may assume a variety of positions, but a forward stride position is recommended.

The knees should be flexed, particularly for long shots where added force is needed.

The trunk should be inclined slightly.

Application of Force. For long shots, the ball should be dropped from the chest to the waist and pushed forward and upward close to the chest.

The thumbs should pull only slightly under the ball and inward. Although many coaches recommend pulling the thumbs sharply under the ball, the result is a marked back spin which tends to diminish the accuracy of the shot. The ball should have little spin.

Knees, hips and ankles should extend as the ball is released.

Follow Through. The entire body should follow through in complete extension toward the basket.

The palms should finish facing toward the basket, thumbs pointing upward and inward.

FIG. 4–19. Two-hand chest or set shot.

USES

The set shot is one of the shots most frequently used from the medium and long areas, although it may be used from any area.

The usefulness of the shot is diminished when the defense is tight and cannot be faked out of position.

Many players prefer this shot for free throws.

Good set shots from medium range can often draw out a zone defense, making way for a fake and pass to a player in a better scoring area.

COACHING SUGGESTIONS

Keep the elbows close to the sides.

Keep wrists and arms in a straight line.

Keep the thumbs behind the ball.

Relax the shoulders and arms. Shoot easily.

Push evenly with both hands.

Shooting consistently to the left of the basket may be corrected by putting the left foot forward.

TEACHING PROGRESSION

1. Shoot from stationary position within 6 or 8 feet of basket, first directly in front, then to the side of the basket.

2. Dribble and shoot from various angles except close to the end line.

CHAPTER 4. BASKETBALL

3. Increase the distance from which stationary shot is taken.
4. Receive pass on the run, dribble and shoot.

SQUAD PRACTICE

Column Formation (Fig. 4–20).   Squad is 3 or 4 feet in front of free-throw line. X^1 shoots, recovers her shot and passes to X^2, who has moved up to X^1's position. X^1 goes to end of line.

Vary positions of team to right or left of the basket and increase distance from basket.

Squad Competition.   Use squad formation as above at each basket. Have squads keep score by awarding 2 points for each goal made and subtracting 1 point for each goal missed. Compare scores at the end of a 3-minute period.

Two Columns on Opposite Sides of Basket (Fig. 4–21). X^1 shoots and goes to end of line B. X^2 recovers X^1's shot, passes to X^3 and goes to end of line A. X^3 shoots and goes to end of line B. X^4 recovers and passes. Thus line A is the shooting line, line B recovers. Change duties after

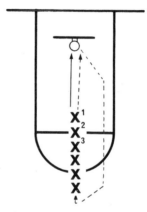

FIG. 4–20. Chest shot, squad practice, in one column.

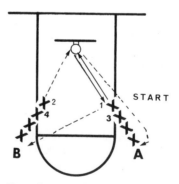

FIG. 4–21. Chest shot, squad practice, in two columns.

CHAPTER 4. BASKETBALL

complete circuit. Add practice in rebounding by having X¹ and X² try to recover the ball after the shot.

Using the same formation farther back from the basket, dribble, then shoot.

The Two-hand Underhand Shot

BODY MECHANICS

Starting Position. The grip is similar to the two-hand underhand pass.

The ball should be held just below the waist close to the body.

The fingers should point downward.

The elbows should be loose to the sides.

The feet may be in forward stride or side stride position, knees flexed.

Application of Force. The ball should be brought upward with a full swing of the arms and extension of the elbows.

The release should come about shoulder high.

The final wrist snap should cause the ball to rotate toward the thrower (back spin).

The effect of the back spin will cause the rebound to fall sharply toward the basket.

Extension of the knees and hips will add force.

Follow Through. With the exception of the shoulder, all joints should be extended.

The palms should be facing, fingers pointed toward the basket.

USES

Some players may prefer the two-hand underhand shot to the chest shot for medium and long-range shooting.

The shot requires time for the player to get set. Close defense limits its use for field goals.

Many players use this shot in free throws.

COACHING SUGGESTIONS

Little time should be spent on this shot except for free throws.

Players who have mastered the shot should not be discouraged from using it, but they should be coached not to rely on it too frequently.

If the shot is made from the forward stride position, the left foot should be forward for shots from the right side of the basket.

The Two-hand Overhead Shot

BODY MECHANICS

Starting Position. The starting position is similar to that of the pass, but the ball may be dropped somewhat behind the head as a loop is desirable.

The head should be back with chin up, eyes fixed on the target.

Application of Force. The parts of the body involved are the same as for the pass, but the swing is forward and upward and the release should come earlier than it does in the pass.

The most effective shooting is done while jumping. The release must be made at the height of the jump.

USE

The shot may be used effectively by a tall player at the post position. The player receives the pass, pivots and jumps, throwing while momentarily in midair.

SQUAD PRACTICE

Column Formation. Squad should be 6 or 8 feet from the basket. Each player in turn shoots from a stationary position. Add a jump, emphasizing a straight jump upward and a shot at the height of the jump.

THE HOOK SHOT

BODY MECHANICS

See the Hook Pass.

USES

This shot may be used effectively, when the defense is close, by turning the side to the basket.

It may be used when dribbling away from the basket.

The shot is useful for the player in the post position.

COACHING SUGGESTIONS

Shoot high and easily.

Relax the arm as the ball is released.

The shot is very difficult to control and should not be taught to beginners.

TEACHING PROGRESSION

See the Hook Pass.

SQUAD PRACTICE

Line Formation Directly in Front of Basket (Fig. 4–22). Players

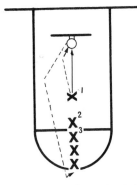

FIG. 4-22. Hook shot, squad practice, in line formation.

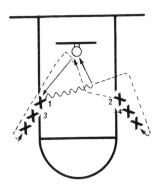

FIG. 4-23. Hook shot, squad practice, in double column formation.

line up, left side to basket. X¹ takes hook shot, recovers it and passes to X², who has moved to X¹'s place. X¹ goes to the end of the line.

Double Column Formation (Fig. 4-23). X¹ bounces or dribbles, then takes a hook shot as she crosses in front of the basket. X² follows to the opposite side to receive rebound, then passes to X³. X¹ and X² go to ends of opposite lines. X³ dribbles to right and shoots; X⁴ recovers. Continue until all have had a turn at shooting.

THE LAY-UP SHOT

BODY MECHANICS

This shot is taken from right or left of the basket; in close, following a dribble or upon receiving the ball on the run. It is a banked shot with a jump, bringing the hand as close to the spot of the bank as possible.

The ball should be caught firmly in both hands before raising it to shoot with one hand.

The player must take the proper stride to get into the basket in this

50 shot. The timing is easier from a dribble than from a pass. The player approaches the basket from a 45-degree angle.

From the right side of the basket the shot should be taken with the right hand, the take-off should be from the left foot about 5 or 6 feet from the basket and to the side. The next-to-last step with the right foot is long. The last step is shorter to assure height in the jump. The left foot, or take-off foot, is planted firmly.

The right knee should be brought up high.

The ball is carried firmly in both hands from the midsection or right side of the body. When it is released high in the jump, the left hand is removed. The right hand reaches as high as possible toward the spot where the shot is to be banked.

The ball should be pushed gently against the backboard.

The release should come at the height of the jump.

The position of the hand as the ball is released depends upon the individual player. For some, it will be easier to turn the hand behind the ball to the inside with the palm facing the backboard. A more recent trend is to release the ball with the hand underneath, simply allowing it to roll off the fingers.

The ball should be placed about 12 inches above and to the right of the basket. When the lay-up shot is from directly in front of the basket, the ball should be placed over the rim.

FIG. 4–24. The lay-up shot, approach from right side of court. A, Ready to take off on left foot, ball in both hands. B, Upward jump, right knee raised, ball lifted in right hand. C, Ball released off finger tips at height of jump.

CHAPTER 4. BASKETBALL

A pass to an offensive player cutting sharply toward the basket may often result in an opportunity for a lay-up shot. However, it is more effective following a dribble. The player can adjust the timing of the stride and jump when she has control of the ball herself.

The shot may be made by crossing in front of the basket from left to right, but in this case a cross body shot is easier to execute than the lay-up.

COACHING SUGGESTIONS

Practice should be given in the take-off first, as many players find it difficult to check the forward momentum and jump upward after the run. Practice should start with two steps only, the first step being the long step and the last the shorter step and take-off.

The jump should be high and directly upward rather than toward the end line. The tendency will be to jump forward and out of the court, sacrificing height and the opportunity to recover the rebound.

The ball must be released as close as possible to the backboard to insure accuracy.

A broad jump tends to rebound the ball too sharply. Practice a short take-off step and height in the jump.

The left-hand or weak-side lay-up from the left of the court reverses the hand and foot positions. The footwork is the most difficult part of the shot from the player's weaker side.

SQUAD PRACTICE

Column Formation (Fig. 4–25). Squad is 4 or 5 feet from basket on right side.

With feet parallel, step on the left foot, jump with right knee raised and shoot. Recover own shot and pass to next player in line. Progress to a two-step approach from a stationary position before spending time on the full stride.

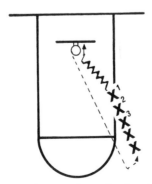

FIG. 4–25. Lay-up shot, squad practice, in column formation.

CHAPTER 4. BASKETBALL

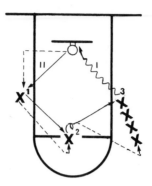

FIG. 4–26. Lay-up shot, squad practice, pass and shoot rotation.

Move back 12 or 15 feet, dribble, then shoot.

Pass and Shoot Rotation (Fig. 4–26). X^3 dribbles, then shoots. X^1 recovers and passes to X^2, X^2 passes to X^4, who should be moving toward basket. X^3 replaces X^1, X^1 replaces X^2, X^2 goes to the end of the line.

X^2 pivots and passes using underhand pass with one or two hands.

Change players to the opposite side of the court to practice shot with left hand from the left side of the court.

THE JUMP SHOT

The jump shot has become one of the most popular in men's basketball today. While it is essentially a two-handed shot, the final push is with one hand (Fig. 4–27).

BODY MECHANICS

Starting Position. The shot is usually preceded by a dribble or a pivot. The feet are brought close together after the stop. The forward foot should be firmly placed and the back foot brought parallel with it. The ball is held in both hands close to the body. The knees are bent.

Application of Force. As the jump is made, the ball is brought above the head. The right hand is behind the ball, the left to the side and toward the front. The eyes are focused on the near rim of the basket. The ball is pushed with the right hand at the top of the jump or on the way down. The jump should be straight upward to give the split-second suspension in the air during which the ball is released. The rim is sighted from under the ball.

Follow Through. The arm is extended toward the basket in the follow through, palm facing downward.

USE

The shot is difficult to defend and can be made from almost any angle.

CHAPTER 4. BASKETBALL

FIG. 4–27. The jump shot.

FREE-THROW SHOOTING

The outcome of a basketball game often depends upon the success or failure of a team in shooting free throws. Every player should be able to score on at least 65 per cent of her attempts.

The choice of the shot depends upon the individual. Many prefer the two-hand set shot. Others prefer the two-hand underhand or the one-hand push. A player does not need a variety of shots. She should discover which one is the most natural for her and practice to perfect it. Most free throws are related to other shooting in basic skills.

Regardless of the type of throw, certain basic principles apply. The stance should be a comfortable forward stride or, in the majority of cases, a side stride. In the side stride position, toes should be placed exactly up to the line but not on or over it. The arms should be relaxed, hanging downward naturally. The ball should be held lightly but firmly in the finger cushions. The eyes should be focused on the front of the rim as soon as all preparations are made.

The shooter should take a deep breath and hold it until after the ball leaves the hand. The trunk is erect, but the knees bend forward slowly until the wrists or forearms touch them. As the knees bend, the heels leave the floor and the weight is over the balls of the feet.

CHAPTER 4. BASKETBALL

Force is obtained for the throw by extension of the knees and a forward, upward swing of the arms with straight elbows. The ball should leave the hands when the body is extended and the arms have reached as near and as high toward the basket as possible.

The shot should be taken with careful aim but without delay. The ball should be arched and dropped through the rim "clean" with practically no spin. If the ball goes to the right of the rim consistently, pull the left foot back; if to the left, change the stance and move the right foot back.

Squad Practice. Free-throw practice may be combined with practice in recovering rebounds. Each player should take five or ten trials before rotating positions. The player should step back from the free-throw line after each free throw is made and approach the line again in a relaxed manner.

Free-Throw Contest. Each player takes 10 to 25 free throws. Rotate the players after every three. The player with the highest total wins. Rebound practice should follow each throw missed.

SQUAD PRACTICE USING VARIOUS SKILLS WITH SHOOTING

Pivot, Dribble and Shoot (Fig. 4–28). Line up two groups on opposite sides of the basket as shown in the illustration. Place a bench or jumping standard in front of each team. X^1 with the ball pivots, dribbles, then passes to X^2, who has pivoted around the obstacle. X^2 dribbles, then shoots. Both try for rebound. Each goes to the end of the opposite line. Use one side only for shooting side.

NOTE: The players pivot and cut toward the inside of the obstacle. Pivots should be away from the obstacle.

Pivot, Dribble and Shoot (Fig. 4–29). X^1 passes to X^2, who pivots, bounces or dribbles, then passes back to X^1, who has cut toward the basket. X^1 shoots, and both try for the rebound. The player recovering the rebound passes to X^3, who continues the drill with X^4 and so on. X^1 and X^2 go to the ends of the opposite lines.

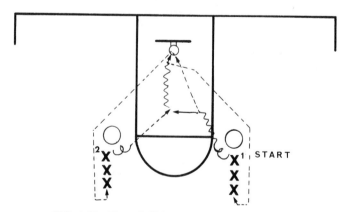

FIG. 4–28. Pivot, dribble and shoot, around obstacle.

CHAPTER 4. BASKETBALL

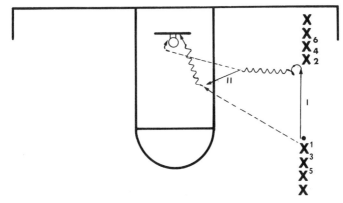

FIG. 4-29. Pivot, dribble and shoot.

FIG. 4-30. Hand-off, dribble and shoot.

Hand-off, Dribble and Shoot (Fig. 4-30). X^1 hands the ball to X^2 when X^2 is directly in line with her. X^2 cuts behind X^1, dribbles, shoots, recovers the rebound and passes back to X^1. X^2 goes to the end of the line. X^1 may remain in her place for several trials, or X^2 may replace her while X^1 goes to the end of the line. The receiver must run close to the passer. In a game situation this makes it possible to screen out a defender who may be attempting to follow.

GAMES FOR SHOOTING PRACTICE

"Twenty-one." Two squads of four or five players each may play at each basket. Use one ball for each two squads. The squads at each basket are in a separate contest.

Put the ball in play by a jump between two players from opposing squads. The two squads must stay within a designated area of the floor near a basket. Both shoot at the same basket.

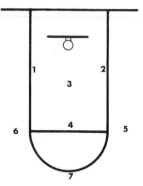

FIG. 4–31. "Risk it."

Each field goal counts 2 points. If a goal is made, the player who made it gets a free throw. If the free throw is successful, she continues to take the free throws until she misses, then the ball is in play. Each free throw counts 1 point.

All basketball rules prevail. The team first scoring 21 points wins.

"Risk It" (Fig. 4–31). Mark seven spots on the floor at the angles indicated by the numbers in Figure 4–31. As many as ten players may compete at each basket. A player starts at spot 1, takes a set shot; if she makes it, she moves to spot 2. If she fails she may "risk it" and try again. If she fails a second time she must start at 1 on her next turn. After a player misses a risked shot, the next player starts. One trial only is allowed at spot 1. A player after making a successful shot at spot 1 continues shooting until she misses. The first player completing the entire circuit wins. After a failure a player need not "risk it" but may await her turn at the spot where the failure occurred.

"Ladder Climb" (Fig. 4–32). Two squads of five or six players each play at each basket. Mark off rungs of the ladder about 2 feet apart

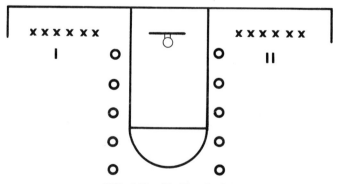

FIG. 4–32. "Ladder climb."

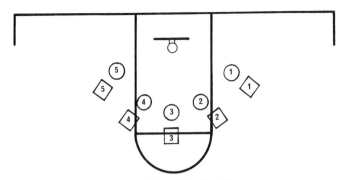

FIG. 4–33. "Hard luck."

toward the sides of the basket and increasingly nearer to the center line. The object of the game is to determine which squad can get its players over the top of the ladder first with a successful shot by each player from every rung on her side of the court.

Each squad should have a ball, but the players must take their turns in regular rotation and alternate shots with the opponents. When a player makes a basket from rung 1 she takes her next shot from rung 2 and so on. Shots may be of any prescribed type, namely, set, push or others of the player's own preference.

"*Hard Luck*" (Fig. 4–33). One squad is placed at each basket as indicated in Figure 4–33. Mark off spots in circles and squares in semi-circle as diagrammed, with squares 2 feet behind the circle spots. The object of the game is to determine which individual player can complete the circuit in the fewest number of shots. Players shoot in turn, taking one shot each turn.

The first shot must be taken from circle 1; if the basket is missed the player has "hard luck" and must drop back 2 feet to the same numbered square. A player may continue shooting from the circles as long as she is successful; if she misses, she falls back to the square and must await her turn. When a basket is made from the square, a player takes her next shot from the circle with the next higher number.

General Coaching Suggestions for Shooting

The ball should be thrown from the finger tips and thumbs rather than from the heels of the hand.

In all shooting, the eyes should be focused on the target, either the rim or the backboard depending on the type of shot.

Players should be coached to shoot quickly from a run or jump without pausing to get set for every shot.

Relaxation is an important factor in successful shooting. Tenseness results in hurling the ball too hard or in pushing harder with one hand than the other.

Practice drills for shooting should be at full speed and should approximate, insofar as possible, game situations after the skills have been learned.

Little time should be given to practicing shots from beyond the 15 to 20 foot radius. Few girls will be able to shoot accurately from beyond that area. Passing to a player better situated should be emphasized.

Shooting practice is essential for all players. Some may shoot less frequently than others, but shooting will give better understanding of the rebound from the backboard for all players.

FAKING OR FEINTING

A feint is a pretense or fake move or throw in a certain direction, followed by a quick shift of the arms or body to an opposite direction.

A successful fake often depends upon the eyes as well as the body. The eyes should not be focused on the intended receiver of a pass.

FAKING

A player who can handle the ball cleverly can make a successful pass even when closely guarded. A fake with the arms, followed by a quick dodge or pivot, will often throw the defensive player off balance.

The pretense to throw is usually made with a quick motion in one direction, followed by a sudden shift and throw to the opposite side. The trunk and body should aid in the deception by rotation to the opposite side from the direction of the pass.

A faking action to one side, followed by a quick change to the original position, often frees the offensive player for a dribble and lay-up shot.

DODGING

Dodging implies eluding an opponent, not only to receive a pass, but to such an extent that, after the pass is received, the receiver is free to shoot or to pass again. This would exclude merely circling an opponent to get in front of her.

The key to successful dodging lies in a quick change of pace and direction. A start should be made in one direction, a sudden stop and pivot or reverse turn in another. It is not necessary to run across the court to dodge, but a few steps in one direction will be sufficient; then the pivot or turn.

The difference between the good player and the average player lies in the ability to control every position of the body without diminishing the speed or effectiveness of play.

CHAPTER 4. BASKETBALL

BODY MECHANICS

Starting Position.   The feet should be in a short forward stride position with the whole foot on the floor. The whole foot makes for better
balance and more flexion of the ankle joint.

The knees should be bent.

The weight should be forward on the toes.

The arms should be at the sides.

Application of Force.   Height is gained by quick extension of all
flexed joints.

Wrists and fingers should be extended.

The arm should swing forward and upward to add power.

The ball should be tapped by the fingers.

COACHING SUGGESTIONS

Timing of the jump is an important factor. The eyes must be focused
on the ball, and the jump should be started just before the ball reaches
the highest point.

The jump must be upward rather than forward.

As soon as the feet strike the floor, the jumper should be in good
balance to participate in the play.

Jumping is an invaluable skill not only for jump balls but also for
shooting, for intercepting high passes or shots and for rebounds from
the backboard.

SQUAD PRACTICE

Individual and Team Jump Ball Contest (Fig. 4–34).   Pair off teams
approximately equal as to height. Opponents face each other in pairs.
Odd numbers are on one squad, evens on the other. A squad leader
tosses the ball between X^1 and X^2. Both jump and attempt to tap ball to
own team. A team wins a point if a member tips the ball toward her

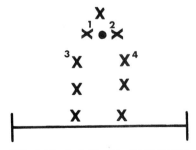

FIG. 4–34.   Individual jumping contest.

CHAPTER 4.   BASKETBALL

own team. In case of a draw, jump again. If the second is still a draw, no point is awarded and the next pair jump.

Jumping Contests Without the Ball. 1. On the top of the backboard, fix a series of tapes, graduated in length. Length of tapes will depend upon age groups. The player who can touch the highest tape wins.

2. The player stands with arm extended over head and makes a mark on the wall with a short piece of chalk. With side to the wall, the player jumps as high as possible, making a second chalk mark at the height of the jump. Measure the distance between the chalk marks to determine the actual height of each jump.

THE REVERSE TURN

BODY MECHANICS

Starting Position. The reverse turn is executed by a quick turn on the balls of both feet, neither of which is moved from the floor.

The feet must be in forward stride.

The weight should be low and the stride moderate.

If the right foot is forward, the turn is to the left; if the left foot is forward, the turn is to the right (Fig. 4-35).

The rear foot does not leave the floor until the turn is completed.

USES

The turn is useful when a player is guarded from directly in front.

The turn may be used at the end of a run to elude an opponent who is trailing. If it is executed unexpectedly, the opponent will probably overrun.

The reverse turn may be used effectively in a screen play.

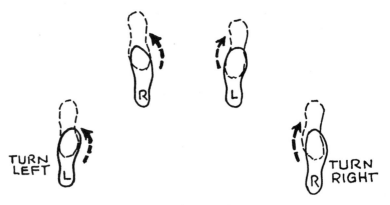

FIG. 4-35. Reverse turn.

CHAPTER 4. BASKETBALL

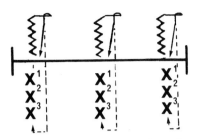

FIG. 4–36. Reverse turn, squad practice.

COACHING SUGGESTIONS

Keep the weight low and on the balls of the feet.
Turn quickly without indicating the attempt in advance.
Keep the weight on the rear foot and turn on the balls of both feet.
Hold the ball close to the body during a turn.

SQUAD PRACTICE

Players in Circle Formation.   On the first signal, players jog around the circle; on the second signal, stop; on third, reverse turn and run in opposite direction. Continue changing directions on each signal thereafter.

Relay Formation (Fig. 4–36). X^1 dribbles, turns and passes back to X^2, then goes to end of line. Competition in this drill is possible by establishing a restraining line and setting the number of bounces in the dribble at three. The squad which is back in position first, with X^1 at head of the line, wins.

PIVOTS

Pivoting is a legal method of changing the position of the body while in possession of the ball. The pivot is an essential factor of all footwork in feinting and dodging with or without the ball.

Pivots are of two general types:

1. Rear pivot.
2. Front pivot.

The body mechanics of both types are similar with the exception of the footwork. Both types may result in a turn of direction in any degree, including a complete circle, provided the pivot foot is kept in contact with the floor.

BODY MECHANICS

Starting Position.   The knees should be bent and the trunk in a crouch position.

CHAPTER 4.   BASKETBALL

The feet should be well spread either in forward or side stride position.

The weight should be on the stationary foot.

The push-off should be given with the ball of the free foot, and the pivot should be made on the sole of the stationary foot.

If the pivot is done while in possession of the ball, the ball should be held in both hands, close to the body.

COACHING SUGGESTIONS

Bend the knees and keep the weight low.

Keep one foot in contact with the floor if in possession of the ball.

Use pivots and turns to elude an opponent. Never run in semi-circular paths or straight lines unless possession of the ball can be gained in no other way.

Pass as soon as the pivot is complete if time is important.

All types of pivots should be mastered.

In faking, pivots in various directions around the same foot may be effective.

TEACHING PROGRESSION

The order of teaching pivots and turns to beginners should be:
1. Reverse turn.
2. Rear pivot, right and left.
3. Front pivot.

Pivots should all be introduced in one or possibly two early lessons and practiced regularly thereafter in combination with passing and shooting.

THE REAR PIVOT

BODY MECHANICS

Starting Position. The rear foot is the pivot or stationary foot from the forward stride position (Fig. 4–37).

If the left foot is forward, the whirl should be to the left and backward.

From a side stride position, either foot may be the pivot foot (Fig. 4–37). However, a shift may not be made from one foot to the other.

USES

The rear pivot is useful when the defensive player is guarding closely from directly in front of the offensive player.

When guarded from in front, a half rear pivot and a quick pass to a teammate trailing results in a legal screen play.

The rear pivot is a basic tactic in good faking. A player may start a rear pivot, check, and return quickly to the original position.

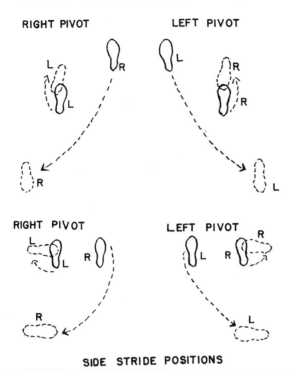

RIGHT PIVOT   LEFT PIVOT

RIGHT PIVOT   LEFT PIVOT

SIDE STRIDE POSITIONS

FIG. 4–37. Rear pivot.

COACHING SUGGESTIONS

Always pivot away from an opponent rather than into her.
Pivot quickly and pass immediately.
Never cross the legs in a rear pivot.
Keep the weight low to maintain balance.
The free foot should be off the floor only an instant to keep good balance.

TEACHING PROGRESSION

1. Explain and demonstrate the movement of the body around the pivot foot.
2. Teach pivots from stationary base on signal first.
3. Run, stop, then pivot without the ball.
4. Dribble, pivot, and pass or shoot. Combine with ball handling, both passing and shooting.

CHAPTER 4. BASKETBALL

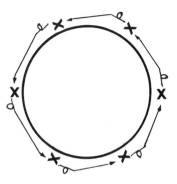

FIG. 4–38. Rear pivot, squad practice, circle formation.

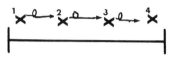

FIG. 4–39. Rear pivot, squad practice, relay formation.

SQUAD PRACTICE

Circle Formation (Fig. 4–38). All players face same direction in a circle. With left foot forward, rear pivot on signal. Change to right foot forward and finally to side stride as in starting position.

Pass ball around circle, using two-hand underhand pass after pivot. Following pivot and pass, return to original position with rear pivot.

Give several balls to each circle and keep all going as rapidly as possible.

Introduce team competition by having teams complete a given number of circuits with a pivot preceding each pass.

Relay Formation (Fig. 4–39). Space players as far apart as possible up to 10 feet; use length of gymnasium if necessary.

X^1 has the ball. X^1 does a rear pivot, then passes to X^2. X^2 pivots and passes to X^3 and so on. As soon as a player passes she sits on the floor. The last player may not sit until she has caught the ball. The first team with all players sitting wins. Use as a relay requiring at least three complete circuits.

The Front Pivot

BODY MECHANICS

Starting Position. From the forward stride position, the forward foot should be the stationary or pivot foot.

The rear foot should swing forward in an arc to achieve the desired degree of change in direction. Although a complete about face may be made, the 90-degree forward pivot blocks out the opponent effectively.

CHAPTER 4. BASKETBALL

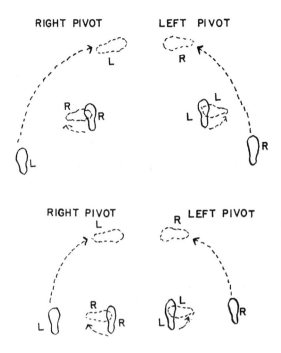

SIDE STRIDE POSITIONS

FIG. 4–40. Front pivot.

The weight should be kept over the pivot foot to maintain balance.

From a side stride position, either foot may be the pivot or stationary foot and the other foot should swing forward (Fig. 4–40).

USES

The front pivot is most frequently used when a guard is at the side. The pivot often causes the opponent to overrun.

The pivot is usually made toward the side line.

The front pivot also makes an effective dodge when not in possession of the ball.

The reverse turn or forward pivot should be used depending on which foot is forward and where the defensive player is located.

COACHING SUGGESTIONS

See suggestions for the rear pivot.

The front pivot should not be used when closely guarded from the front; charging may result.

CHAPTER 4. BASKETBALL

See Rear Pivot.

Shuttle Formation (Fig. 4–41). Place bench, standard or a player 8 or 10 feet in front of each team as indicated by squares in Figure 4–41.

1. X^1 dribbles, jumps to a side stride stop, pivots forward, then passes to X^2. X^1 goes to end of her line. X^2 repeats, passes to X^3 and goes to the end of her line.

2. Same formation but use forward stride stop. If player lands with right foot forward, use forward pivot and pass. If left foot is forward, use one-quarter reverse turn and pass.

Combination of Forward and Rear Pivots (Fig. 4–42). Use two-hand underhand pass or any other pass easily controlled by the player.

X^1 and X^3 are about 15 feet apart, X^2 stands 10 feet to the right of X^1 and about 5 feet ahead of her. X^3 passes first to X^1 coming forward to meet the pass. X^1 does a front pivot and passes to X^2. X^2 does a 90 degree rear pivot, then passes to X^4. X^1 goes to line 2, X^3 to 1 and X^2 to the end of line 3. Move as soon as the pass is completed. Move players farther apart. Have each player dribble, pivot and pass.

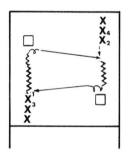

FIG. 4–41. Dribble, pivot and pass, squad practice.

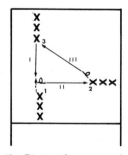

FIG. 4–42. Pivot and pass, squad practice.

All defense is based upon individual skills both in man-to-man defense and in the zone defense. The defensive posture of the player requires good balance and a proper stance at all times. In most situations, the outside foot, or the foot closest to the side lines, should be to the rear. The inside foot should be forward. Inside and outside are determined by an imaginary line from basket to basket.

Some players will find it more natural to take a stance with the right foot forward and right hand up, left at the side.

INDIVIDUAL DEFENSE AGAINST AN OPPONENT WITHOUT THE BALL

BODY MECHANICS

Starting Position. The knees should be bent so that the body is slightly crouched. This position makes it possible to slide across the floor with the offensive player. The arms should be down but the hands should be out from the sides.

The weight should be on the balls of the feet and evenly distributed.

The eyes should follow the ball and the opponent.

If the ball is a safe distance from the basket, it is unnecessary to play the opponent too closely. She should never be allowed to get too far away. A close defensive position is more susceptible to screens and fast breaks by the offensive player who fakes well.

Against a faster opponent, the defensive player should allow the offensive player more latitude when away from the basket. Guarding should be alert but more relaxed in this situation than normally.

Following the Opponent. The position of the defensive player must be such that she places herself between her opponent and the basket and toward the inside of the court. Certain exceptions are made in the defense against the player in the post position.

The footwork of the defensive player is most important. She can often keep herself in position by a series of slides and small steps, moving with her opponent, never before her.

COACHING SUGGESTIONS

The defensive player will have to learn to anticipate the movement of the offensive player and to follow her a split second after the direction of her move is apparent.

The stance is important. If the defender's feet are parallel, it is easier to fake her out of position.

The position should be aggressive but relaxed, not stiff.

A good shooter should never be free to receive a pass in a medium scoring area from the basket and have time to throw an unguarded set shot.

CHAPTER 4. BASKETBALL

Keep Away. Arrange players in squads of six or eight, each squad divided into two groups. One group is given the ball, or a toss-up may be used to put the ball in play. The group gaining possession of the ball passes it to its own members until it is intercepted by an opponent. When a group loses the ball, each member should then trail an opponent as her guard to try to regain possession. All opponents should be guarded at all times when a group is on the defensive.

INDIVIDUAL DEFENSE AGAINST AN OPPONENT WITH THE BALL

BODY MECHANICS

Starting Position. The stance is similar to the position for defense against an opponent without the ball, but the body should be low except when under the basket.

The hands play an important part in guarding the opponent. The inside hand should be up, arm extended (Fig. 4–43). The other hand should be slightly out from the side. Eyes should be focused on the midsection of the opponent's body. Fakes are more easily detected if the opponent's body is the focal point of vision. The ball is followed with peripheral vision.

A good defensive player will fake with the hands and try to put a hand on the ball to get a tie ball.

The defensive player should avoid jumping when it only appears

FIG. 4–43. Individual defense against an opponent with the ball.

CHAPTER 4. BASKETBALL

that a shot may be attempted. The player with the ball may fake a shot, **69** then dribble around a jumper.

When the offensive player with the ball is near the basket, guarding should be close, no more than a foot away.

Following the Opponent. If the player with the ball attempts to fake a pivot, the defender should not move her feet until she is sure of the opponent's direction.

The opponent should not be lost after a shot. The defender should go for the rebound with the opponent.

INDIVIDUAL DEFENSE AGAINST THE PIVOT PLAYER
(POST POSITION)

An individual defense against the player in the post position is one of the most difficult defensive assignments. The defensive player should be as tall as the post player and faster, if possible. In general, the defender must play to prevent a pass from reaching the player in the post position within the area of the free-throw lane.

If the pivot player is in a low post area, near the basket, the defender should slide into a position in *front* of her. If the pivot player is in a high post position near the free-throw line, the defender should play to the post player's side where the ball is being played. The inside foot should be behind the post player.

If the pivot player succeeds in receiving a pass in the high post position, the defender should slide behind her immediately.

The player in the post position should not be crowded too closely from behind or from the side. The offensive team then can set up a screen more easily.

SQUAD PRACTICE

Double Lines (Fig. 4–44). X¹ dribbles, feints, then pivots to pass to X⁴. D¹ moves forward to meet X¹, taking care not to block her progress

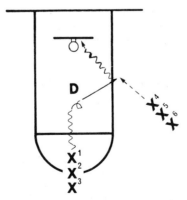

FIG. 4–44. Individual defense against an opponent with the ball, squad practice, in double lines.

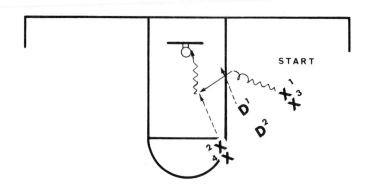

FIG. 4–45. Individual defense against an opponent with the ball, squad practice, in three lines.

in the dribble. D^1 follows X^1 until X^1 has chosen to pass or shoot. If X^1 passes to X^4, D^1 goes to the basket with her.

If D^1 switches over to X^4 too soon, X^1 may keep the ball and shoot. All go in for the rebound.

Three Parallel Lines (Fig. 4–45). X^1 dribbles toward the basket, fakes, then pivots to pass to X^2, who advances when X^1 does. If D^1 moves over toward X^2 too soon, X^1 may keep the ball and shoot. X^2 dribbles and shoots if she receives the ball. All go in for rebound. X^1 goes to a position behind X^4, D^1 goes behind X^3 and X^2 moves behind D^2.

INDIVIDUAL DEFENSE AGAINST THE REBOUND

BODY MECHANICS

When the ball has left the hands of the shooter, the defender should turn her back on the offensive player and get into the position the shooter normally would want. The defender should be between her opponent and the basket.

The turn will often result in a legal screen against the shooter. The defensive player should take a crouch position, feet spread, to get ready for a jump. Hands should be out from the sides.

The shooter will have to go to either side around the defensive player.

As the ball rebounds, the defensive player should jump forward and high to recover the ball. Often if she is unable to catch the rebound, she can at least tip it toward the side line.

SQUAD PRACTICE

Column Formation (Fig. 4–46). X^1 takes a long shot from about the free-throw line using a prescribed shot or one of her choice. D^1 comes forward with one arm raised, guarding from several feet in front of X^1. As soon as the shot has left X^1's hands, both go in for the rebound. D^1 keeps her position between X^1 and the basket. D^1 goes to the end of the defender's line, X^1 to the end of the offensive line.

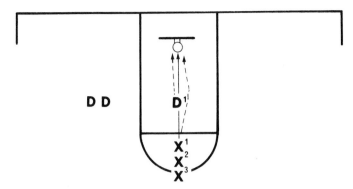

FIG. 4–46. Individual defense against the rebound, squad practice.

INDIVIDUAL DEFENSE AGAINST THE DRIBBLE

BODY MECHANICS

The defender keeps her position between the dribbler and the basket by slides. The inside hand snaps at the ball. The body is better balanced if the inside hand is used to flick at the ball.

The defender moves parallel with the opponent in the same direction. An attempt should be made to force the dribbler to the side line without blocking.

During the dribble, the defender should be 3 or 4 feet from the offensive player. As the last bounce is taken, the defender should close the gap to about 1 to 3 feet, depending upon the distance from the basket.

COACHING SUGGESTIONS

Avoid coming in head on as this will usually result in a blocking foul against the defender.

Avoid bodily contact in attempting to divert or tie up the ball.

Breaking up the dribble is not a primary consideration. Position of the body and hands come first.

Avoid standing still. Retreat if necessary to be in position for the pass or shot that must follow the dribble. A dribble is dangerous only if the defender has allowed the offensive player to get between her and the basket.

SQUAD PRACTICE

Double Relay Formation (Fig. 4–47). X¹ dribbles straight ahead. X² moves parallel with her to get ahead of her without crossing in front or impeding her progress. X² should assume a defensive position and slide ahead of X¹. Each goes to the end of the opposite line when the play is completed. Line 1 dribbles, and line 2 plays the defensive position. Change duties and methods of defending.

CHAPTER 4.   BASKETBALL

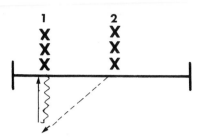

FIG. 4–47. Individual defense against the dribble, squad practice.

GENERAL COACHING SUGGESTIONS FOR INDIVIDUAL DEFENSE

Master all the elements of individual guarding tactics, particularly footwork and hand positions. All players should learn aggressive defending.

Take defensive positions at least 3 feet away from the offensive player except when a short or medium shot is being attempted. This position makes it easier to anticipate a pivot or to intercept a pass.

Take small steps and slides to keep the weight well under control.

On a tie ball in defense territory, tip the ball toward the side lines rather than toward the goal.

Shift quickly to offense when a teammate has possession of the ball.

Pass toward the side lines when the offensive has been gained near the opponents' basket or on a rebound.

OFFENSE TACTICS

A team is on the offensive whenever any member of the team is in possession of the ball. The climax to the offense is a successful field goal. The pass, the dribble, the pivot and other tactics are all basic skills of individual and team offense as well as shooting.

Every player on the team is important to the offense. Players stationed in the back court are an essential part of the offense, particularly on the fast break.

"LOSING" THE OPPONENT

BODY MECHANICS

Starting Position. Keep knees easy, weight on the balls of the feet, one foot forward.

The arms should be relaxed and close to the body.

From the starting position get underway fast. Speed and deception will help to lose the opponent.

CHAPTER 4. BASKETBALL

When near the center line, face in or out to be in position to start for the basket with a quick pivot or feint.

Footwork. The clever offense player must master the following tactics to enable her to evade a defense player:

1. Change of pace.
2. Dodging and change of direction.
3. Reverse turn.
4. All pivots.
5. Faking.

GETTING INTO THE SCORING AREA

Cutting is the most effective individual offensive tactic in getting into a good scoring position. An offensive player can often fake in the direction of the side line, then cut sharply to the basket on the inside of the defender to receive a pass. A change of pace or direction often gives the offensive player the single advantage she needs. The cutter should start her drive after the passer has control of the ball. If the cut is too early, the cutter should drift to the side line, then return to position for another attempt.

Screening is an offensive maneuver that legally prevents a defender from following too closely. It is basic to offensive team play. The offensive player, taking advantage of a screen by her teammate, needs a good set shot. The screen will provide the necessary protection.

The various types of screen plays are described in the section on team offense.

REBOUND PLAY

LONG SHOTS

The rebound player may remain back a few feet to determine the direction of the ball, then run to a spot to recover it. The long shot normally has sufficient force to rebound farther from the basket than the short shot.

A tall player may stand near the basket and jump high to retrieve the ball.

The important element in rebound play is timing. Players should practice tossing the ball against the backboard to study the angles of rebound.

WHEN REBOUND IS CONTROLLED

The offensive player who controls or who regains the ball may:

1. Try to tap the ball toward the basket.
2. Tip the ball back to another offensive player.
3. Catch the ball and shoot or dribble away to begin a new attack.

In general, the offensive player who shoots should not follow for a rebound when:

1. She is shooting parallel with the end lines.
2. She is moving away from the basket.
3. Her shot will carry her off the floor.

GENERAL COACHING SUGGESTIONS FOR INDIVIDUAL OFFENSE PLAY

Learn to shoot quickly and easily with one or both hands.

Avoid the common foul of charging, *i.e.*, moving into a defensive player whose course or position is established.

Avoid long passes. Short passes should be the basis of the attack.

Know when to dribble. The most useful situations for dribbling are:

When teammates are closely guarded.

When the space in front is clear.

When the ball can be moved into an area for a close-in shot.

(A pass is a chance to lose the ball by an interception by an opponent.)

Know when to fake or pivot, then dribble. Situations in which a pivot should precede the bounce are:

When guarded from the front.

When the defense player is moving toward the player with the ball.

All players should learn to shift quickly from defense to offense.

Passes should be taken on the run. A player should not pass to a stationary teammate or to one off balance.

Adjust the speed of a pass to the speed of a teammate and to her position.

SECTION III: TEAM TACTICS

DEFENSE BY TEAM

There are many types of team defense which may be used, all of which are derived from a man-to-man system, a zone system, or a combination of the two.

MAN-TO-MAN (PLAYER-TO-PLAYER) DEFENSE

The man-to-man defense is both the easiest and the hardest defense to maintain. The basic assignment for the defensive player is simpler in the man-to-man than in the zone. Each defensive player is assigned an offensive player whom she must guard as closely as possible when her team does not have the ball. But to do this effectively requires speed, quick reflexes, endurance and a thorough mastery of the individual defensive tactics, and the ability to anticipate the play of the opponent.

As far as the team is concerned, players should guard those equal to them in ability, thus reducing inequalities in height and skill which may work against the defending team. Players should assist their teammates by telling them when they are about to be the victims of a screen play. Shouting "screen left" or "screen right" can often defeat this elementary offensive tactic.

The main advantage of the man-to-man defense is that it hinders the passing of the offensive team to a greater extent than the zone. The defender should play her opponent "loosely" until the last bounce of a dribble. Then she should close in with her arms extended in order to obstruct the pass or shot which must follow. Care must be taken that the player in possession of the ball is not fouled. It is the likelihood of blocking or personal contact resulting in a foul which makes the man-to-man defense so exacting and difficult for the unskilled player.

In addition to hampering a passing attack, the man-to-man defense has several other advantages. It defines clearly each player's responsibility and makes her more dependent on the player she is guarding than on the overall movement of players on the floor (though this may not be ignored). Also, the man-to-man defense allows each player to develop a sense of motivation and pride, since she alone is responsible for the play of her opponent. (The zone defense offers the opportunity for each defender to place the blame on a teammate when there is a score.) Finally, the man-to-man defense is more flexible than the zone, adapting more readily to the particular physical and strategic peculiarities of the opposing team.

The man-to-man defense is also demanding. In addition to the care which must be taken to avoid fouling, the defender must be quick to realize when to switch as the result of a screen and when not to. If a switch will result in extreme inequalities of height or ability, it should be avoided if at all possible.

BODY MECHANICS

The general principles of man-to-man team play are:

Maintain a balanced crouch position. The outside hand, the one nearer the side lines, should be kept low and back, while the other hand should be raised high and forward.

Play the ball carrier and potential pass receiver "tight." Break up the pass play. Use constant pressure to force bad passes and prevent good shots.

Never turn the back on the ball. Use side vision to keep eyes on both opponent and ball. If the opponent slips behind the defender she may reach back and feel lightly to make certain of her position. (Some referees may call a foul for this, despite the explicit statement in the

CHAPTER 4. BASKETBALL

rules that personal contact should not be penalized unless roughness has resulted.) Persistent contact must be avoided.

Play those not close to the ball "loosely." The best position places the defender where she is between the basket and her opponent and in a good position to steal passes.

PICK-UP DEFENSE

A less formal variation of the man-to-man defense is the pick-up defense. The individual tactics are the same, but players are not assigned specific players to guard. They take the player nearest them when the ball is brought down court. The disadvantages of this defense are that it may result in costly confusion, and it prevents the defense player from learning to guard any one player skillfully.

ZONE DEFENSE

The basic principle in zone defense is the opposite of that used in the man-to-man. Rather than being assigned a specific player to guard, a defender is given a specific area for which she is responsible. This defense requires a keen sense of team play in order to succeed. The defender must anticipate not what any one player may do but what the entire opposing team may do. The defender must know at all times the situation on the entire court and be able to move intelligently in relation to the ball, the basket and offensive players in her zone.

The zone defense operates on the principle that a player is not dangerous unless she is in the scoring area. Therefore, it concentrates on that area. This defense is most effective against a driving, dribbling attack, since it allows the defenders to group or "collapse" around the ball carrier. Unfortunately, the dribbling attack is not often used in girls' basketball when number of bounces is limited. On the other hand, the zone is strengthened by the inability of most girls to shoot accurately from outside the area which the zone protects.

The defensive players may be stationed at any position on the court as the needs of the team require. However, the four defenses described below are among the simplest and strongest versions of the zone defense.

BOX ZONE DEFENSE

This is probably the easiest of the zone defenses to learn, and it is one of the most effective. The four players are stationed symmetrically beside the key—two close to the basket and two near the free-throw line (Fig. 4–48). This distributes the players fairly evenly over the critical playing area. Shifting to the strong side of the court is not difficult in this formation, as the simple box formation is maintained (Fig. 4–49).

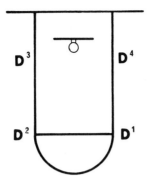

FIG. 4–48. Box zone defense.

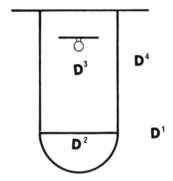

FIG. 4–49. Box zone defense, shift to strong side.

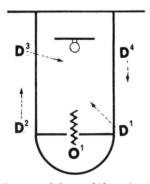

FIG. 4–50. Box zone defense, shift against center drive.

While this formation provides a good defense against the team which shoots from the outside, it is vulnerable to an attack down the middle (Fig. 4–50). In this case, D^1 (or D^2) moves to cover the dribbler while D^2 (or D^1) moves parallel to the dribbler to intercept a possible pass. D^4 moves directly in front of the dribbler, while D^3 moves to intercept a possible pass. At no time should both D^1 and D^2 or both D^3 and D^4

CHAPTER 4. BASKETBALL

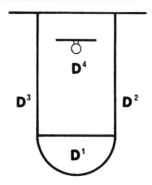

FIG. 4–51. Diamond zone defense.

move to cover the ball handler. This will result in dangerous holes in the defense, allowing the dribbler to pass off to a teammate in a position to shoot.

DIAMOND ZONE DEFENSE

The diamond zone places one player at the head of the key, one under the basket, and one on each side of the lane (Fig. 4–51). It is a strong defense against drives down the lane, but it is vulnerable on each side of the basket near the end line. The shift to the strong side of the court is complicated and must be practiced slowly at first (Fig. 4–52).

Generally, the tallest player will take the D^4 position. The fastest and most agile player will take the D^1 position and attempt to steal passes.

TRIANGLE AND ONE DEFENSE

In the event that the opposing team possesses one outstanding player, a modified zone should be employed. This defense places two

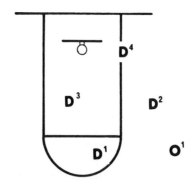

FIG. 4–52. Diamond zone, shift to strong side.

CHAPTER 4.   BASKETBALL

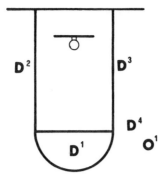

FIG. 4–53.   Triangle and one zone defense.

players on each side of the lane under the basket and the third at the head of the key. The fourth, D^4, is presumably the best defensive player on the team and is assigned to guard the outstanding opponent on a man-to-man basis (Fig. 4–53).

The three zone players will shift less in response to O^1 and more in relation to the three remaining offensive players.

CENTER-POST ZONE DEFENSE

This formation is for use by teams with a tall, skillful defensive player. It keeps her near the basket most of the time. It is also useful against a team whose strategy is to shoot from close to the basket, or a team with strong players under the basket.

One player is located at the head of the key while the other three remain close under the basket (Fig. 4–54). D^4 is the tallest player. On the shift to the strong side of the court, D^2 moves up to the free-throw line and D^1 moves toward the ball. D^4 shifts very little (Fig. 4–55). When the ball is in the middle of the court, D^4 moves up in the lane to cover the space in front of the basket (Fig. 4–56).

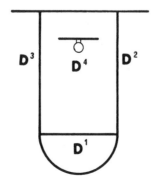

FIG. 4–54.   Center-post zone defense.

CHAPTER 4.   BASKETBALL

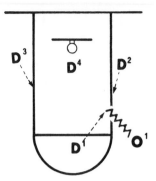

FIG. 4–55. Center-post zone defense, shift to strong side.

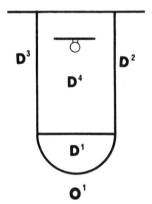

FIG. 4–56. Center-post zone defense, shift against center drive.

General Coaching Suggestions for Zone Defense

Put two players on the player in possession whenever possible. Those defenders not involved in "doubling up" must fall off and protect the areas most susceptible to attack.

Attempt to steal the ball from the player in possession. If that is not possible, attempt to tie up the ball to create a held-ball situation.

Keep the ball toward the side lines. Force the offensive player into a bad pass or shot position.

Learn to anticipate offensive plays and to move quickly.

TEAM OFFENSE

The objective of all offensive play is to work the ball into position for a good shot. This is true against both the man-to-man and the zone defenses. The methods used to work the ball into an advantageous position against the man-to-man defense are quite different from those used against the zone defense.

CHAPTER 4. BASKETBALL

FIG. 4–57. A screen.

STRATEGY AGAINST A MAN-TO-MAN DEFENSE

The purpose of the man-to-man defense is to keep each offensive player covered by a defender. Therefore, the best offensive strategy is the one which separates the offensive player from the opponent whose duty it is to guard her. This is achieved most successfully by a "screen." The simplest form of a screen play is one in which the player in possession of the ball uses a teammate to obstruct the path of her defender, thus freeing her for a shot or a pass (Fig. 4–57).

OUTSIDE SCREEN

This is the simplest screen play (Fig. 4–58). O¹ passes to O² and then comes around the outside of O² for a hand-off. D¹ is either blocked by

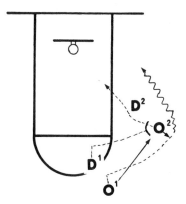

FIG. 4–58. Outside screen.

CHAPTER 4. BASKETBALL

O² or must take costly steps to go around her. *After* D¹ has been screened, O² moves toward the lane to take a possible pass from O¹. (NOTE: O² must wait until D¹ has been screened before moving toward the lane. A foul may be called if the screener is in motion when contact occurs.)

INSIDE SCREEN

This effective play starts with a pass from O¹ to O². O¹ then places herself close to D², obstructing her attempt to follow O², who has the ball (Fig. 4–59). O² must be careful to move toward the lane at the proper instant. If she moves too soon, the screen will not have been set and D² will discover the screen and move around it.

Once O² has taken advantage of the screen, O¹ has the option of driving toward the basket and receiving a pass from O². This is called a cutaway screen (Fig. 4–60). In this case, the defense will probably switch, with D¹ moving to cover O² and D² to O¹.

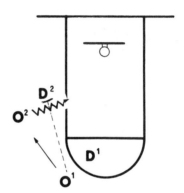

FIG. 4–59. Inside screen.

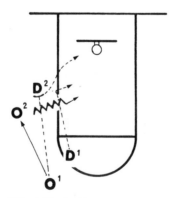

FIG. 4–60. Inside screen, cutaway.

CHAPTER 4.   BASKETBALL

This maneuver employs the basic principles of the previous screen plays, but it involves three players instead of two. O^1 passes to O^3 and then sets a screen on the defender of O^2. O^2 breaks toward the basket, passing on the inside of O^3 and receiving the ball from O^3 (Fig. 4–61). This play may be reversed, with O^2 passing to O^3 and then setting an outside screen for O^1, who breaks past O^3 toward the basket. In either case, if D^3 tends to switch and leave the post player clear, she should fake a pass to O^2 (or O^1) and then go for the basket herself.

SPLITTING THE POST

This play is designed to create an easy lay-up situation. O^1 runs to a high post position at the free-throw line. O^3 passes to O^1, and O^2 comes by immediately for a hand-off and a lay-up (Fig. 4–62).

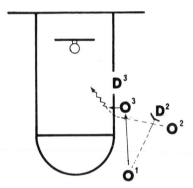

FIG. 4–61. Triangle cut.

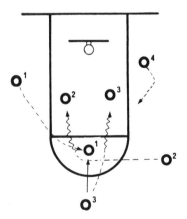

FIG. 4–62. Splitting the post.

CHAPTER 4.   BASKETBALL

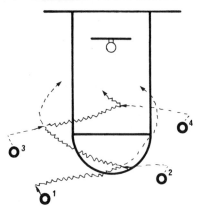

FIG. 4–63. Four-man weave offense.

The post player has the option of handing off to either O² or O³, or of keeping the ball and moving in for a shot.

For correct timing, O² *must* pass the post position ahead of O³.

FOUR-MAN WEAVE OFFENSE

The entire team participates in this series of moving screens designed to move the ball toward the basket for an easy shot (Fig. 4–63). O¹ dribbles to her right and hands off on the outside to O². O² dribbles back to the left toward the basket, handing off on the outside to O³. O³ does the same for O⁴, who does the same for O², *etc*. This is a difficult maneuver and should be practiced first without any motion toward the basket. The responsiblity for correct timing rests with the person receiving the pass.

The play does not have to be carried under to the basket to be successful. Any player who is free after receiving a hand-off should shoot.

General Coaching Suggestions for
Man-to-Man Offense

Always look for the opportunity to free a teammate by screening her defender.

Employ a fake whenever possible. A rapid change of direction will make the defender commit herself and facilitate dribbling or passing around her.

Keep the plays simple. Make one play follow another. Do not waste time "setting up" for the next play.

Use your teammates as screens. Handling the ball as an individual greatly simplifies the job of the defender.

Act quickly to take advantage of a screen. Delay will allow the defender to cover her player despite the screen.

The underlying purpose of the zone defense is to cover the crucial playing area with an even distribution of players. Therefore, it must be the objective of the offense to upset this even distribution, either by overloading or by deception, in order to clear a player for a good shot. Playing against a zone defense requires more of a sense of team playing than does the screen strategy used against a man-to-man defense. The players must act together, rather than waiting for one another to set a screen.

The purpose of overloading is to put more offensive than defensive players in an area, thus preventing the defense from covering every player. The purpose of deception against the zone is to allow the player in possession of the ball to draw two or more defensive players toward her, thus freeing her teammates for a shot. These tactics may be used in various methods against the four basic types of zone defense discussed earlier.

OFFENSE AGAINST THE BOX ZONE DEFENSE

The box zone may be attacked in two ways, both of which exploit the box zone's weakness down the lane.

Deception. This strategy calls for O^1 to drive toward the basket with the ball. O^1 receives a pass from O^2 at the free-throw line, then dribbles toward the basket. As she approaches the basket, O^1 may either shoot or, if either D^3 or D^4 have moved to guard her, pass to O^3 or O^4 in the clear (Fig. 4–64).

This play calls for a quick decision on the part of O^1, who must accurately decide whether she should shoot or pass to a teammate in a better position.

Overloading. O^1 passes to O^2 and takes a position close to O^4. At the same time, O^4 runs to the far side of the basket, overloading the area of D^3 (Fig. 4–65). O^2 may now shoot, dribble or pass to any of her three teammates.

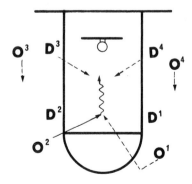

FIG. 4–64.   Deception against box zone defense.

CHAPTER 4.   BASKETBALL

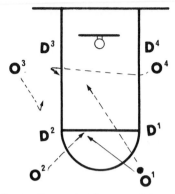

FIG. 4-65.   Overloading against box zone defense, first method.

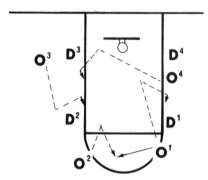

FIG. 4-66.   Overloading against box zone defense, second method.

All movements in this play must be executed quickly and simultaneously in order to take the defense by surprise. Delay will allow the defenders to cover adequately the overloaded area.

Another method of overloading the box zone is to place O^1 and O^4 on the opposite sides of the key (Fig. 4-66). If done quickly enough, this maneuver will certainly place one offensive player in the clear for a pass from O^2 and a shot.

OFFENSE AGAINST THE DIAMOND ZONE DEFENSE

The weakness of the diamond defense along the end line under the basket should be exploited.

Deception.   This play is similar to the deception used against the box zone defense, except that in this instance O^1, the player driving for the basket, approaches from the side of the key rather than down the lane. As she nears the basket, she will have the option of shooting or passing to O^3 or O^4, who will be clear if O^1 has properly decoyed D^2 and D^3 (Fig. 4-67).

CHAPTER 4.   BASKETBALL

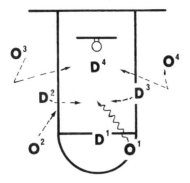

FIG. 4–67. Deception against diamond zone defense.

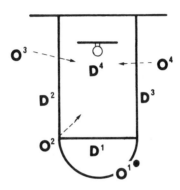

FIG. 4–68. Overloading against diamond zone defense.

Overloading. O³ and O⁴ should run near the basket, looking for a pass from O¹. O² should go to the middle of the lane below the free-throw lane (Fig. 4–68).

O², O³ and O⁴ should be careful not to come too close together. They can be easily defended against when bunched.

OFFENSE AGAINST THE TRIANGLE AND ONE
ZONE DEFENSE (OVERLOADING)

O⁴ takes a middle post position while O² and O³ go to the center of the lane. All three may take passes from O¹ (Fig. 4–69).

Note that O¹ is being played man-to-man and may need a screen by O⁴ if she has trouble getting the pass away. Once again, O², O³ and O⁴ must avoid being too close together. Otherwise, they will be easily guarded.

The spread-out nature of the defense and the presence of D⁴ playing man-to-man make a deception attack less valuable against the triangle and one than against the box or the diamond.

CHAPTER 4. BASKETBALL

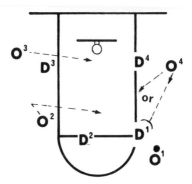

FIG. 4–69. Overloading against a triangle and one zone defense.

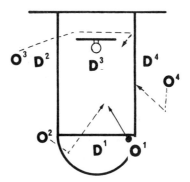

FIG. 4–70. Attacking the center-post zone defense.

OFFENSE AGAINST THE CENTER-POST ZONE DEFENSE

O⁴ runs to a middle post position while O² moves to the center of the lane and O³ goes under the basket (Fig. 4–70). O² or O⁴ receive the pass from O¹ and may either shoot or pass to O³ if they are being closely guarded.

This play involves both overloading and deception. The players overload the right side of the court, but they also have the shoot-pass option to O³.

Because she has farther to go than her teammates, O³ should be the first player to move. O² and O⁴ should not reach their positions until O³ is underneath the basket.

GENERAL COACHING SUGGESTIONS FOR OFFENSE AGAINST ZONE DEFENSES

The principles of the zone offense are:

1. Proper timing. All players must reach their designated positions together, otherwise the defense will be able to adjust.

CHAPTER 4. BASKETBALL

2. Proper execution of the shoot-pass option on the deception plays. The player in possession of the ball must be able to judge whether the defense has collapsed sufficiently upon her to free her teammates for a shot.

3. Rapid moves. Passes, shots and changes of position must be executed as fast as possible before the defense has a chance to adjust to the new situation. A player who must stand and wait for a pass will have lost the advantage of deception or overloading.

4. Knowledge of the weakness of the defense. Players that tend to group around the ball handler are vulnerable to deception plays. Players that tend to play the position rather than the ball are vulnerable to overloading plays.

SPECIAL SITUATION OFFENSES

OUT-OF-BOUNDS PLAYS

From under Opponents' Basket. Normally, there will be little difficulty putting the ball in play from under the opponents' basket. However, in the case of a full court press, the offensive team should retain four players in the back court, one of whom will put the ball in play. The tactics employed to put the ball in play may be the same as those discussed in the following paragraphs, the only difference being that the offensive team should pass frequently once it has received the ball in order to move the ball into its own court.

From under One's Own Basket. Putting the ball in play under one's own basket should be designed to score points. The play in Figure 4–71 begins with a slap on the ball by O^1. This sends O^4 to her right for a pass after a fake left. O^4 then passes to O^2 (for whom O^3 has provided a screen) for a shot. O^2 must be careful not to reach her position before O^4 is prepared to pass to her. Otherwise, she will be covered by D^2 or D^3.

A similar play calls for O^4 to move to her right and O^3 to back up

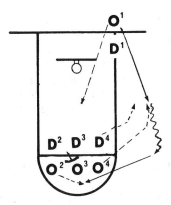

FIG. 4–71. Out of bounds under one's own basket, first example.

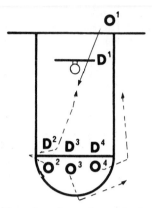

FIG. 4–72. Out of bounds under one's own basket, second example.

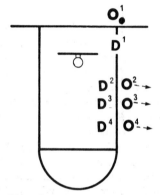

FIG. 4–73. Out of bounds under one's own basket, third example.

when the ball is slapped. O^2 fakes to her left and then drives for the basket (Fig. 4–72).

If the defense is especially strong against out-of-bounds plays, then the three players may line up parallel to the side lines and to one side of the basket (Fig. 4–73). A quick move to the right as the ball is slapped will free one of them for the in-bounds pass.

To be consistently effective, these plays should be interchanged and used from both sides of the basket. If, for example, in Figure 4–72, D^2 anticipates the fake by O^2, then O^2 should drive directly around the outside of D^2 on the next play.

SPECIAL DRILLS FOR OFFENSE AND DEFENSE

Defensive Formation Drill (Fig. 4–74). Three squads each stand in diamond zone formation, the points toward the center. The leader,

CHAPTER 4. BASKETBALL

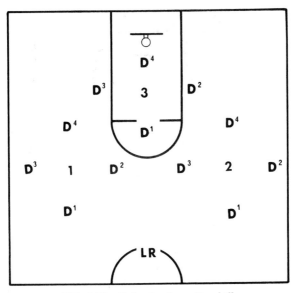

FIG. 4–74. Defensive formation drill.

LR, stands in the center of the court facing the formations. All players assume the defensive stance.

1. On signal "Forward," raise right hand, left hand down at side, and slide or hop forward. On signal "Back," retreat backward, hands at sides.

2. On signal "Right," raise right hand, left hand down at side, and slide to the right.

3. On signal "Left," raise left hand, right hand down at side, and slide to the left.

The leader should signal "Stop" after each maneuver and change direction frequently.

Hand-off Drill (Fig. 4–75). Players move in pairs. Four or five squads can start from the same end line. O^1 has the ball. O^1 starts with a dribble several steps ahead of O^2. At the end of her dribble, O^1 pivots and hands the ball to O^2 who has caught up with her. O^2 dribbles, pivots and hands the ball to O^1. Continue the length of the court. The player receiving the hand-off should always start a step or so after her partner.

Pass-and-Run Offensive Drill (Fig. 4–76). Use squads of three or more in each corner of a half court. X^1 and X^3 start passes in clockwise direction. As soon as each player receives the ball, she passes to the head of the next line, then runs to the end of the same line. Players should move rapidly up in the line when the pass and run has been executed by the player at the top. Shorten the sides of the square for inexperienced players.

Advanced players may use the same drill with four balls, one at the head of each line. The pass-and-go situation should be continuous.

CHAPTER 4. BASKETBALL

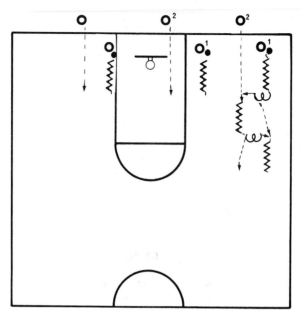

FIG. 4–75.   Hand-off drill.

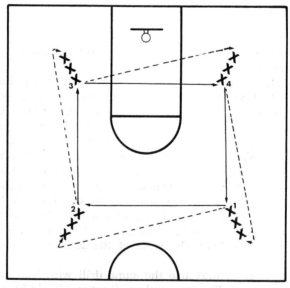

FIG. 4–76.   Pass and run offensive drill.

CHAPTER 4.   BASKETBALL

DEFENSE

In general, height in at least two players is an advantage, provided they are able to move quickly. At least one tall defensive player is needed to handle rebounds and to guard the post player. A short defender with speedy footwork is better than a tall, slow one, as she can often move quickly enough to intercept passes before the ball reaches the intended receiver.

Defensive players must have endurance and determination in covering an opponent.

Defensive players should be steady and reliable at all times. Any slip-up in play by one defender means a shot at the basket for an opponent.

While the chief function of the defensive players in their own back court is to prevent the opponents from scoring, they must be able to change to the offense and to get the ball across the center line to their own front court.

OFFENSE

Height is not essential to the offense except in the post position. A tall player who can shoot is always a threat.

Clever footwork by the offensive players is more important than height in getting into scoring position. Speed and aggressiveness are important to the offense.

Consistent shooting is a requirement for a successful team. All players should practice shooting as often as any other basketball fundamentals, even though some players may stay fairly regularly in a team's back court and not rove.

Offensive players must be able to shoot quickly while moving rather than taking time for a set shot.

All players should understand the use of the screen play.

All players should consider themselves offensive or defensive in terms of possession of the ball rather than as a position.

Offensive players must learn to fake their opponents out of position, then cut quickly for the basket.

Offensive players must be able to get away from their opponents and to keep as free as possible.

Offensive players must learn to take advantage of all openings, getting there at the exact instant to receive a pass.

When awarded the ball out of bounds, offensive players should get going rapidly to prevent the defense from getting set.

WHEN TAKEN	REGULATIONS	WHAT HAPPENS IF REGULATIONS NOT FULFILLED
	Jump Ball (Toss-up)	
	a. Time out taken by official.	
	b. Time in when ball tapped by one player.	
	c. Ball tossed between opponents.	Repeat
	d. Jumpers stay in own half of circle until ball is tapped	Out-of-bounds opponents
	e. Ball must be tapped after reaching highest point.	
	f. Must not be caught	
	g. Not tapped more than 2 times by one jumper	
	h. No replay by jumper until ball touches floor, basket, backboard or another player	
	i. Ball must be tapped by one jumper	Repeat
	j. Other players outside restraining circle until ball tapped	Out-of-bounds opponents or no penalty
1. After tie ball 2. After double violation 3. After opponents send ball out of bounds 4. Question as to who sent ball out of bounds 5. At the beginning of each quarter 6. After last free throw following double foul 7. Beginning of each extra period in tie game 8. Ball touches official on court 9. After time out with no player in possession of ball 10. When ball lodges in supports of basket except on free throw	k. Taken in center of nearest restraining circle, between players involved, except in case of injury or disqualification	Repeat
	a. Taken between opponents in center of middle restraining circle	Repeat
	b. Taken between opponents in center of nearest restraining circle	Repeat

CHAPTER 4. BASKETBALL

WHEN TAKEN	REGULATIONS	WHAT HAPPENS IF REGULATIONS NOT FULFILLED
	Free Throw	
	a. Time out taken	Goal shall not count, opponents out of bounds. If violation on first of 2 free throws, penalty follows second
	b. Must shoot within 10 seconds of receiving ball	
	c. Must not touch floor on or beyond free-throw line	
	d. Forward fouled must take own free throw unless injured or disqualified	Goal counts unless error found before ball put in play. Out-of-bounds opponents. If found in time, goal does not count; out-of-bounds opponents

1. Individual fouls with personal contact: blocking, charging, holding, pushing, tripping, personal contact in guarding, obstructing, tagging, unnecessary roughness	a. Free throw for opponents. Made or missed ball put in play from out of bounds by forward taking free throw
2. Threatening eyes of opponent in possession of the ball.	b. Against player in act of shooting. Goal made counts, 1 free throw awarded. Goal missed, 2 free throws
3. Delaying the game by: failing to jump when ordered to, failing to keep 3 feet from out-of-bounds play, failing to report change of number, delaying game in any unnecessary way	c. Against forward before shooting, goal made does not count, 1 free throw for forward
4. Unsportsmanlike conduct (May be a disqualifying foul)	d. Against teammate of forward in act of shooting, goal counts and made or missed 1 free throw for team fouled
	e. By forward in act of shooting goal does not count, 1 free throw opponents
	f. By teammate of forward in act of shooting, goal does not count, 1 free throw opponents

CHAPTER 4.   BASKETBALL

WHEN TAKEN	REGULATIONS	WHAT HAPPENS IF REGULATIONS NOT FULFILLED
	Free Throw (Continued)	
5. Opponent interfering with ball or forward during free throw	Goal counts if made, 1 free throw awarded. If goal missed, 2 free throws	
6. Team fouls of: failing to provide scorers with names and numbers of players at least 2 minutes before playing time, more than 5 time outs, entering game after disqualification, coach or spectator on court without permission, coach or spectator showing disrespect for officials or players, coaching from side lines	Free throw made or missed, out of bounds for player shooting. Goal counts	
	Out of bounds (Throw-in)	
	a. Player with ball must stand at the correct spot outside boundary line	Repeat
	b. No other player closer than 3 feet to boundary line, if out of bounds is limited to less than 3 feet	
	c. Player with ball may not touch any part of boundary line	Out-of-bounds opponents
	d. May not hold ball more than 5 seconds	

CHAPTER 4.   BASKETBALL

WHEN TAKEN	REGULATIONS	WHAT HAPPENS IF REGULATIONS NOT FULFILLED
Out of bounds (Continued)		
1. Jump ball violations (see jump ball — toss up)		
2. Ball handling violations: handling the ball, intentionally kicking ball, striking ball with fist, traveling with ball, combining any bounce, juggle, limited dribble, holding ball more than 5 seconds on court		Out-of-bounds opponents at side line opposite spot where violation occurred
3. Division line violations: touching division line or touching floor beyond division line with any part of body		Out-of-bounds opponents at intersection of side line and division line. Double violation, jump ball center circle
4. Three second lane violation: player without the ball remaining in free-throw lane for more than 3 seconds when her team is in possession of the ball in opponent's court		Out-of-bounds opponents at side line opposite spot where violation occurred
5. Out-of-bounds violations: causing ball to go out of bounds, carrying ball in bounds from out of bounds, immediately replaying ball from out of bounds, holding ball more than 5 seconds, placing foot on wall while holding ball, leaving court and returning at a better place, touching boundary line while holding ball		Out-of-bounds opponents on boundary line opposite spot where violation occurred. Double violation, jump in nearest restraining circle

CHAPTER 4.   BASKETBALL

WHEN TAKEN	REGULATIONS	WHAT HAPPENS IF REGULATIONS NOT FULFILLED
Out of bounds (Continued)		
6. Field goal violations: Shooting for basket from out of bounds		Goal does not count — out-of-bounds opponents at side line
Throwing for own basket from back court		Goal does not count, shot recovered by teammate — out-of-bounds opponents
Interfering with ball or basket while ball is descending toward basket (goal tending)		Violation by defense: goal awarded to offensive team; defensive team puts ball in play. Violation by offense: goal does not count; defensive team puts ball in play.
7. Free-throw violations: Touching floor on or beyond free-throw line or restraining circle before ball has touched ring or backboard or has entered basket, holding ball more than 10 seconds on line for free throw, wrong player taking free throw, player extending her arms into an adjacent area		Violation by offensive player: goal does not count; defensive team puts ball in play. Violation by defensive player: goal counts if made; if missed, the throw is repeated; offensive team puts ball in play. Violation on first free throw, penalty awarded after second

CHAPTER 4.   BASKETBALL

Miscellaneous

1. Disqualification:
   a. Player disqualified after 5 fouls must leave game
   b. Player must leave game after single disqualifying foul

2. Defaulted game
   a. Taken when: A team fails to appear

       A team is not ready 15 minutes after game called

       A team is not ready to play within 1 minute at second half or after time out

       A team fails to play after instructed to do so by official

       A team fails to have 6 players ready to start and 5 to continue

       A coach or team follower refuses to heed official's instructions to leave gymnasium

   b. Score of defaulted game, 2–0, or the existing score if defaulting team is behind

3. Discontinued game
   a. Taken when: Spectators show unsportsmanlike conduct

       After 2 suspensions of not more than 5 minutes

   b. Score of discontinued game, 0–0

4. Time out, time in
   a. Time out is taken when: The ball is dead and the team in possession of the ball requests it for not more than 1 minute

       A foul is called

       A jump ball is called

       Substituting, 30 seconds per team

       Game is suspended

       Official requests it for any reason

   b. Time in is taken: On a jump ball as soon as the ball is tapped

       On throw-in when player on court touches ball

       On a missed free throw as the ball, which has touched the ring, touches a player on the court

CHAPTER 4. BASKETBALL

HOCKEY

SECTION I. INTRODUCTION

HISTORY

There is every reason to believe that hockey is of Greek origin, although the only evidences of that fact today are the figures of "hockey players" in old Greek friezes. Some writers prefer to consider "hurley," an old Irish game, the first reference to which is found in the will of the Irish king Cathair Mor in 148 A.D., as the forerunner of hockey. An early Scotch game known as "shinty" was in all probability the direct ancestor of the modern game. In London the same game was known as "hackie," while in Wales during the same period the game of "bandy" bore a close resemblance to the ancestor of hockey.

Early in the nineteenth century the regulations concerning the playing of the game of hockey began to appear in standardized form. To quote from the Reverend A. E. Bevan, an English writer of that period, "Hockey was played twenty to a side, with an Indian rubber ball, about the size of a cricket ball, but cut in angles all around, so that it should not bounce equally. Our weapons were light oak sticks, often weighted with lead to give greater driving power as a goal might be scored from anywhere in the field, the half circle not being in existence. There was no limit, to the best of my recollection, to the field of play, except as far as the goal line was concerned. Should a player come in on the wrong side (*i.e.*, the left side) as you were dribbling down, you were at liberty to hit him across the shins, and if one of your own players was following up closely, instead of shouldering the ball he could apply kindly but hurtful attentions in the same way."

In 1885 women took up the sport with the formation of teams in the women's colleges of Oxford and Cambridge. From that moment on, hockey has grown increasingly popular with women of all countries.

The first hockey in the United States was played in 1900 when an English team played a Staten Island team, which, incidentally, was composed of English players. The following year Miss Constance Applebee demonstrated the game at Harvard Summer School, and that fall found her teaching the ladies at Wellesley, Smith, Mt. Holyoke, Vassar, Radcliffe and Bryn Mawr the pleasures and difficulties of a game called hockey.

Club hockey, for players not in school, appeared the same year in Philadelphia, and shortly a well-established tournament was underway with four clubs participating in the league.

A few years later a group of Philadelphia players, with Miss Applebee at the helm, crossed to England to play hockey. In 1921 England sent its first team to the United States to coach and to play "even as far west as Madison, Wisconsin." The following year saw the formation of the United States Hockey Association. Under its leadership, hockey in the United States has developed rapidly and soundly. There are clubs and associations scattered all over the country; there are interclub, intercity, sectional, national and international tournaments under its guidance; there are umpiring conferences for the purpose of improving standards of officiating; there is technical material available to members and nonmembers; there are untold services which the U.S.F.H.A. performs to spread the story of hockey to the four corners of the country and beyond.

Hockey has taken great strides forward since the days when the rules stated that "no player shall wear hat-pins or sailor or other hard-brimmed hat." Players need no longer be concerned about that "one unforgivable sin of a skirt which dips at the back," nor is there any need for them to remember that "knickerbockers and not petticoats should be worn under the skirts." Hockey has kept abreast of the times both as to rules and as to costume, and its ever-increasing popularity proves that it is winning the place in the hearts of American women that English women have long accorded it.

An International Federation of Women's Hockey Associations was founded in 1927 with eight member countries. The 1963 Federation Conference was held at Goucher College, Towson, Maryland, under the auspices of the U.S.F.H.A. Teams from sixteen countries participated. At the present time, 27 countries are members of the I.F.W.H.A., another indication of the growth in popularity of the game called hockey.

EQUIPMENT AND ITS CARE

Personal Equipment. Each player should be provided with a pair of regulation hockey shoes. The cleated rubber soles of these shoes make it possible to grip firmly and are indispensable to running, stopping and starting. The proper type of shoe helps to prevent accidents caused by slipping. Shoes with leather or metal cleats are prohibited by rule.

Any suitable gymnasium costume will serve as a hockey costume.

102   The tunic is suggested as the most acceptable and comfortable type. It is also recommended that players have warm-up pants or ski pants for colder weather.

All players should be provided with shin guards and encouraged to wear them. More advanced players, particularly of school age, are prone to consider it sporting to take bumps on the shins and so decline to wear guards. As a protection both to the school and to the individual, all players should be required to wear them.

The goalkeeper should be provided with special chest protector, pads and shoes. She cannot be expected to face hard shots at the goal or to use her feet properly unless she is adequately protected for her position. Instep protectors are also strongly recommended. The goalkeeper should be particular about being warmly dressed but should avoid bulky clothes which might hamper her movement.

All players wearing glasses should be encouraged to play without them or to wear a glasses guard, shatterproof glasses or contact lenses.

Playing Equipment.   In choosing a stick a player should check for the following points:

1. The stick should have good balance, it should feel right to the player.

2. The grain of the wood should follow the curve of the head of the stick.

3. The toe of the stick should have rounded corners.

4. The handle of the stick should be springy and should have rubber inserts. A rubber grip over the handle is most satisfactory.

5. A player should be able to grip the stick comfortably. A stick with a handle too large for the player to grip easily causes the finger muscles to become cramped.

6. The stick should weigh between 18 and 20 ounces.

7. The stick should come approximately to the player's hip when held upright.

There are no "left-handed" sticks in hockey.

The ball for a match game should be a regulation one, made of cork and string with a stitched leather cover, and weighing between $5\frac{1}{2}$ and $5\frac{3}{4}$ ounces. Practice balls of the composition type are satisfactory for stickwork periods but with the exception of the Clingford ball should not be used in a game.

Care of Equipment.   A coat of floor wax or varnish will give the needed protection to the stick and will maintain resiliency in the wood.

If the stick should splinter, the rough edges should be taken off with sandpaper and the stick bound with tape. When a stick requires retaping, the old tape should be removed first so that the balance of the stick will not be upset by too much additional weight.

At the end of the playing season, the stick should be stored in a dry, cool place. The stick should be waxed before storing.

After being used, balls should be repainted so that they will be ready for use again when needed. If the balls were used on a muddy field they should be washed before painting. A quick-drying lacquer is suggested as a suitable paint. Care must be taken not to apply too heavy a coat or the lacquer will dry in bumps and the ball will lose its roundness.

It is suggested that match balls and practice balls be painted in different colors, especially if there is any possibility that players will mix them. White is required for match balls; practice balls can be painted orange or red.

Additional Equipment. Any group playing hockey should have at least one set of pinnies so that it is possible to have the teams on the field marked with distinguishing colors. If pinnies are numbered it will help in quickly spotting any player out of position. Such a device is also helpful to the teacher in the first few lessons before the names of the players have been learned. An additional aid is to have pinnies of one color for the forwards and another color for the backs.

A ball-drying rack is a useful piece of equipment. The rack, consisting of a board 1 inch thick and as large as necessary, is made by driving twopenny nails about ¼ inch into the board in 1-inch squares. The tops of the nails should be cut off after they have been driven into place. Each painted ball can then be placed on a 1-inch square of nails to dry.

A grip for holding balls while painting them saves many exasperating moments.

Such a grip is obtainable at sporting goods stores or can be made by turning a ¼-inch piece of wire in a vise, shaping it like a pair of tongs.

The Field. The field (Figs. 5–1 and 5–2) should be a rectangle 50 to 60 yards wide and 90 to 100 yards long.

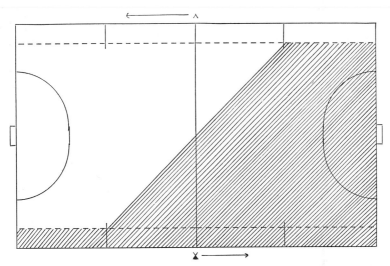

FIG. 5–1. As the umpires stand at the center line facing one another across the field, each is responsible for that half of the field to her right and for the entire alley on her side of the field.

CHAPTER 5.   HOCKEY

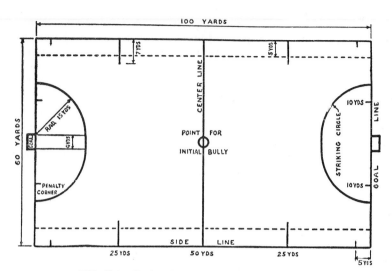

FIG. 5–2. Hockey field (Williams and Brownwell).

The surface should be turf, well trimmed and even. The field should be marked as in Figure 5–2. Most marking is done with a lime and water preparation which eats into the sod and makes it impossible to grow grass there again. Consequently the lines become ruts in the field. More satisfactory preparations, but more expensive ones, are a whitening or a prepared chalk and oil.

The field should be reseeded in the early spring and should be mowed frequently during the period of rapid growth. If the grass is allowed to grow long at the beginning of the spring season, by fall there will be knobby tufts all over the field, which even good rolling will fail to eliminate. Frequent spring rollings, especially after rains, are necessary.

In order to be certain that the field is laid out squarely, the following procedure can be used. From one corner of the field mark 3 yards along the goal line and 4 yards along the side line. If the field is square a line joining these two points will measure 5 yards.

OFFICIALS

There should be two umpires for each hockey game. One umpire cannot be expected to cover the entire field efficiently. Each umpire is responsible for the following:

1. Calling all fouls and imposing all penalties within her territory.
2. Calling all out of bounds in her territory.
3. Calling all goals in her half of the field.
4. Calling time out if necessary.
5. Cooperating with the other umpire to make the game run smoothly.

CHAPTER 5. HOCKEY

The umpire on the side of the field with the timers and scorers is responsible for recognizing substitutes and for blowing the whistle at half time and at the end of the game. Each umpire may start the center bully for one half of the game or may blow for the center bully after a goal has been scored in her half of the field.

Each umpire should follow play up and down the field in her section. She should travel from her own goal line to about the 25-yard line of the opposite goal. She should keep on a line with the moving ball or, better still, slightly ahead of the ball. She should keep off the field of play, except when scrimmage is close in front of the goal, when she should cut back of the goal line in order to get a clearer view. She should clearly indicate with arm signals the penalty which she imposes. She should see that all penalties are properly taken. The umpires should refrain from awarding any penalty if the offending team would gain advantage by stopping play for the penalty. "Whistle holding" is an important part of officiating.

An umpire should remember that she is there to guide the play and that to overofficiate a game is as serious in many ways as to underofficiate.

THE GAME

The game of hockey is played with 11 players on a team, 5 of whom are forward line players, 3 halfbacks, 2 fullbacks, and 1 goalkeeper. The game is played in half-time periods varying from 15 minutes to 30 minutes. The usual playing time for adult teams is 25-minute halves.

The game is started with a center bully, after which the ball is in play. The object of the game is to send the ball into the opponents' goal for a score. A field goal scores 1 point; a penalty goal scores 1 point.

SAFEGUARDS IN TEACHING OF HOCKEY

COMMON TYPES OF INJURIES

Injuries include:
Bruised shins from inadequate protection and careless playing.
Body injuries from the stick or ball, most frequently due to careless playing or inadequate training.
Sprained ankles or knees from playing on slippery ground when improperly equipped or from lack of training in the fundamentals of starting, stopping, changing direction.
Charley horse, torn muscle fibers or strained ligaments caused by the lack of a warm-up period before strenuous playing.
Colds, grippe, *etc.*, owing to lack of proper care after overheating.

Suggestions to the Teacher for Helping
to Prevent Injuries

Select proper playing equipment:
Provide an adequate supply of shin guards.
See that there are sticks of different weights and lengths.
Provide necessary special equipment for the goalkeeper, such as pads, shoes and chest protector.
Provide glasses guards where necessary.
Provide for care of equipment and field:
See that the sticks and shin guards are in good condition.
Arrange for adequate rolling, marking and raking of the field.
Check costume and personal equipment:
Be certain that shin guards and cleated shoes are worn.
Check personal costume as to suitability and warmth.
See that glasses guards are worn where necessary.
Encourage the wearing of a jacket between halves.
Be sure that the goalkeeper is warmly dressed.
Stress thorough knowledge of skills:
Teach the fundamentals of stick, body and ball control.
Review the fundamental rules of the hygiene of exercise.

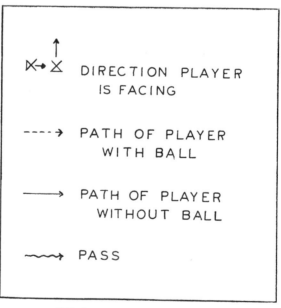

FIG. 5–3. Key to hockey diagrams.

CHAPTER 5. HOCKEY

THE DRIBBLE

BODY MECHANICS

Starting Position.   The stick should be ahead of and slightly to the right of the player. The top of the stick should be inclined forward and the blade of the stick should face forward.

The left hand should be at the top of the handle with the right hand 1 or 2 inches below it. Players with strong, supple wrists may prefer to have hands together at the top of the stick. This is not recommended for beginners. The thumbs of both hands should be toward the ground.

The left wrist should be well bent and should lead—the back of the left hand and the palm of the right hand should face in the direction of the hit. (This allows for good wrist action which is so essential in hockey technics.)

The left elbow should lead, should be held slightly away.

The trunk should be inclined slightly forward.

In a close dribble, the ball should be carried a little ahead of and outside of the right foot.

In a loose dribble, the ball should be carried more directly ahead of the right foot, at a distance varying from 1 to 3 feet.

Application of Force.   A series of sharp taps imparts momentum to the ball.

The hands work together, imparting momentum to the ball by means of flexible wrist action on the stick.

The ball should be hit from directly behind.

Follow Through.   There should be a very slight follow through of the stick in the direction of the tap.

USE

Used to carry the ball while running.

COACHING SUGGESTIONS

Use the wrists. Most of the power in the dribble comes from pliable wrists.

Look up. Look up before you pass or dodge. Locate your teammates, your opponents and yourself.

Keep the ball close. It is then under control and in position for a pass or dodge.

Keep the ball ahead of and outside of the right foot. This position is necessary in order to dribble in a straight line.

CHAPTER 5.   HOCKEY

Lead with the left elbow and left wrist. This will keep the ball to the right and prevent it from getting mixed up with the feet.

TEACHING PROGRESSION

1. Demonstrate and explain the dribble.
2. Dribble slowly in a *straight line* walking or running.
3. Dribble in a straight line running at full speed.
4. Dribble and pass—push, drive, flick or scoop.
5. Receive a pass from the right or left and dribble on.
6. Dribble, pass and receive.
7. Dribble in a circle.

SQUAD PRACTICE

Shuttle Formation (see Fig. 2–6). Columns are 30 feet apart. X^1 dribbles to X^2 opposite, leaves the ball and goes to the end of that column. X^2 dribbles to X^3 and so on. This can be used as a relay.

Shuttle Formation (see Fig. 2–6). Columns are 50 feet apart with a center mark 25 feet from the first player in each column. X^1 dribbles to the center mark and passes the ball to the opposite X^2, then goes to the end of that column. In the same way the ball is returned to X^3.

Single Column Formation (see Fig. 2–1). Players line up along any line, the side line, the striking circle or the end line. Dribble along this line one at a time.

Circle Formation (see Fig. 2–13). Six to eight players in a circle standing a little more than arm and stick distance apart. X^1 starts with the ball, dribbles clockwise around the outside of the circle and, when she returns to her place, passes to the player on her left, X^6. Use as a relay with circles of equal size.

Single Column Formation (see Fig. 2–1). Set up posts or any other obstacles in a column 5 feet apart. Players line up in column 10 feet from the first post. X^1 dribbles in and out between the posts and returns the ball to X^2. X^1 then goes to the end of the column.

Dribble and Pass. In twos, threes, fours and fives.

CARRYING POSITION

BODY MECHANICS

Starting Position. The left hand should be at the top of the handle, with the right hand no more than 2 inches below it.

The arms should be fairly straight, the left arm should be diagonally across the body toward the right.

The stick should be carried with the head toward the ground, hitting surface forward, in a position of readiness for use.

CHAPTER 5. HOCKEY

Used to carry the stick while running.

COACHING SUGGESTIONS

Let the stick swing naturally with the arms. If this is done, the stick will not impede the progress of the player. The stick should be a part of the player, not an extra appendage.

Carry the stick in a relaxed position until ready to use it.

Carry the stick with the head toward the ground. In this position it is quickly available for use, there is little danger of "sticks" when the stick is brought into position and no time is lost in bringing the stick to the ball.

Give some practice in running while carrying the stick.

Give some practice in bringing the stick into action from this position.

PASSING

THE PUSH PASS

BODY MECHANICS

Starting Position. The stick should be in front of the player and at approximately right angles to the ground. The top of the stick should be inclined forward in the direction of the pass, the hitting surface in contact with the ball.

The left hand should be at the top of the stick and the right hand 3 to 4 inches below it.

The back of the left hand and the palm of the right hand should face in the direction of the stroke.

The trunk should be inclined forward.

The right foot should be forward with the weight on it.

The ball should be ahead of and slightly outside of the right foot.

Application of Force. The stick should be placed behind the ball. There should be no backswing.

Momentum is imparted by pushing forward with the right hand, pulling back with the left hand and stepping into the stroke in the direction of the pass.

The feet should be in a forward stride position.

Follow Through. The stick should follow through in the direction of the pass.

USES

Used for passing and shooting.

Used when a quick accurate pass or shot is needed.

CHAPTER 5. HOCKEY

Used as a pass to the right in the triangular pass.

Used as a square or backward pass. (Position of ball in relation to feet should be changed accordingly. See chart, p. 139.)

Used to save time.

Used on a free hit.

COACHING SUGGESTIONS

Place the stick behind the ball; there is no backswing. This minimizes the time required to make the stroke.

Step into the stroke! The body weight is especially necessary behind this stroke because there is no backswing.

Use the wrists! Wrist action is important in that it adds force and gives direction to the stroke.

Keep the hands apart! This makes leverlike action of the stick possible.

For a pass to the right the ball should be outside of the right foot, the body twisted to the right, but the toes should be pointed straight ahead.

For a backward pass the ball should be behind the right foot and the body twisted well to the right, toes pointing ahead.

TEACHING PROGRESSION

1. Demonstrate and explain the push pass.
2. Push and field, using a straight-ahead push, then a right push.
3. Dribble and push straight ahead for accuracy and for distance.
4. Dribble and push to the right for accuracy and for distance.
5. Dribble and pass, using push pass.

SQUAD PRACTICE

Double Line Formation (see Fig. 2–9). Form facing lines, 15 to 20 feet apart. Push the ball back and forth, stopping it before returning it.

Single Column Formation (see Fig. 2–1) Dribble from 25-yard line, push into goal, recover own ball and go to the end of the column.

Single Column Formation (see Fig. 2–1). Columns stand side by side, 15 feet apart, facing in opposite directions so that the players are standing right shoulder to right shoulder. Practice the right push back and forth.

Single Column Formation (Fig. 5–4). Players line up 5 yards from and parallel to the goal line. Dribble and push toward the goal. To make for greater accuracy, decrease the space in the goal by putting an obstacle in the right half of it. Players recover own ball and go to the end of the column.

Column and Line Formation (Fig. 5–5). Players line up in three rows as indicated in the diagram. X^{1}s dribble until opposite X^{2}s, and then pass with a right push pass. X^{1}s run on straight ahead and come in

CHAPTER 5. HOCKEY

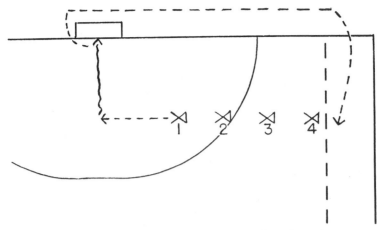

FIG. 5-4. Push pass, squad practice, single column formation.

behind X²s, who then dribble and push to X³s and come in behind that line. X³s dribble and push to X¹s.

THE DRIVE

BODY MECHANICS

Starting Position. The stick should be held in front of the player and at right angles to the ground, with the hitting surface toward the left foot.

The left hand should be at the top of the handle and the right hand directly below it.

The trunk should be inclined slightly forward.

The shoulders and toes should point forward to prevent obstruction.

The feet should be in an easy side stride position.

The ball should be in front of the body, somewhat nearer the left foot than the right and about 8 inches from the player.

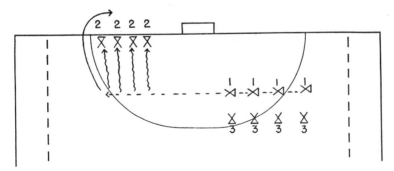

FIG. 5-5. Push pass, squad practice, column and line formation.

Application of Force. A quick backswing followed by a forward swing through the ball, hitting it from directly behind, imparts momentum to the ball. At the moment of contact the stick should be at right angles to the ground.

Both arms should be straight at contact and the wrists locked to prevent "sticks" in front.

A final snap of the wrists just before contact with the ball adds force to the stroke.

Follow Through. The body weight should be transferred into the stroke by shifting the weight forward to the left foot.

There should be a follow through of the stick in the direction of the drive. This should be checked below shoulder level.

USES

Used as a long hard pass or shot.
Used as a centering pass from the wing.
Used as a hard shot at goal.
Used as a long through pass by a back.
Used as a clearing pass from goal.
Used as a corner hit.
Used as a free hit.

COACHING SUGGESTIONS

Hands together at the top of the stick! This gives a longer lever and makes for a freer stroke.

Step into the stroke! This gets the body weight behind the ball and adds force to the stroke.

Keep the eye on the ball! Watch the ball until it is actually hit.

Keep the stick below the shoulder! To avoid "sticks" behind, bend the right elbow. To avoid "sticks" on the follow through, lock the wrists at the end of the stroke.

In a drive to the right, the right foot should be forward and the ball just *back of the heel.*

Keep the toes and shoulders pointing straight ahead to avoid obstruction.

TEACHING PROGRESSION

1. Demonstrate and explain the drive.
2. Drive for accuracy, then for accuracy and distance.
3. Dribble and drive for accuracy, then for accuracy and distance.
4. Drive to the right.
5. Field and control a ball moving toward you, change direction with a drive.

CHAPTER 5. HOCKEY

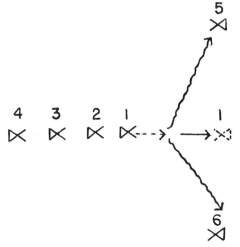

FIG. 5–6. Dribble and diagonal drive, single column formation.

SQUAD PRACTICE

Double Line Formation (see Fig. 2–9). With lines facing, 25 feet apart, drive back and forth, stopping the ball before returning it.

Single Column Formation (see Fig. 2–1). Drive from the edge of the striking circle at a target placed in the goal. Add a dribble before the drive. Dribble parallel to the goal line and drive right toward the goal. Dribble down the left alley and center with a right drive.

Single Column Formation (Fig. 5–6). Dribble and drive diagonally. X^5 and X^6 stand 20 feet apart and 40 feet beyond X^1. X^1 dribbles and drives either to X^5 or X^6 and then runs on through to start another column opposite to and facing the first one. Excellent passing practice.

Single Column Formation (see Fig. 2–1). There can be any number of players to a column. First player in each column should be at the edge of the striking circle, facing toward the goal. First player in each column dribbles and drives at goal, recovers her own ball, passes it back to the next player and goes to the end of the column.

THE SCOOP

BODY MECHANICS

Starting Position. The stick should be held well in front of the player at a sharp angle to the ground, the hitting surface facing upward.

The left hand should be at the top of the handle, the right hand well down the handle with the thumb on top.

The palm of the right hand should face upward.

The trunk should be inclined well forward.

CHAPTER 5. HOCKEY

The right foot should be forward with the weight on it.

The ball should be about 2 feet in front of and slightly to the right of the right foot.

Application of Force. The toe of the stick should be placed under the ball. There is no backswing.

Momentum is imparted by an upward and forward movement of the stick, pulling upward and forward with the right hand and pushing down with the left hand.

The top of the handle of the stick should be kept to the left of the body.

Follow Through. There should be a short, quickly checked follow through in the direction of the scoop.

The body weight should follow forward.

USES

Used as a dodge over an opponent's stick.

Used as a shot at goal.

Used on a heavy field when it is difficult to make the ball roll.

Used as a short pass.

Generally used in connection with the dribble.

COACHING SUGGESTIONS

Lay the blade of the stick well back before scooping. This must be done if the ball is to be lifted.

The scoop is most easily learned on a stationary ball or on a ball moving in the same direction as the player.

Raise the ball only slightly from the ground. A high scoop is a waste of time and is more easily intercepted than a low scoop.

Don't use the scoop excessively. The scoop is a slow stroke and easily anticipated.

Beginners tend to push forward too much on the scoop with the result that the ball rolls back over the stick.

Keep the follow through of the stick low.

Get well down behind the ball.

TEACHING PROGRESSION

1. Demonstrate and explain the scoop.
2. Scoop for accuracy from a stationary position.
3. Run up to a stationary ball and scoop.
4. Dribble and scoop.
5. Field, control and scoop a ball moving in the opposite direction.
6. Dodge an oncoming opponent using a scoop.
7. Dribble and dodge an opponent with a scoop.

CHAPTER 5. HOCKEY

Practice scooping at any stationary object.

Single Column Formation (see Fig. 2–1). Place balls 20 feet ahead of the first player in each column. X¹s run up to the ball, scoop it, pick it up in a dribble, reverse direction with a clockwise turn, leave the balls on the field and return to the end of the column.

Single Column Formation (see Fig. 2–1). Dribble and scoop. Each X¹ is in possession of a ball. Directly in front of and 25 feet away from X¹ in each column is an obstacle over which the player must scoop. X¹s dribble, scoop over the obstacle, reverse direction with a clockwise turn, scoop over the obstacle again, dribble back to X²s and go to the end of the column.

Relay with Leader Formation (see Fig. 2–2). Leader stands 20 feet in front of X¹. Leader rolls or hits ball to X¹. X¹ fields the ball, scoops it back to the leader and goes to the end of the column.

Shuttle Formation (see Fig. 2–7). X¹ dribbles the ball, X² comes forward to tackle. X¹ avoids the tackle with a scoop and dribbles on to X⁴, leaves the ball there and goes to the end of that column. X² goes to the end of the opposite column. X⁴ then dribbles, avoiding X³ as she tackles.

THE FLICK

BODY MECHANICS

Starting Position. The stick should be held approximately at right angles to the ground. The hitting surface should face forward away from the player.

The left hand should be at the top of the handle, the right hand well below it.

The back of the left hand and the palm of the right hand should face in the direction of the stroke.

The trunk should be inclined forward.

The right foot should be forward with the weight on it.

The ball should be slightly ahead of the player and outside of the right foot.

Application of Force. The stroke should be started as the push pass and followed immediately by a sudden turnover of the stick, imparting spin to the ball.

The hitting surface should turn from right to left toward the ground at the end of the stroke.

Follow Through. There should be a follow through of the stick in the direction of the pass.

The blade of the stick should be facing the ground at the end of the stroke. If less spin is to be imparted, the toe of the stick should point upward.

The body weight should be transferred into the stroke.

CHAPTER 5.   HOCKEY

Used as a pass.
Used as a shot at goal.

COACHING SUGGESTIONS

Let this stroke develop naturally from the push pass.
Emphasize the use of the wrists and the spin of the ball.
Be sure that the turnover comes as a part of the stroke and not as the follow through. If it comes as part of the follow through, the ball will not leave the ground.
Keep the follow through low.
Get the body weight behind the stroke. This is important since there is no backswing.

TEACHING PROGRESSION

1. Demonstrate and explain the flick.
2. Practice the flick from a stationary position.
3. Dribble and pass with a flick.
4. Dribble and shoot with a flick.
5. Dribble and avoid an oncoming opponent with a flick.

SQUAD PRACTICE

Couple Formation. Flick back and forth.

Circle Formation (see Fig. 2–13). Eight to ten players form a circle, stick and arm distance apart. Flick to any member of the circle, calling the name of the player for whom the pass is meant.

Single Column Formation (see Fig. 2–1). Columns line up outside the striking circle. Dribble and flick into goal. Start the players from various points along the striking circle in order to get different angles on the shot.

Double Column Formation (see Fig. 2–8). Dribble and flick to the nonstick side of a stationary opponent. Two columns, 20 feet apart. Squad leader 20 feet beyond the first player in each column. Each player in the left column with a ball. X^1 dribbles forward and flicks to her partner. The flick should be started well before reaching the position of the squad leader. Have the squad leader advance to tackle in order to make timing more difficult.

"Teacher and Class" Formation (see Fig. 2–5). Players line up 15 to 20 feet in front of the "teacher." Teacher flicks to X^1, who fields the ball and returns it with a flick. Players continue to flick back and forth until X^5 receives the ball. X^5 dribbles to the teacher's place. The teacher goes to the head of the line and play continues.

Couple Formation. (Fig. 5–7). Partners line up opposite a row of stakes set 10 feet apart as indicated. (Other obstacles can be used.)

CHAPTER 5. HOCKEY

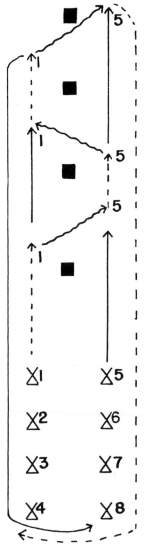

FIG. 5-7. Flick, squad practice, couple formation.

The first two players dribble and pass between the stakes with a flick and return to the end of the columns as the second couple starts.

GENERAL COACHING SUGGESTIONS ON PASSING

Look up before passing, but keep your eye on the ball as you hit it.
Pass diagonally ahead. Beginners tend to pass too straight.
Pass through spaces rather than directly to a player.

CHAPTER 5.   HOCKEY

Pass farther ahead to a player receiving from the left than to a player receiving from the right.

Use short quick passes wherever possible.

Pass so that the ball can be picked up on the run.

Do not run in the direction of your own pass.

Pass easily when near the goal you are attacking. This is especially important for halfbacks taking free hits in that territory.

Practice passing while running at top speed.

Practice passing to a player who is running at top speed.

Practice passing from any position for accuracy and for distance.

Pass toward the side line when the ball is near the goal you are defending.

Pass toward the center of the field when the ball is near the goal you are attacking.

After intercepting a pass, change the direction of your pass.

Avoid making the direction of the pass obvious.

A forward, as a rule, should not pass until she is about to be tackled. As in all rules there are exceptions. For example, a forward, having successfully tackled back, should get rid of the ball at once.

A back should get rid of the ball quickly after having gotten control of it. If a back keeps the ball too long her forwards will be marked and chances of getting a pass through to them will become less.

NOTE: All strokes as analyzed here started from the ideal position for that stroke. Such a position can well be used for teaching and analyzing the stroke. In actual playing, the ideal position is seldom reached before the stroke is made. Players differ as to their particular method of making any stroke, but unless this individual difference violates any of the mechanical or kinesiological principles underlying the stroke, such methods should not be changed.

GENERAL TEACHING PROGRESSION FOR PASSING

1. The dribble.
2. The push pass.
3. The drive.
4. The scoop.
5. The flick.

GENERAL SQUAD PRACTICE FOR PASSING

Dribble and Pass. In twos, threes, fours and fives, using a special pass or any kind of pass. Start the ball with the center player, with the player on the right, with the player on the left. Groups should move down the field in a line.

Single Line Formation (see Fig. 2-5). With five players in forward line formation, practice dribbling and passing against five defensive players.

Double Column Formation (Fig. 5-8). Formations and distances

CHAPTER 5. HOCKEY

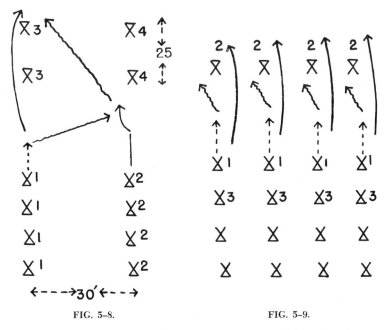

FIG. 5–8.   FIG. 5–9.

FIG. 5–8. Combined technics, squad practice, couple formation.
FIG. 5–9. Combined technics, squad practice, single line formation.

should be as indicated in the diagram. X^1 and X^2 are the forward line players. The first two forwards start down through the first two defense players. Second forward couple starts as the first couple goes on through the second defense set. Excellent practice for learning to pass to the nonstick side of an opponent and for passing before being tackled.

Single Line Formation (Fig. 5–9). Line X^1 should be 25 yards from line X^2, and line X^3 should be directly behind X^1. X^1s dribble the ball, and on signal pass to X^2s and run on beyond that line. X^2s dribble, pass to X^3s and go behind that line. Encourages players to keep close contact with the ball in order to be able to pass on signal.

TACKLING

THE LEFT-HAND LUNGE

BODY MECHANICS

Starting Position. The stick should be carried across the body about waist height, with the left hand at the top of the handle and the right hand slightly below it.

The tackler should be on her opponent's right.

CHAPTER 5.   HOCKEY

Application of Force. The right hand should throw the stick to the ground, to the left, and in front of the opponent's ball.

The path traveled by the head of the stick should be diagonally toward the ground.

The left hand should retain its grip at the top of the handle.

The left elbow should be straight, the wrist firm and the thumb up the back of the handle in order to add strength to the stroke.

The left foot should be forward with the weight on it.

Follow Through. There should be no follow through of the stick.

The body should follow through with a step on the right foot.

USES

Used as a tackling stroke when the opponent is on the tackler's left.

Used as a tackling stroke when the opponent is coming straight on.

Used as a saving stroke to prevent the ball from going over the side line or the goal line.

Used as a shot at goal following a rush.

Used as a dodge to tap the ball beyond the opponent's reach.

Used as a pass when a long reach is needed.

Used as a counterattack after a circular tackle.

COACHING SUGGESTIONS

This is an important stroke and should be mastered by all players.

Aim just ahead of the ball, not directly at it.

Use your reach! Tackle can be made from slightly behind rather than waiting to catch up to your opponent.

Keep the arc of the stick low. Beginners tend to raise the head of the stick before releasing it and thus often commit the foul of "sticks."

Keep the left elbow straight on the reach.

When tackling from behind opponent, be careful to avoid tripping.

Timing the stroke is most important. The stick should contact the ball when it is free from the opponent's stick.

TEACHING PROGRESSION

1. Demonstrate and explain left-hand lunge.
2. Practice left-hand lunge without the ball.
3. Practice left-hand lunge on a stationary ball.
4. Practice left-hand lunge on a ball rolled by the coach.
5. Practice left-hand lunge on a player dribbling slowly.
6. Practice left-hand lunge on a player dribbling at full speed.
7. Overtake a player dribbling and use a left-hand lunge to tackle.

SQUAD PRACTICE

Couple Formation. Player on the left dribbles and player on right tackles with a left-hand lunge.

CHAPTER 5. HOCKEY

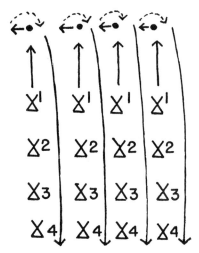

FIG. 5-10. Left-hand lunge, squad practice, column formation.

Single Column Formation (see Fig. 2-1). Squad leader is opposite first player and 10 feet off to her left. Squad leader rolls ball diagonally toward the players. X¹ runs forward in the same direction in which the ball is moving, taps it backward with a left-hand lunge, recovers the ball, dribbles it back to the squad leader and goes to the end of the column. X² then starts.

Couple Formation. Player on the left dribbles with loose dribble. Player on the right tackles with a left-hand lunge, tapping the ball diagonally backward to recover it.

Column Formation (Fig. 5-10). Balls placed on the ground 15 feet in front of the first player in each column. On signal all X's run forward, lunge at the balls to tap them toward the left. Each player recovers her own ball, dribbles in a clockwise position and goes to the end of her column. X²s follow.

THE CIRCULAR TACKLE (Figs. 5-11 and 5-12)

BODY MECHANICS

Starting Position. The stick should be held as in the dribble or the push pass, the left hand at the top of the handle and the right hand 2 or 3 inches below it.

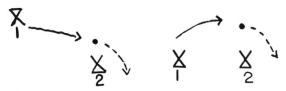

FIG. 5-11. Circular tackle, starting position.

FIG. 5–12. Circular tackle, to tackle when she is on opponent's left.

The tackler should be ahead of her opponent and to her left, or coming toward her opponent diagonally from the left. In Figure 5–11, X^1 is the tackler.

Application of Force. The stick should be turned toward the ball. The tackler should either push the ball to her opponent's right and finish off by dribbling, or the tackler should start the dribble immediately without the preliminary push.

Follow Through. There should be *no* follow through.

USES

Used to tackle an opponent when she is on the tackler's right.

Used to tackle an opponent coming diagonally toward the tackler from the left.

COACHING SUGGESTIONS

Get ahead of the opponent before attempting to tackle. It is possible to avoid body contact when the tackle is started from this position.

Turn the stick toward the ball before starting the tackle. The stick should be turned before the tackler herself starts to turn.

Do not attempt to circular tackle until the ball is off the opponent's stick.

Carry the ball well around beyond the reach of the opponent's stick.

CHAPTER 5. HOCKEY

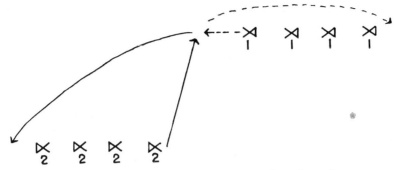

FIG. 5–13. Circular tackle, squad practice, column formation.

TEACHING PROGRESSION

1. Demonstrate and explain the circular tackle. Emphasize turning the stick before the body is turned and getting ahead of the opponent before starting the tackle.
2. Run in the same direction as a moving ball and push it sharply to the right.
3. Dribble and reverse direction on signal, turning sharply to the right.
4. Practice circular tackle with partner dribbling slowly.
5. Practice circular tackle with partner dribbling at full speed.
6. Practice circular tackle coming in at an angle from the left.

SQUAD PRACTICE

Column Formation (Fig. 5–13). Each X^1 should have a ball. The first X^1 dribbles forward. The first X^2 comes in to tackle with a diagonal circular tackle. Players go to the end of the opposite columns. X^2 takes the ball with her.

Couple Formation. Use couple formation, starting X^2s somewhat ahead so that each X^1 must overtake and pass her partner before tackling. Change positions.

Single Column Formation (see Fig. 2–1). Squad leader stands to the left of the column to roll the ball or hit it out in the same direction in which the player runs. X^1 starts as soon as the ball is hit, comes even with the ball, turns the stick well around toward the right and pushes the ball sharply to the right. She recovers her own ball, dribbles it back to the squad leader and returns to the end of the column.

THE STRAIGHT TACKLE

BODY MECHANICS

Starting Position. The stick should be held at approximately right angles to the ground, the handle of the stick slightly farther from the player than the head.

The left hand should be at the top of the handle, the right hand 3 to 4 inches below it.

The feet should be in a forward stride position, the weight on the forward foot, preferably the right one.

The trunk should be inclined forward.

The tackler should be slightly to the right (stick) side of and facing her opponent.

Application of Force. The stick should be placed in front of the oncoming ball in order to block it. There should be a pushing into the ball rather than a hitting at it.

Follow Through. There should be *no* follow through of the stick or of the body.

USE

Used to tackle an opponent approaching head on.

COACHING SUGGESTIONS

Get the body weight behind the tackle or the stick position will be insecure and the dribbler will be able to run through the tackler.

Keep your eye on the ball! Be alert for a dodge or a pass on the part of the dribbler.

Block the ball rather than merely hitting at it wildly.

Stay slightly to the right of the dribbler in order to be on her stick side.

Time the tackle for a moment when the ball is not in contact with the dribbler's stick.

Make the tackle unexpected.

Keep the hands well apart on the stick in order to insure a good firm position.

TEACHING PROGRESSION

1. Demonstrate and explain the tackle.
2. Tackle an opponent dribbling slowly.
3. Tackle an opponent dribbling at full speed.
4. Tackle an opponent attempting to avoid the tackle.

SQUAD PRACTICE

Single Line Formation (see Fig. 2–4). Players form three lines. Lines 1 and 2 should be 25 feet apart and facing, line 3 directly behind line 2. Players in line 2 dribble straight ahead toward the opposite players in line 1. These players advance to tackle. Line 2 moves to the rear of line 1 and players from line 1 dribble toward those in line 3.

Line Formation (Fig. 5–14). Line 1 should be 20 yards from the first player in line 3. Players in each line 10 yards apart. Line 1 advances,

CHAPTER 5. HOCKEY

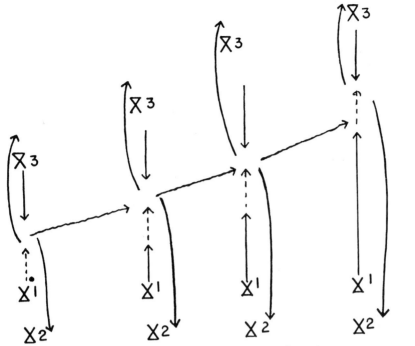

FIG. 5-14. Straight tackle, squad practice, line formation.

the ball in possession of the player on the left. The right end player in line 3 advances to tackle. Whether or not she tackles successfully, the ball is given to the second player in line 1 and the line continues dribbling and passing. No defense player should advance to tackle until her opponent has the ball and is dribbling. Line 1 takes the place of line 3, and line 3 goes behind line 2. Line 2 then starts to dribble through.

THE JOB

BODY MECHANICS

Starting Position. The job should be started with the stick in carrying position.

The tackler should be on a level with and to the left of her opponent. (May also be done facing opponent.)

The left hand should be at the top of the stick throughout the stroke, in the left job.

The left elbow should be straight and the wrist firm.

The weight should be carried over the left foot, which should be forward.

The trunk should be inclined.

Application of Force. The stick should be pushed with a straight arm directly at the ball, in a series of quick little jobs.

The hitting surface of the stick should face upward.

Follow Through. There should be *no* follow through of the stick.

The body should follow through with a long step in the direction of the jobs.

USES

This is primarily a spoiling stroke. It is used as such to tackle an opponent from the left or from straight on.

Used to shove the ball into goal following a rush.

Used to tip the ball beyond the reach of an opponent.

Used whenever a very long reach is needed.

COACHING SUGGESTIONS

The right job is executed in the same manner as the left job except that the right hand is shifted to the top of the handle and controls the stroke. The tackler should be on opponent's right.

Aim at the ball.

Avoid touching the opponent's stick.

The left job can be used from either the left or right side of an opponent. If used from the left there is little danger of obstruction, if from the right there is great danger. The right job is a better stroke from the right side.

Keep the arm straight and firm.

Lay the blade well back.

The job is at best a weak stroke and should only be resorted to in an emergency.

TEACHING PROGRESSION

1. Demonstrate and explain the job.
2. Job at a stationary ball.
3. Job at a ball moving in the same direction as the player.
4. Tackle an opponent from the left using the job.
5. Tackle an opponent head on using the job.
6. Job at a ball moving in any direction.

SQUAD PRACTICE

Single Column Formation (see Fig. 2–1). Each player in turn runs and jobs at a stationary ball.

Single Column Formation (see Fig. 2–1). Squad leader standing to the left of the column rolls the ball forward. X¹ runs forward to job at the ball, pick it up in a dribble, return it to the squad leader and go to

CHAPTER 5. HOCKEY

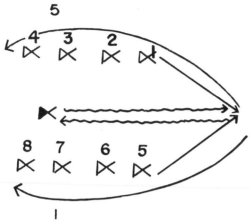

FIG. 5-15.   Left job, squad practice, couple formation.

the end of the line. The same practice can be done with the ball coming at right angles to the players.

Couple Formation (Fig. 5-15).   Partners should be about 10 feet apart. The ball should be rolled out between partners by the squad leader. As the ball is rolled, the first couple starts forward to recover it. X[1] attempts a left job and X[5] a left-hand lunge. The ball is hit back to the squad leader, each player going to the end of the opposite column.

THE RIGHT CUT

BODY MECHANICS

Starting Position.   The right cut should be started with the stick in carrying position, the hitting surface facing forward.

The tackler should be even with the opponent and on her left.

The stick should be reversed in position so that the toe points toward the ground. The right hand should turn the stick as it swings slightly to the left on the backswing. The arms should *not* cross.

The right hand should slide up the handle to a position directly below the left as the stick is swung to the left.

The weight should be carried over the right foot, which should be forward.

The trunk should be inclined forward.

Application of Force.   The stick should be swung sharply to the right.

The swing should be made chiefly with the wrists.

The toe of the stick should be snapped to the ground in front of the moving ball.

Follow Through.   There should be no follow through of the stick.

CHAPTER 5.   HOCKEY

The body should follow through with the weight coming on to the left foot.

Used to tackle when opponent is on tackler's right or even with her.

COACHING SUGGESTIONS

Aim slightly ahead of the moving ball. This makes it possible to avoid contact with the opponent's stick.

Hold the stick firmly when it touches the ground. At best this is a weak stroke.

Reverse the stick position! This must be done at the beginning of the stroke.

Keep the elbows straight. This adds reach to the stroke.

The tackler should be even with or slightly ahead of her opponent. Don't attempt this stroke when behind the opponent. The foul of bodily contact is apt to result.

The left halfback should know this stroke.

TEACHING PROGRESSION

1. Demonstrate and explain the right cut.
2. Practice the right cut without the ball.
3. Practice the right cut on a rolling ball.
4. Practice the right cut with partner dribbling slowly.
5. Practice the right cut with partner dribbling at top speed.

SQUAD PRACTICE

Couple Formation. Partner on the right dribbles, partner on the left attempts a right cut. Emphasize blocking the ball with the toe of the stick and a quick pulling back of the stick in order to avoid tripping the dribbler.

Single Column Formation (see Fig. 2–1). Squad leader stands to the right of the first player in the column. Squad leader rolls the ball out and the players, one at a time, go out to block the ball with a right cut, recover the ball, dribble back to the squad leader and go to the end of the column.

Shuttle Formation (see Fig. 2–6). 1. X^1 hits the ball to X^2. X^2 changes the direction of the ball with a right cut, recovers the ball, passes it to X^3, who repeats what X^2 did. Each player goes to the end of the column after passing the ball.

2. Players stand in shuttle formation 30 to 40 yards apart (Fig. 5–16). An obstacle is placed halfway between the first players in each column. X^1 dribbles to the obstacle, uses a right cut to pass it, recovers

FIG. 5-16.   Right cut, squad practice, shuttle formation.

the ball, dribbles to X^5. X^5 repeats. Each player goes to the end of the opposite column after passing the ball.

THE RIGHT-HAND LUNGE

BODY MECHANICS

Starting Position.   The right-hand lunge should be started with the stick in the normal carrying position.

The tackler should be even with or slightly behind her opponent and on the opponent's left.

The stick should be reversed in position, the right hand doing the turning as the stick is swung to the left on the backswing. The right hand should be shifted to the top of the handle and the left hand to the middle as the stick is reversed.

The weight should be carried over the right foot, which should be forward.

The trunk should be inclined forward.

Application of Force.   The stick should be swung sharply to the right, the left hand throwing it and the right hand guiding it. (This stroke is similar to the left-hand lunge except that the hand position and the stick position should be reversed.)

The thumb of the right hand may or may not be extended up the handle of the stick.

The toe of the stick should hit the ground in front of the ball.

Follow Through.   There should be *no* follow through of the stick.

The body weight should follow through onto the left foot.

USE

Used to tackle an opponent from the left.

COACHING SUGGESTIONS

This is the weakest of all tackling strokes, therefore its use should be discouraged except as a last resort.

It is possible to get a long reach with this stroke, and it is therefore feasible to use it when all other strokes fail.

Keep the right elbow straight. This adds reach and firmness to the stroke.

CHAPTER 5.   HOCKEY

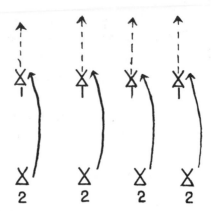

FIG. 5–17. Right-hand lunge, squad practice, line formation.

TEACHING PROGRESSION

1. Demonstrate and explain the right-hand lunge.
2. Practice the right-hand lunge without the ball in order to get the correct shift of grip.
3. Practice the right-hand lunge with partner dribbling slowly.
4. Practice the right-hand lunge with partner dribbling at top speed.

SQUAD PRACTICE

Couple Formation. Practice the right-hand lunge with partner dribbling slowly and then rapidly. Emphasize the change of grip and a quick pull back of the stick after the stroke in order to avoid tripping the opponent.

Line Formation (Fig. 5–17). Each player in line 1 has a ball. X¹s start to dribble on signal. On a second signal all X²s start to overtake opponents and tackle with a right-hand lunge. Reverse positions when returning, X²s dribbling and X¹s tackling.

Later have X¹s attempt to avoid the tackle by pushing the ball slightly ahead just as the opponent's stick comes down to block it. Reverse positions when returning.

GENERAL COACHING SUGGESTIONS ON TACKLING

Play the ball, not the opponent.
Go in to tackle with the stick down.
Keep the body and stick away from the opponent.
Be careful of obstruction.
Use the tackling stroke best suited to the immediate situation. Beginners often attempt to get into position for a left-hand lunge for all tackles.

CHAPTER 5. HOCKEY

TACKLER		OPPONENT ON RIGHT	OPPONENT ON LEFT
Running in the same direction as opponent	Even with opponent	Left job Right cut Right-hand lunge	Left-hand lunge Right job
	Slightly behind opponent	Right-hand lunge	Left-hand lunge
	Slightly ahead of opponent	Circular tackle	Left-hand lunge
Coming head on toward opponent		Straight tackle – Left-hand lunge – Left job – Right job	

Advance to tackle as soon as your opponent has the ball.

When a successful tackle has been made, get rid of the ball quickly or your opponent will tackle back.

Don't give up if the first attempt fails.

GOALKEEPING

BODY MECHANICS

Starting Position. The goalkeeper should stand about 2 feet in front of the cage, slightly to the left of the center.

The stick should be carried in any position below the shoulder. Many goalkeepers prefer to carry the stick in the right hand, holding it about halfway down the handle.

The knees should be easy.

The feet should be in a short side stride position.

The trunk should be inclined slightly forward.

Application of Force. The ball should be stopped full on the pads with the knees together and slightly bent. The goalkeeper should meet the ball in that position.

Follow Through. The goalkeeper should lean forward into the clearing kick or drive which follows the stop.

There should be a follow through of the kicking leg in the direction of the kick. The foot should be kept close to the ground to prevent a lofted ball. The ball should be met with the side of the big toe in a clearing kick.

Goalkeepers often carry the stick in the right hand in order to be able to reach out farther to deflect a shot.

USE

Used by the goalkeeper to prevent a goal from being scored.

CHAPTER 5.   HOCKEY

Adjust the position in the cage depending upon the angle of approach of the ball.

Clear to the side with a kick or a drive after stopping the ball.

Use the stick to clear only if the ball has first been stopped. The safest clear is parallel to and close to the goal line. Practice without a stick.

If necessary to kick on the fly, the inside of the instep or the top of the instep should be used.

Use the stick for deflecting balls which cannot be stopped with the feet.

Use the hands for stopping high balls.

When clearing a ball on the fly, push the foot into it rather than kicking at it.

When hard pressed use any legal means of stopping the ball.

Clear the ball quickly.

TEACHING PROGRESSION

1. Stopping the ball with both feet and clearing to the side with a kick.
2. Stopping the ball with one foot and clearing with a kick.
3. Steps 1 and 2, but clearing with the stick.
4. Reaching with the stick to stop and clear.
5. Stopping lofted ball with hand and clearing with kick or stick.
6. Stopping and clearing using any of the above methods while being rushed.

SQUAD PRACTICE

Column Formation (Fig. 5–18). 1. Players line up at the edge of the circle with two players stationed at A and B to recover clearing passes. Goalkeepers in the cage about 2 feet in front of the goal line and slightly to the left of the center. X[1] dribbles into the circle and shoots. Goalie stops and clears using any of the suggested methods. She attempts to clear to either A or B. This practice can be varied by placing the shooting players at different angles around the circle and by varying the position of the receivers. X[2] follows X[1] and so on down the line, each player going to the end of the line after shooting.

2. Same as preceding, except that couples approach the goal dribbling and passing and both players rush any shot at goal.

Players in Groups of Threes. Same as above with the three players advancing and rushing.

A goalie can be stationed in the cage during any shooting practices in order to help her in goalkeeping and at the same time to make it more difficult to shoot.

Single Player or Groups of Three or Four. Practice kicking a tennis

CHAPTER 5. HOCKEY

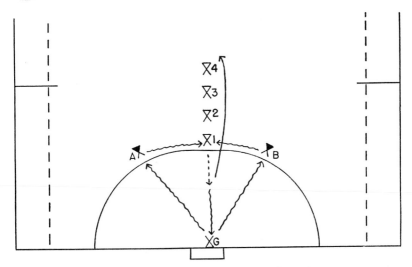

FIG. 5–18.   Stopping and clearing, squad practice.

ball or other soft ball of similar size at targets placed in varying positions. This develops accuracy and is a good indoor practice.

FIELDING

BODY MECHANICS

Starting Position.   The left hand should be at the top of the handle of the stick.

The right hand should be 6 to 8 inches below the left.

The body weight should be carried over the forward foot. Either foot may be forward.

The trunk should be inclined slightly forward.

Ideally the body should be directly in line with the oncoming ball.

Application of Force.   The stick should be at a slight angle to the ground, the top of the handle nearer the player than the head of the stick. The hitting surface should be toward the ball.

The stick should "give" as the ball touches it in order to stop the ball dead.

Follow Through.   There should be no follow through.

USE

Used to stop a moving ball and gain control of it.

COACHING SUGGESTIONS

Keep your eye on the ball! Watch the ball until it is actually on the stick. An easy ball can be missed by looking up too soon.

134   Fielding with the stick is the most efficient method of stopping the ball. The ball may also be fielded with the hand:

1. Keep the fingers toward the ground and the palm of the hand in line with the ball. This method is often used in stopping the ball on a corner hit.

2. The ball may be fielded in the air with the hand but must be dropped immediately.

Beginners should use the stick only in fielding.

TEACHING PROGRESSION

1. Demonstrate and explain fielding with the stick.
2. Practice fielding a slowly moving ball.
3. Practice fielding a hard-hit ball.
4. Practice fielding a ball while running toward it.
5. Practice fielding with the hand.

SQUAD PRACTICE

Double Line Formation (see Fig. 2–9).   Hitting and fielding practice combined. Partners hit the ball back and forth. The ball must be fielded before being returned. Vary the distance between the lines.

Shuttle Formation (see Fig. 2–6).   X¹ hits the ball to X², who fields

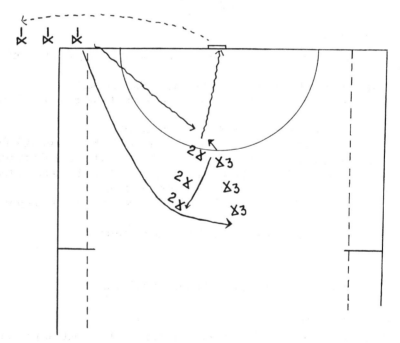

FIG. 5–19.   Fielding, squad practice, column formation.

CHAPTER 5.   HOCKEY

it and returns it to X³. Each player goes to the end of the column after hitting the ball.

Single Column Formation (see Fig. 2–1). Squad leader standing to the left of the column hits the ball forward. X¹ runs after it, fields it with a left-hand lunge, dribbles it back to the squad leader and goes to the end of the column. X² follows.

Column Formation (Fig. 5–19). Two columns stand opposite the goal and facing it, one column along the goal line in position for a short corner hit. Each X¹ with a ball. X¹ passes to X³ who stops the ball with her hand, steps back and lets X² shoot. X² follows her shot, recovers ball and dribbles to the end of column 1. X¹ goes to the end of column 3, and X³ goes to the end of column 2. Repeat practice from other side of goal. Same practices may be used for long corners.

THE ROLL-IN

BODY MECHANICS (see section on roll-in, p. 159)

Starting Position. (right-handed roll). The stick should be held in the left hand outside of the side line.

The ball should be held in the fingers of the right hand.

The right knee should be bent almost to the ground.

The left foot should be forward with the left knee well bent.

The trunk should be inclined forward.

Application of Force. The right arm should be swung backward, then forward, the hand releasing the ball when the arm is at right angles to the ground. (Similar to an underhand pitch in baseball.)

If more force is desired in the roll-in, it can be started with the feet together and a step forward taken onto the left foot.

Follow Through. The arm should follow through in the direction of the roll.

USE

Used to put the ball in play after it has gone out of bounds over the side line, unless sent out by members of each team.

COACHING SUGGESTIONS

Keep the hand close to the ground on the release in order to prevent the ball from bouncing.

Keep the stick in your hand! This is necessary in order to make the roll-in legal.

Keep the direction of the roll-in from being obvious.

Vary the direction of the roll-in.

Take the roll-in quickly.

Right halfbacks should learn to roll with the left hand.

CHAPTER 5. HOCKEY

1. Demonstrate the roll-in and explain the rules.
2. Practice the roll-in for distance.
3. Practice the roll-in for distance and accuracy.
4. Practice deceptive roll-ins.

Practice the different types of roll-ins (see section on roll-ins for suggestions).

Column Formation (Fig. 5–20A). 1. One column is along the side line and the other column diagonally ahead facing in the opposite direction. Each X¹ has a ball. X¹s roll to partners in X² column. X²s return the ball.

2. Same formation as preceding, except that all players face in the same direction (Fig. 5–20B). X¹ rolls the ball to X⁵, who is moving for-

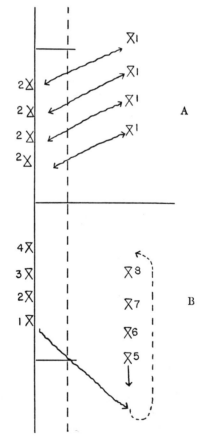

FIG. 5–20. Roll-in, squad practice, column formation.

CHAPTER 5. HOCKEY

then rolls the ball. When all the balls have been rolled by one column, the players face in the opposite direction and the balls are then rolled by the column which received the first time.

THE BULLY

BODY MECHANICS

Starting Position. The left hand should be at the top of the stick, the right hand 6 to 8 inches down the handle.

The feet should be in an easy side stride position.

The weight should be carried on the balls of the feet.

The knees should be easy.

The trunk should be inclined slightly forward.

Application of Force. The bully consists of carefully controlled movements of the wrists and forearms, moving the stick to hit alternately the ground on her side of the ball and the opponent's stick three times.

The stick should be moved close to the ball so as to avoid waste movement and in order to be ready to play at the completion of "groundsticks."

Follow Through. There should be *no* follow through in the bully.

USES

To put the ball in play:
At the start of the game and after half time.
After a goal has been scored.
When the attacking team sends the ball over the opponent's goal line without score.
When opponents send the ball over the side line or over the goal line.
When play is resumed after time out unless there was a corner, roll-in, or free hit previously called.
When a member of the defending team, from beyond the 25-yard line, sends the ball over her own goal line.
When a member of the defending team, within her own striking circle, willfully fouls or commits a foul which prevents a goal from being made. (Penalty bully.)
After a double foul.
After a penalty bully with no score.

COACHING SUGGESTIONS (see also p. 168)

Speed on the bully is important.
Stand fairly close to the ball.

CHAPTER 5. HOCKEY

Keep the stick close to the ball.

Use the wrists.

Study your opponent's tactics in the bully.

Develop different bullies and learn to use them.

All players should be given some practice in the bully.

TEACHING PROGRESSION

1. Demonstrate stick and body position for the bully. Explain the rules.

2. Practice the different types of bullies.

3. Practice the bully with inners and center halfback in proper position.

4. Practice the bully with wings and center halfback in proper position.

5. Practice with complete forward line and center halfback.

SQUAD PRACTICE

Couple Formation. Practice the different types of bully. Each player should be allowed to secure the ball after the bully before allowing her to compete for possession of the ball.

Groups of Fours (Figs. 5–21 and 5–22). Line up the four players as center, center halfback and inners; or center, center halfback and wings. Each team scores 1 point if the ball is sent to a member of her team

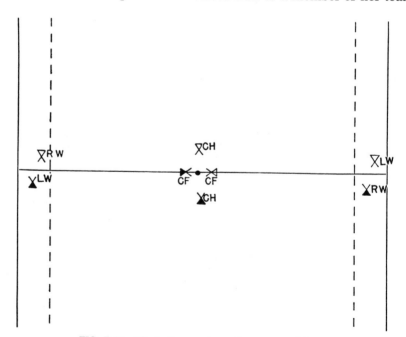

FIG. 5–21. The bully, squad practice, groups of fours.

CHAPTER 5. HOCKEY

COMPARATIVE CHART OF STROKE AND TACKLE POSITIONS

STROKE OR TACKLE	HANDS	FEET, BALL AND STICK
Dribble	Slightly apart	
Drive	Together	
Right drive	Together	
Push	Slightly apart	
Right push	Slightly apart	
Scoop	Slightly apart	
Flick	Slightly apart	
Left hand lunge	Left hand only	
Circular tackle	Slightly apart	
Left job	Left hand only	
Right job	Right hand only	
Right cut	Together	
Right hand lunge	Right hand only	
Straight tackle	Slightly apart	

＊ BEST POSITION.

CHAPTER 5. HOCKEY

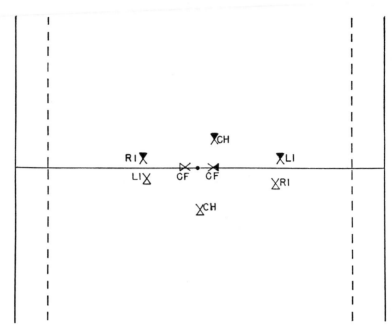

FIG. 5–22. The bully, squad practice, groups of fours.

after the completion of the bully. Rotate positions of the scoring team after each score. If a team fails to score after three trials rotate positions of that team.

Groups of Sixes. Line up a forward line and a center halfback for each team. A team scores 2 points if the ball is sent directly to the wing after the completion of the bully from either the center forward or the center halfback. A team scores 1 point if the ball is sent to either inner. Rotate positions as in Groups of Fours.

Throughout the rest of this section the terms "defending" and "defense" apply to the team *not* in possession of the ball at any given moment. The terms "attacking" and "offense" apply to the team in possession of the ball at a given moment. On the field there is a constant shifting of a team from defense to offense and vice versa, making necessary a constant shift in the use of tactics.

DEFENSE TACTICS (INDIVIDUAL)

TACKLES

All tackles belong under defense tactics. In addition to knowing the various types of tackles, players should know when to use each kind to its best advantage. The various tackles have been previously discussed.

USE

Tackling back is a counterattack on an opponent who has made a successful tackle.

METHODS

Any legal stroke may be used for tackling back.

COACHING SUGGESTIONS

A player should tackle back as soon as the ball has been taken from her. If any time is lost in tackling back, the opponent will either be too far away to make the attempt worthwhile or will have passed the ball.

A forward should not go far out of her position in an effort to tackle back or she will run into her own line of backs and upset their play.

Should a player be successful in tackling back, she should pass at once and then return to her own position on the field.

Forwards especially should be trained in tackling back. Too often forwards leave all the work of defense to the backs and thereby weaken the defensive strength of the team and throw too much work on their backs.

Tackling back is an especially important tactic for the forwards when their backs are hard pressed.

Tackle back within reaching distance of an opponent.

GOALKEEPING

(For a complete analysis of goalkeeping see p. 131, Section II.)

In Figure 5–23, when a shot is made from angle A, the ball passing over any part of line WZ will enter the goal. The goalkeeper must then be prepared to cover all of line WZ.

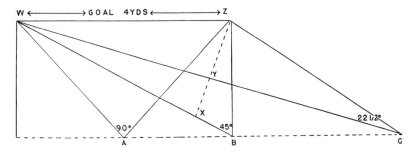

FIG. 5–23.   Areas which must be covered by the goalie when ball approaches from various angles.

CHAPTER 5.   HOCKEY

When a shot is made from angle B, the ball passing over any part of line XZ will enter the goal. The goalkeeper must be ready to cover line XZ.

When a shot is made from angle C, the ball passing over any part of line YZ will enter the goal. The goalkeeper must cover line YZ.

CLEARING

USES

A hard hit by the backs or goalie or a kick by the goalie to clear the ball out of the scoring area and get the ball to the forward line.

METHODS

Any legal stroke may be used for clearing. A hard drive, push or a kick (by the goalie) are the best methods.

COACHING SUGGESTIONS

Clear diagonally down the field toward the nearer side line.

Clear immediately—it is dangerous to play with the ball when it is near the goal.

Clear to a member of your team if possible.

Make the clearing pass the beginning of an attack.

Clear through a space, if possible, don't just hit at the ball.

Beginning right fullbacks frequently clear across the goal because it is difficult to get turned around to clear toward the right side line.

Wild or uncontrolled clearing passes are apt to result in the foul of dangerous hitting.

Goalkeepers have the privilege of kicking the ball or advancing it while within the striking circle. They should be coached to use these privileges.

GENERAL COACHING SUGGESTIONS FOR INDIVIDUAL DEFENSE TACTICS

A team on the defensive is not in possession of the ball; its first concern should be to get the ball.

If a player cannot actually get possession of the ball she can at least hurry her opponent's pass, shot or dodge.

Act quickly—otherwise the moment for acting may pass.

Play your position, don't attempt to tackle any player who has the ball. A player doing this soon wears herself out and upsets her own team.

Cooperate with the rest of the team.

Study your opponent's methods of play and try to anticipate her moves.

CHAPTER 5.   HOCKEY

If you are not immediately concerned with a tackle, try to place yourself in an advantageous position for intercepting a pass by the opposing team. Forwards can do a great deal in the way of covering spaces.

Advance to tackle as soon as your opponent has the ball.

If you fail on the first attempt, don't give up, try again.

Play to get the ball and start your team on the attack.

Keep out of the goalie's way.

OFFENSE TACTICS (INDIVIDUAL)

DRAWING

USES

Used primarily by a forward line player with the ball to force a member of the opposing team to move out of her position to tackle.

Used by a forward without the ball to draw an opposing back out of position and so make a space through which the ball can be passed.

METHODS

Keep possession of the ball until the opponent is about to tackle (forwards).

When being closely marked draw out of position to left or right, taking the marking player with you.

COACHING SUGGESTIONS

Draw the opponent away from the direction in which the pass is to be made. If the right inner is carrying the ball and wishes to pass to the left she should move slightly to the right, take the left fullback with her, and pass before being tackled.

If a forward fails to keep the ball until she has drawn an opponent to tackle her, the opposing team is stronger because one of its backs is free.

Beginners tend to pass the ball as soon as it is received or else to carry it so long that a tackle is made.

A forward should not attempt to draw if she receives the ball when well behind her own forward line.

DODGING

USES

Used to evade an opponent and maintain possession of the ball.

Used especially by a forward well ahead of her own line.

Used sometimes by a back to get free for her pass.

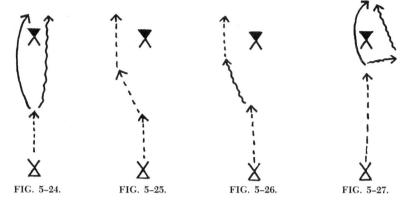

FIG. 5–24.   FIG. 5–25.   FIG. 5–26.   FIG. 5–27.

FIGS. 5–24, 5–25, 5–26 and 5–27.   Methods of dodging.

METHODS

Pass the ball to the nonstick side of the oncoming opponent (dodger's right), run around to the stick side (dodger's left) to recover the ball (Fig. 5–24).

Pull the ball well toward the opponent's stick side (dodger's left) and continue (Fig. 5–25).

Scoop the ball over the opponent's stick (Fig. 5–26).

Dribble toward the opponent's stick side (dodger's left), reverse the stick and tap the ball to the right, pass it around the opponent's nonstick side (dodger's right) and go around the opponent's stick side (dodger's left) to recover (Fig. 5–27).

COACHING SUGGESTIONS

A pass is generally better than a dodge because the ball is advanced more rapidly by passing than by dribbling.

In a dodge the ball should be hit lightly so that it can be easily and quickly recovered. A hard hit on a dodge will send the ball beyond recovery distance and very likely into the opposing backs.

Backs should seldom take time to dodge.

Excessive dodging emphasizes individual rather than team play. Hockey is a team game.

The dodge should be started just before the opponent tackles.

The direction of the dodge must not be made evident.

THROUGH PASSING

USES

Used by backs to pass the ball through a space on the forward line so that a forward can run ahead to pick up the pass rather than standing and waiting.

CHAPTER 5.   HOCKEY

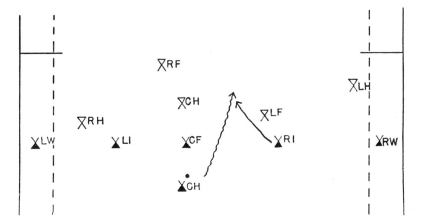

FIG. 5–28. Through pass by a back.

Used by forwards in passing through a space between opposing backs so that another forward can run on to pick up the pass.

METHODS

Through Pass by a Back (drive).   Figure 5–28 shows the right inner moving out of position to draw the left fullback with her, thereby making a space through which the center halfback can pass.

Through Pass by a Forward (push or flick).   Can be used most successfully when the opposing backs are caught standing squarely. Figure 5–29 shows a through pass from the left inner to the left wing.

COACHING SUGGESTIONS

Through passes are effective in increasing the speed of the forward line. There is no danger of a forward slackening her pace if the ball is sent ahead of her.

A through pass must be accurately placed or it will go too far and into the backs or too close to one of them so that it is intercepted.

A through pass by a forward line player is most effectively used if the forward first draws her opponent out and then passes.

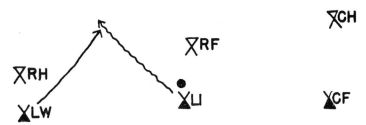

FIG. 5–29. Through pass from left inner to left wing.

Through passes must go farther to the right of an opponent than to the left.

SHOOTING

USE

Used as a means of scoring goals.

METHODS

Any legal stroke may be used in shooting. (A shot for goal, in order to score, must have been touched by the stick of a member of the attacking team inside the striking circle.)

COACHING SUGGESTIONS

Shoot from any position and learn to shoot on the run.

When approaching the goal from the center, aim for the right corner.

If approaching the goal alone, dribble in quite close and try a flick or a scoop or a push.

The best point of aim in shooting is the inner goal post.

Angles of shot are important. As the angle between the approach and the goal becomes more acute, the space through which the ball must pass, in order to score, becomes smaller (see Fig. 5–23).

Vary the type of shot used. Don't always try a hard shot; it is the tricky unexpected shot which often scores.

If there is any opening, shoot as soon as the ball is in the striking circle.

A shot for goal should always be rushed.

Beginners tend to carry the ball too far into the circle before shooting.

Look up to locate the goal before shooting.

Remember that the goalie can cover the right side of the goal (shooter's left) more easily than the left side of the goal.

Draw the goalie off balance and shoot past her.

Don't give up if the first shot fails.

PICKING UP PASSES (Fig. 5–30)

USE

Used to gain control of a pass.

METHODS

The receiver, in picking up a pass, should be facing in the direction in which she wishes to run. She should get the ball on her stick and

FIG. 5–30. Foot position while waiting for a pass. Pass coming from right. Pass coming from left.

deflect it in the proper direction without actually stopping the movement of the ball.

COACHING SUGGESTIONS

Don't stop a pass when picking it up, merely deflect it in the proper direction.

In picking up a pass from the left, the ball should roll across to the stick side of the receiver, or the receiver should get around so that the ball is on her stick side before attempting to pick it up.

A pass from the left, to be easily controlled, should be well ahead of the receiver. This makes it possible for her to increase her speed to pick up the ball rather than slowing up for it.

The ideal position in which to receive a pass is with the feet pointing toward the opponent's goal.

The receiver should run toward a pass which is not traveling fast enough to reach her.

The receiver should run in toward a pass if an opponent is advancing to intercept.

In picking up a pass from the right, the receiver should get it on her stick just ahead of her right foot.

Easy and correct receiving of passes depends a great deal upon the accuracy of the passer.

Beginners tend to stand facing their own goal while waiting for a pass and so find it difficult to pick up the pass without obstructing or without first stopping the ball.

CHAPTER 5.   HOCKEY

To send a ball to a teammate.

METHODS

Any legal stroke may be used as a pass.

COACHING SUGGESTIONS

Pass farther ahead to a player receiving from the left than to a player receiving from the right.

Use diagonal passes rather than straight passes or square passes.

Learn a variety of passes and when to use each most effectively.

Make use of every opportunity for through passing.

The ball progresses more rapidly by passing than by dribbling.

GENERAL COACHING SUGGESTIONS ON INDIVIDUAL OFFENSE TACTICS

When the ball is once in possession of your team it should not be lost until a goal has been scored.

All players, backs as well as forwards, should be able to execute any offense tactic. The whole team attacks, not just the forwards.

Players should know a variety of offense tactics and know when and how to use them.

It is harder to initiate an attack than it is to break one up, therefore the team attacking has a more difficult play than the team defending.

Wings should pass the ball toward the center when near the 25-yard line so that it will be near the scoring area.

SECTION III. TEAM TACTICS

Team tactics apply to those tactics which are used by the team as a whole or by various combinations of players in contrast to those tactics which are used by a single player.

DEFENSE TEAM TACTICS

MARKING

Marking applies to the backs of the team on the defense. Each back is normally responsible for a definite forward line player on the opposing team. Whenever a forward next to the one for whom a given back is responsible has the ball, that back should mark her forward. The term "marking" means staying close enough to a forward to intercept a pass to her or to be able to tackle immediately should she gain possession of the ball.

For example, when the right inner has the ball, the center halfback and left halfback of the opposite team should mark their forwards, namely the center forward and right wing. The left fullback should be tackling the right inner or attempting to.

The value of marking lies in the fact that in such a position the backs concerned are in readiness for whatever may happen. In a marking position the back makes it difficult for the opposing forward, in possession of the ball, to pass to advantage. A back who knows when to mark and when not to gives the entire team a feeling of confidence. A back who fails to mark at the proper time can disrupt the play of the entire defending team.

The one exception to this theory of marking is the left fullback, who stands in more of a covering position when the center forward has the ball because this back is responsible for the center forward should she elude the center halfback. Backs not marking should be in covering positions.

All backs should mark, closely or loosely, when in the circle, the type of marking depending upon the position of the ball.

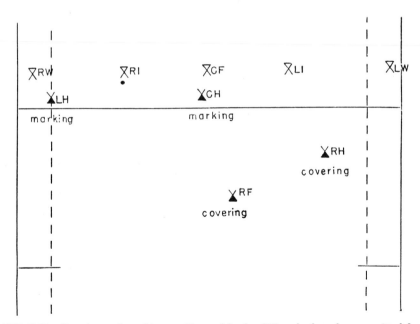

FIG. 5–31. Covering and marking positions of backs. (LF and other players omitted for clarity.)

The value of covering lies in the added strength which such a position gives to the defending team. The covering backs are in position to block various angles of passing which might otherwise be open to the attacking team, and they are in position to make quick interchange possible. The center halfback does little or no covering. A back should assume a covering position when the ball is on her side of the field. The covering back acts as a "safety" man. Covering and interchange are interdependent.

INTERCHANGING

Interchange is a shifting of positions by the backs when one of the backs on that team has been left behind and is temporarily out of play. Any interchange should be initiated by the covering fullback. The halfback on the side of the field with the covering fullback shifts to the fullback's position as soon as the interchange is started.

Sometimes a covering back can reach a long through pass to the wing more quickly than the halfback. When this is done the halfback should take on the inner left by the fullback. The fullback must be careful not to be lured out of position by *any* ball coming in her direction.

Interchange When Left Wing Passes the Right Halfback (Fig. 5–32). For example, the left wing has dodged past her right halfback and is coming down the field toward the circle. The left fullback, in covering position, goes over to the wing and the left halfback comes in to the position left open when the fullback shifted.

Interchange When Center Forward Passes the Center Halfback (Fig. 5–33). If the center forward outdistances her center halfback, the left fullback, because she is on the center's stick side, is responsible for her, and the left halfback comes in to the position she leaves open. If the center forward goes on past the left fullback, then the left halfback must take her on.

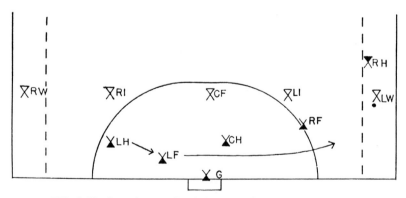

FIG. 5–32.   Interchange when left wing passes the right halfback.

CHAPTER 5.   HOCKEY

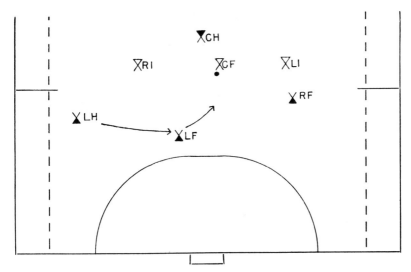

FIG. 5–33. Interchange when center forward passes the center halfback.

Interchange When Right Inner Passes the Left Fullback (Fig. 5–34). If the right inner leaves the left fullback behind, the right fullback comes over to her and the right halfback moves into the position left open by the fullback.

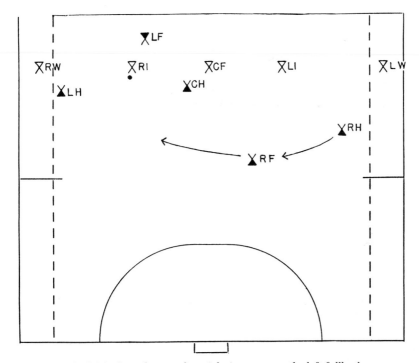

FIG. 5–34. Interchange when right inner passes the left fullback.

The value of interchanging lies in the fact that it makes it possible to cover up the loss of a back left behind by concentrating the strength of the defense in that section of the field where the ball happens to be, and by leaving free that forward on the opposing line who is farthest from the ball at that particular moment.

INTERCEPTING

Intercepting is a method by which the team on the defense gains possession of the ball. Although one player alone intercepts, that player must feel that the whole team is moving with her. If this were not true, no player would feel free to move out of her position toward the ball.

Timing is important, not only for the player who is doing the intercepting but for the entire team. The interceptor must move in at exactly the right moment, when the ball is out of control of any player on the opposite team. The members of her team must adjust their positions to cover any gap which might be left. Split-second timing is essential for the entire team.

Once a player has been successful in intercepting, her teammates should get into position to receive her pass or to back her up.

COVERING SPACES

The term "covering spaces" means blocking all possible angles of pass so that the team in possession of the ball finds it impossible to get a pass through. Covering spaces is the duty of the entire team on the defense, both forwards and backs. Forwards can do a great deal more of this than they generally do, especially on free hits and roll-ins. The backs necessarily cover spaces when the opposing forwards are progressing with the ball, but when the opposing backs are in possession of the ball the forwards should quickly get into covering positions.

When any player is in possession of the ball, there is a limited number of directions in which a pass can be sent if it is to be worth anything to the team. These are the spaces which must be covered by the defending team in order to intercept the pass.

GENERAL COACHING SUGGESTIONS ON DEFENSE TEAM TACTICS

The team on the defense must be quick to shift position in relation to the position of the ball.

Beginners tend to crowd up to where the ball is and so leave many free spaces through which a pass can be sent without any danger of its being intercepted.

Beginners tend to pass directly to a player so that the defending team is more apt to mark players than to cover spaces.

It is difficult to lay down hard and fast rules in the use of defense team tactics. Play the game and the tactics will come. When the for-

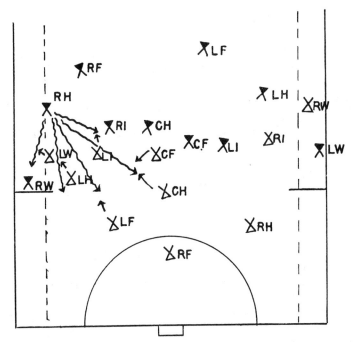

FIG. 5–35. Covering positions of forwards when opposing right halfback is in possession of ball.

wards on your team have the ball, covering is important; when the opposing forwards have it anywhere between the circles, marking and covering are important; when the opposing forwards have the ball in the circle, marking is important. In teaching defense tactics, present marking first, then covering and last interchanging.

There are many possibilities in the tactics used by the defending team, but the important thing is that there be a general plan of defense, understood by all and participated in by all. Remember that diagonal lines of defense are the most effective, and that when one back moves they all move.

Marking = Man to man
Covering Spaces = loose - play spaces

OFFENSE TEAM TACTICS

TRIANGULAR PASSING

Triangular passing is, as the name implies, a passing tactic used by two forwards to eliminate an opposing back from play. It might be called a two-player dodge. Successful triangular passing requires great accuracy and perfect timing. Passing too soon will give the back a chance to intercept and carrying the ball too long will give the back a chance to tackle.

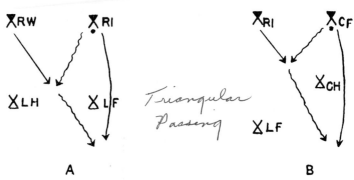

FIG. 5–36. *A*, Triangular pass with backs sqaure. *B*, Triangular pass with backs diagonal.

If the right inner has the ball, the left fullback is advancing to tackle and the left halfback is marking, the triangular pass, as shown in Figure 5–36*A*, can be used to eliminate the left fullback from play. Figure 5–36*B* shows the center forward and the right inner using the triangular pass around the center half.

The value of triangular passing lies in the fact that the opposing defense is weakened, at least temporarily, by the loss of one of its backs. Triangular passes, properly executed while the forward line is progressing down the field, make it possible to cover a great deal of ground quickly without giving the opposing backs a chance to tackle.

TEACHING PROGRESSION

1. Receive a pass and return the ball at once to the player who sent it.
2. Practice the triangular pass with stationary opponent in front of player starting with the ball.
3. Practice the triangular pass with single opponent advancing to tackle player with ball.
4. Practice the triangular pass with two stationary opponents.
   Opponents standing squarely.
   Opponents standing diagonally.
5. Practice the triangular pass with two tackling opponents.

SQUAD PRACTICE

Couple Formation. 1. Practice passing and receiving while progressing down the field.
2. Stationary opponent stands in front of the player on the left, who starts with the ball (Fig. 5–37). X¹ dribbles almost to X³, passes to X², runs around her opponent and receives a return pass.
3. Same as preceding, except that X³ advances to tackle as soon as X¹ starts to dribble. This adds a more difficult timing situation.

CHAPTER 5. HOCKEY

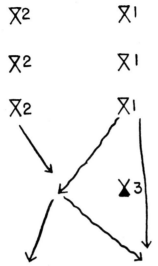

FIG. 5-37.   Triangular passing, squad practice, couple formation.

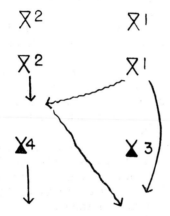

FIG. 5-38.   Triangular passing, squad practice, couple formation.

4. Stationary opponents stand in front of both X^1 and X^2 (Fig. 5-38). X^1 dribbles the ball toward X^3, passes to X^2, goes around X^3 to receive a return pass. When opponents stand squarely, the first pass should be square. When opponents stand diagonally, the first pass should be diagonal. Sometimes, with opponents standing squarely, the first pass can be a through pass.

BACKING UP

Backing up applies to the duties of the backs when their forwards are in possession of the ball. The halfback line should follow their

FIG. 5–39. Backing-up position when right inner is in possession of ball.

forwards down the field, ready to intercept a pass should an opposing back tackle successfully, ready to pick up a clearing pass, and ready to shoot if opportunity arises.

The fullback on whose side of the field the ball is should assist in backing up but should not progress down the field as far as the halfbacks. The other fullback should be in a covering position.

Note that in the positions indicated in Figure 5–39 the halfback line is playing on diagonals rather than on a straight line. Playing squarely, even when attacking, is dangerous because at any time the team may shift from attack to defense and the square position makes through passing easy to accomplish.

Backing up is important because it adds strength to the attack and because with the backs in that position it is more difficult for the opposing backs to get a pass through to their forwards should they gain possession of the ball. The backing up required of the halfbacks makes those positions the most taxing on the team.

RUSHING

Rushing concerns the forward line players only and only after a shot for goal has been attempted. Every shot at goal should be quickly followed in by one or more players. The player shooting should follow her own shot because of the possibility of the goalie returning the ball along the same line of flight. The shooting forward should normally be supported by one other forward.

When the center forward shoots, the left inner should rush with her. When either inner shoots the opposite inner should rush, the center forward dropping back slightly within the circle. If a wing shoots, the center forward should rush with her. The forwards not rushing any given shot should be inside the striking circle fairly close to the goal, unless they are wings, in which case they should be near the edge of the circle.

It is impossible to lay down and adhere to strict rules on rushing. The combinations above are so listed because, in each case, the pair of forwards rushing are most likely to cover angles of rebound from the goalie. It is often the follow-up shot which scores the goal because it comes quickly, because it comes from close in, and because the goalie is apt to be caught off balance from a previous save.

GENERAL COACHING SUGGESTIONS ON OFFENSE
TEAM TACTICS

The team on the offense must be quick to take advantage of any breaks in the game.

Forwards should space themselves well across the field and not collect around the ball.

Triangular passing is the strongest offense tactic which can be used by forwards.

Backing up is vital. Halfbacks should be coached to follow their forwards well down the field, to the edge of the circle. One fullback, the one on the side of the field where the ball is, should follow almost that far.

A shot at goal should always be rushed.

SECTION IV. FORMATION PLAYS

(For rules and regulations concerning these formation plays, see analytical chart, page 180.)

THE FREE HIT

THE ATTACKING TEAM

A free hit is awarded for a foul committed anywhere on the field except by a member of the defending team within her own striking circle.

The team to which the free hit is awarded should, in order to gain real benefit from this penalty, take the hit quickly. The free hit should be taken by the back nearest the ball at the time, preferably a halfback. However, when a free hit is awarded the attacking team at the side edge of the circle, time is often saved if a wing takes the hit.

No member of the attacking team may stand closer than 5 yards

CHAPTER 5. HOCKEY

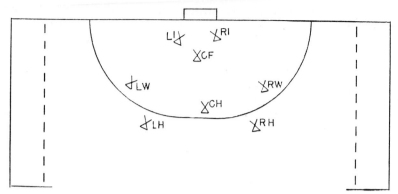

FIG. 5–40. Right and left inners rushing, center forward back, wings near edge of circle, and halfbacks in backing-up positions.

to the ball. No member of the attacking team should stand in an off-side position. The forwards of the attacking team should endeavor to draw the opposing backs out in order to make spaces through which a pass can be sent. Naturally the forwards near the player taking the free hit will be closely marked, and it will be practically impossible to get a pass directly to one of them. That is why they should draw out of position somewhat.

The player taking the free hit should do so quickly before all her teammates are marked and before all spaces are covered. She should not fail to look up to locate her teammates before passing. A free hit taken near the player's own goal should be played toward the nearest side line and sent well down the field. A free hit near the opponent's goal should be centered. The flick or scoop may not be used on a free hit.

THE DEFENDING TEAM

The forwards of the defending team should place themselves so that they cover all possible angles of pass. They should, if possible, get to a position between the opposing forward line and the player taking the free hit. They should cover the spaces which the other forward line attempts to make.

The backs of the defending team near the player taking the free hit should mark the opposing forwards. The remaining backs should stand in covering positions ready to intercept a through pass should one be attempted. All backs should be between the forward for whom they are responsible and the goal they are guarding.

The defending team should remember that frequently, especially in the opponent's half of the field, the free hit may be played to a back. Forwards of the defending team must be on the watch for this. No player of the defending team should be closer than 5 yards to the ball.

CHAPTER 5. HOCKEY

THE ATTACKING TEAM

The roll-in is awarded when the ball is sent over the side line off the stick of one or more players of the same team.

The roll-in should, if properly played, be a decided advantage to the team to which it is awarded. Generally speaking, the right or left halfback takes the roll-in, although if it occurs near the circle of the opponent's goal it is well to let the wing take it.

The general tactics of the attacking team are the same as for the free hit, namely, to make spaces through which the ball can be rolled. The inner on the side of the field where the roll-in is being taken should play out fairly close to the alley line. If she should receive the ball she should pass immediately and then get back to her proper position in the forward line. Near the opponent's goal it is not advisable for the inner to go out. Here she should stay closer to the center of the field and nearer to the scoring area. All players of the attacking team should be in an onside position in the field of play, and no member of the team may stand within the alley.

The player taking the roll-in should not make the direction obvious. It is best to play the ball well down field when the roll occurs near the player's own goal. The player taking the roll-in should get back onto the field of play at once.

THE DEFENDING TEAM

The backs opposing the forwards near where the roll-in is being taken should mark their forwards, staying between them and the goal these forwards are attacking. They should be ready to start forward as soon as the ball is released in order to intercept the roll. The backs on the far side of the field should be in a covering position.

The forwards of the defending team should place themselves in position to cover possible angles of pass and to block spaces made by the opposing forwards. Here again, the forwards should be between the player taking the roll-in and the forwards to whom she is rolling. No member of the defending team may stand inside the alley while the roll is being taken.

SUGGESTED ROLL-INS

Near the Attacking Team's Goal:

1. A long roll up the alley, almost parallel to the side line, such that the wing can run ahead to pick up the ball (Fig. 5–41).

2. A short roll to the inner, who is near the alley line, so that the inner can pass well down the field to the wing (Fig. 5–42).

CHAPTER 5.   HOCKEY

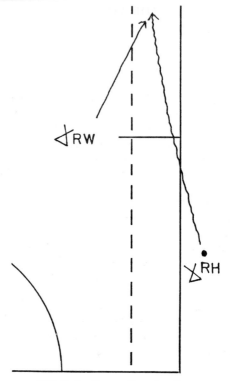

FIG. 5-41. Long roll up the alley.

In Midfield:

1. A roll to the inner, who is near the alley line, a pass back to the halfback who rolled the ball followed by a pass from her to the wing (Fig. 5-43).

2. A roll to the center forward, who plays the ball either to the right or to the left side of the field (Fig. 5-44).

3. A roll to the center halfback or the right fullback, who immediately sends the ball to the wing or inner on the far side of the field (Fig. 5-45).

Near Opponents' Goal:

1. A roll from the wing to the inner, who is near the edge of the circle (Fig. 5-46).

2. A roll from the wing to the left halfback, who passes to the center forward in the circle (Fig. 5-47).

Generally speaking, when near the opponent's goal roll toward the center of the field in order to get the ball into the scoring area. This is comparable to a centering pass. When the roll occurs near the player's own goal, the ball should be sent well down the field and kept out in the alley.

CHAPTER 5. HOCKEY

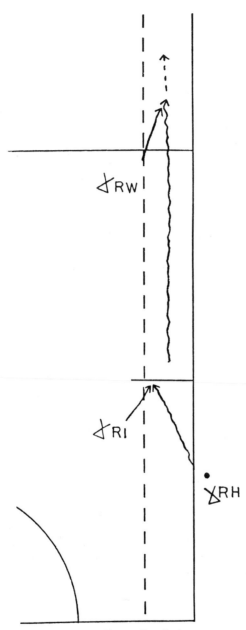

FIG. 5–42.   Short roll to the inner.

CHAPTER 5.   HOCKEY

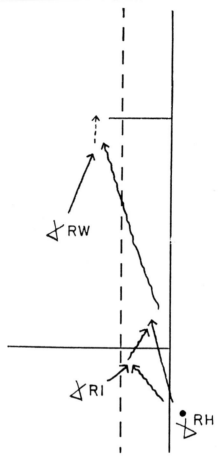

FIG. 5–43. Roll to the inner, in midfield.

THE SHORT OR PENALTY CORNER

The short or penalty corner is awarded for a foul committed by a member of the defending team within her own striking circle, for illegal substitution, or when a member of the defending team intentionally sends the ball over her own goal line from any position between the goal line and the nearer 25-yard line.

THE ATTACKING TEAM

The attacking team, with the exception of the wing taking the corner hit, must be outside the striking circle. The forwards should line up around the edge of the striking circle somewhat off center toward the side from which the hit is coming. They must remain out-

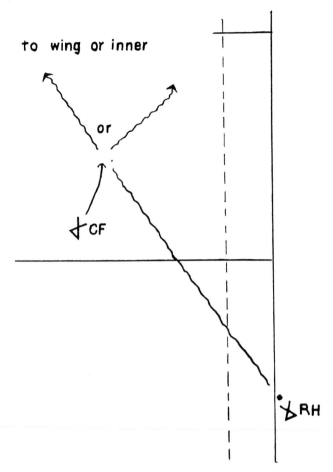

to wing or inner

or

CF

RH

FIG. 5-44. Roll to the center forward, in midfield.

side the circle until the ball is hit. The ball must be stopped by a member of the attacking team or touched by a member of the defending team before a shot at goal is made.

The halfbacks of the attacking team should play well up the field toward the circle in a backing-up position, ready to pick up the pass if it should go beyond the forwards or ready to tackle the opposing backs if they should intercept the pass. Occasionally the center halfbacks find an opportunity to shoot or to stop the ball for the center forward to shoot. The center halfback should therefore be at the edge of the circle.

The wing taking the hit may stand in any position she chooses, provided the ball remains on the goal line no closer than 10 yards to the nearer goal post. Any stroke may be used on a corner hit. No other player may stand closer than 5 yards to the ball.

CHAPTER 5. HOCKEY

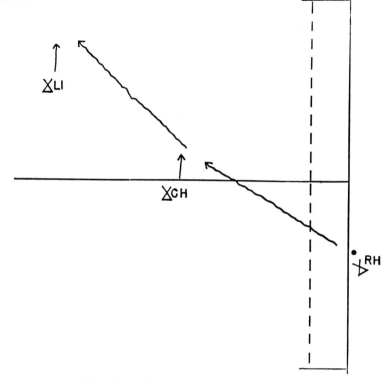

FIG. 5–45. Roll to the center halfback, in midfield.

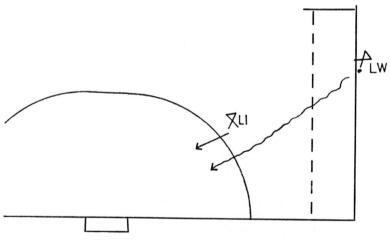

FIG. 5–46. Roll from the wing to the inner.

CHAPTER 5. HOCKEY

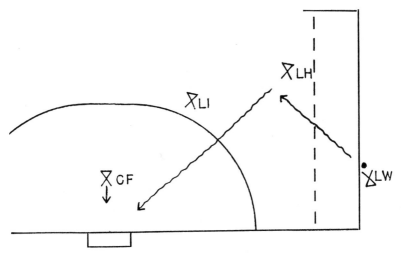

FIG. 5–47.   Roll from the wing to the left halfback.

The forwards should start to move as soon as the ball is hit, going into the circle if the ball is moving ahead of them. Many a good shot at goal has been lost because the forwards wait for the ball to come to them rather than going on to meet the ball.

The corner hit should be angled across the circle toward the far inner so that the forwards will have a chance to pick it up as they advance. The corner hit should be a clean, well-directed drive sent so that it rolls quickly over the ground without bouncing. The wing taking the hit should come back into play at once or she will find herself in an offside position.

The fundamentals in all corners are correct position, accuracy in the hit, control by the receiver and speed by the player shooting.

THE DEFENDING TEAM

Six members of the defending team, generally the backs and goalie, should line up behind the goal line, no player closer than 5 yards to the ball. Each back should stand opposite the forward for whom she is responsible, except the halfback on whose side the hit is being taken. It is best to stand slightly to the opponent's stick side. The left halfback has an excellent opportunity to intercept the pass when the right wing takes the corner hit if she reaches out with a left-hand lunge. She should therefore place herself as close to the wing as is permitted. No back should be in the cage with the goalie. The goalie needs an uninterrupted view of what is going on and a chance to shift her position within the goal without interference.

The other five players of the defending team must stand behind the nearer 25-yard line until the ball has been touched by a second player or until it goes outside of the striking circle.

1. Hit by the left wing to the right inner, who stops the ball with her hand for the center forward to shoot.

2. Hit toward the inner on the near side of the circle.

3. Hit toward the inner on the far side of the circle.

4. Hit from left wing to center halfback, who stops the ball with her hand for the center forward to shoot.

THE LONG CORNER, OR CORNER

The long corner, or corner, is awarded when a member of the defending team, from any position between the goal line and the nearer 25-yard line, unintentionally sends the ball over her own goal line.

THE ATTACKING TEAM

The attacking team should follow the same line-up and tactics as for the short corner. In this corner, however, the ball should be 5 yards from the corner on either side line or the goal line, but the wing taking the hit may stand in any position she chooses. If the ball goes between the goal

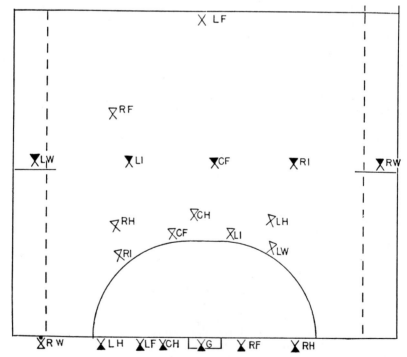

FIG. 5–48. Line-up for long corner hit by right wing.

CHAPTER 5. HOCKEY

of sides.

THE DEFENDING TEAM

The line-up and tactics of the defending team are essentially the same as on the short corner.

THE BULLY

A center bully is taken at the beginning of the game, at the start of the second half and after each score.

There is no attacking and defending team on the bully, but each team should be ready to combine either for offense or defense as soon as the bully is completed.

Every player on the team should know how to bully, the goalie not excepted. There are nine times, exclusive of the penalty bully, when a bully is awarded on the field, and it may fall to the lot of any player to participate in one.

The following discussion will be concerned with the center bully on the 50-yard line but may be adapted with only slight variations to any bully on the field.

POSITION OF PLAYERS

All players, except those taking the bully, must be nearer to their own goal than to the opponent's goal. The players taking the bully must face the side lines squarely. The center halfback should back up

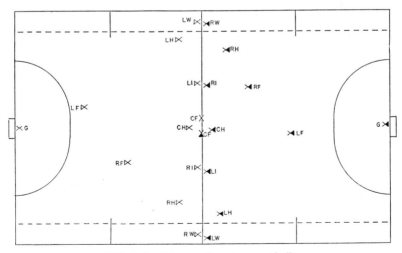

FIG. 5–49.   Line-up of two teams at bully.

CHAPTER 5.   HOCKEY

the bully as closely as the rules allow, standing slightly to the left of the ball. The right fullback should play almost on a line with the center halfback. The left fullback should be in a covering position.

CHANGES AT COMPLETION OF THE BULLY

Both forward lines should cross the center line as soon as the bully is completed. Many forwards tend to hang back to see what will happen and in that way handicap their own team by not being ready for a pass. If, at the completion of the bully, the ball is passed diagonally ahead and the forwards have failed to cross over, there will be no one ready to receive the pass.

The halfbacks and fullbacks of the team losing the bully should immediately shift to marking and covering positions. The halfbacks of the team securing the bully should back up the forward line, and the fullbacks should shift up and down the field depending upon the position of the ball.

SUGGESTED BULLIES

1. The center forward reverses her stick, taps the ball back toward her own goal a very short distance, changes her stick and hits *to the right inner*, who, in the meantime, has crossed the center line and is starting downfield (Fig. 5–50).

2. The center forward reverses her stick and taps the ball back *to her own center halfback*, who opens out the game with a pass to one of the wings (Fig. 5–51).

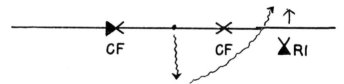

FIG. 5–50. Bully, center forward to the right inner.

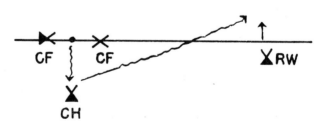

FIG. 5–51. Bully, center forward to the center halfback.

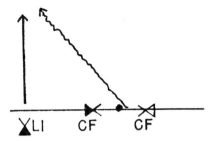

FIG. 5–52. Bully, center forward to the left inner.

3. The center forward steps or jumps back, pulling the ball with her, and then hits *to her left inner*, who has already crossed the center line. In this bully special care must be taken not to move the feet before the bully is completed and not to obstruct the opposing center forward by turning the body or shoulder toward the left inner (Fig. 5–52).

4. If the opposing center forward continually attempts to hit the ball straight ahead, lift the stick and let her hit to your own center halfback.

5. If the ball is caught between the sticks of both center forwards, press against the opponent's stick and lift slightly to cause the ball to jump the stick and roll free.

THE PENALTY BULLY

The penalty bully is awarded for a willful foul by a member of the defending team within her own striking circle, or for a foul by a member of the defending team within her own striking circle, said foul preventing a goal from being scored. The penalty bully concerns only the two players participating. The general bully regulations such as ground-sticks three times and facing squarely must be fulfilled. All members of both teams, except the two participating in the bully, must be beyond the nearer 25-yard line.

The bully is over when a goal is scored, when the defending player commits a foul, when the defending player sends the ball out of the striking circle onto the field, or when the attacking player sends the ball over the goal line without score.

The bully is taken on the penalty bully mark between the player who committed the foul and any member selected from the opposite team. The goalkeeper loses all privileges during a penalty bully, and she may not take time to remove her goal pads.

NOTE: No attempt has been made in this section to give all regulations concerning the various penalties. It is suggested that a current rule book be consulted because of the frequent changes in the rules.

SECTION V. POSITION PLAY

THE FORWARD LINE

The forward line consists of five players, the left wing, the left inner, the center forward, the right inner and the right wing. The halfback line consists of a left halfback, a center halfback and a right halfback; the fullback line of a left fullback and a right fullback. The goalkeeper, in the goal cage, is the eleventh member of a hockey team.

The forward line players, as stated previously, should learn to receive the ball with feet pointing in the direction they intend to run. This not only enables them to get away to a quicker start but it also frequently prevents the foul of obstruction by turning. Passes should be sent to the forwards so that they do not have to turn around to pick them up, but so that they can continue on down the field without breaking stride or slackening speed.

Interchange of position between forwards is generally considered as a sign of weakness on the part of some player. There are occasions when it seems that interchange is necessary, but those result chiefly from the failure of one forward to stay in her position or to keep up with the rest of the forward line. If, for example, the right inner is behind the rest of the forwards and a pass comes to her position, it is permissible for the wing to come in for it and then to continue on in the inner's place. In this case the inner should recover in the wing position and both continue until the play is completed.

Forwards frequently make the mistake of slowing up when they see a pass going beyond them and into the backs. They should learn to continue on, stick down in order to tackle the back or at least to hurry her pass. Forwards should make every possible effort to reach a pass meant for them.

A forward, picking up a pass behind her own line, will find it a good move to pass to the inner or wing on the far side of the field. This inner is generally unmarked. A sudden change of direction of this sort will often temporarily disorganize the opposing defense.

It is more difficult to initiate an attack than it is to break one up. The forward line is necessarily responsible for initiating attack, once they have the ball in their possession. It is only through close cooperation with one another that the forward line is at all able to carry through an attack to its ultimate goal, namely a score. Individual stars on the forward line should be discouraged.

THE CENTER FORWARD

The center forward must be fast, unselfish, versed in individual tactics, skilled in the bully and a leader of the forward line.

CHAPTER 5. HOCKEY

She must be able to pass equally well to the left and the right in order to keep the play well distributed.

She must be able to dribble well, shoot well and pass well.

She must know when to rush a shot at goal and when not to.

She has the most persistent of the opposing backs against her, and all her skill is needed to outwit this opponent.

The center forward must learn that her position is in the center of the field, and she should confine herself to that area. A roving center forward throws the whole forward line off balance and weakens the attack.

The center forward should lead her team in the attack. When on the defense she should bring the line back so that there will not be too great a distance between the forwards and the backs when the opposing forward line has the ball.

THE RIGHT AND LEFT INNERS

The inners are the connecting links between the center forward and the wings. They should be skilled in the same tactics, fundamentals and technics as the center forward. They will find their positions somewhat easier to play than that of center forward because the diagonal position of the opposing backs leaves one inner unmarked, except when in the circle.

The inners should not think that every pass coming their direction belongs to them. If the ball is moving rapidly and diagonally, it is often best to let it go on to another player. This is especially true if the ball is behind the inner.

Inners should get out toward the alley line for the roll-in unless this occurs close to the goal they are attacking. Most inners have difficulty in picking up passes from the right and should learn to get the stick around to meet the pass facing the goal they are attacking.

Inners should veer toward the center when approaching the striking circle. An inner in possession of the ball and ahead of the forward line should cut toward the circle immediately.

The right inner gets many excellent opportunities to shoot, and since she is naturally in a good shooting position she should learn to make her shots count. The right inner should combine with the right wing or the center forward in the use of triangular passes.

The left inner must learn to get her shoulders around and step in close to the ball when attempting a shot at goal or a pass to the right. She should be able to do this while running straight ahead. The left inner is in a much more difficult position from which to shoot than is the right inner. The best shot for the left inner is toward the inside goal post on the far side of the goal. The left inner should combine with the left wing or center forward in the use of triangular passes. Inners should learn to reverse the field by passing to the other inner or wing on the far side of the field.

CHAPTER 5.   HOCKEY

As a general rule, whenever one inner shoots for goal the other inner should rush the shot.

The Right and Left Wings

The wings should be fast, good dribblers, and possessed of a drive which will carry the ball from the alley well toward the center of the field. They should be able to execute such drives while running at top speed.

The wings act chiefly as ball carriers, but their work does not stop there. They should cooperate with the inners in the execution of triangular passes; they should be ready to take a free hit or roll-in occurring near the goal which they are attacking; they should be quick in getting near the alley line for a roll-in; and they should be ready to take corner hits on their side of the field.

Wings have very little opportunity to shoot, their work at the circle being mostly that of backing up. However, should a wing find herself in possession of the ball and ahead of the rest of the forward line, she should not hesitate to cut toward the circle and carry the ball in herself for a shot at goal. This is especially true in a situation in which the covering fullback is not playing deep in defensive territory.

Wings should learn to center the ball at the 25-yard line. This calls for a clean-hit, diagonally forward pass which can be picked up by any one of the three inside forwards near the edge of the circle. If a wing finds that she has carried the ball well beyond the 25-yard line, the centering pass should be made diagonally backward, unless there is an opening for a square pass parallel to the goal line.

On long or short corners, the wings are responsible for the hit. Again, a good clean drive is necessary. The wing taking the corner hit must get back onto the field quickly or she will find herself offside.

In order to play the position of wing as it should be played, the player *must* stay out in the alley. If a wing wanders it not only disorganizes the forward line but it makes it easy for the opposing backs. Bunched forwards are more easily taken care of than forwards well spread out across the field. The right wing, by staying out in the alley, not only draws her opposing halfback out with her, but makes it impossible for that halfback to tackle her with her strongest tackle, namely the circular tackle.

The left wing has the more difficult side of the field to play. Most passes come to her on the right so are not very easy to pick up; she has difficulty in evading her opposing halfback who is in position to use the strongest tackling stroke, namely the left-hand lunge, and she will find it difficult to center from the left side of the field. In order to center well from this side, the wing must carry the ball close to her. The left wing can either overrun the ball and center with a right drive, or she can pull the ball back, get herself turned around and center with a regular drive. Both these methods, easy as they may sound, need a great deal of practice for perfection.

CHAPTER 5. HOCKEY

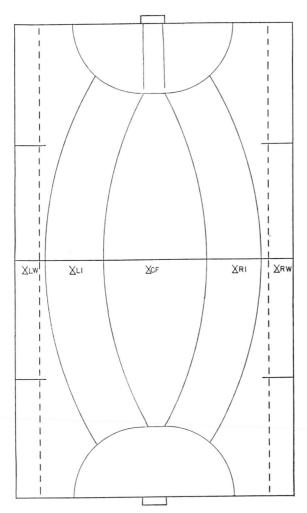

FIG. 5–53. Territory covered by the different forwards.

THE HALFBACK LINE

The halfbacks play more of a combined attacking and defending game than any of the other players on the field, and for that reason they must be tireless. The right and left halfbacks participate in, but do not initiate, interchange.

The halfbacks should never be caught standing in a straight line; diagonal defense is the strongest. When their forward line has the ball they should follow up the field, ready to shift immediately should the opposing line gain possession of the ball.

It is the constant shifting of position from backing up to defending

FIG. 5–54. Position of the halfback line when the opposing forward line has the ball.

which makes the position of the halfback the most strenuous on the field. Any halfback who cannot keep up this shifting during the entire game should not be in that position.

Many a good halfback spoils her play by dribbling the ball too long, thereby giving the opposing backs a chance to get organized and mark the forwards. A halfback carrying the ball is easy prey for a forward tackling back. Get your stick on the ball, control it, look up and then pass!

THE CENTER HALFBACK

The center halfback plays one of the most exacting positions on the field. In the first place, the center halfback is responsible for the opposing center forward and must, in spite of temptations to wander,

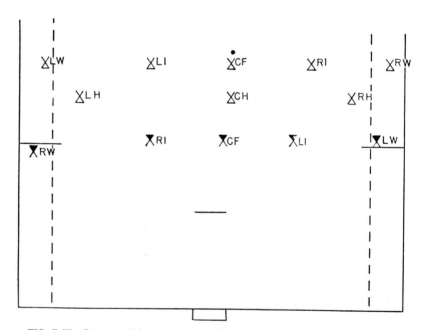

FIG. 5–55. Position of the halfback line when their own forwards have the ball.

CHAPTER 5. HOCKEY

stay with her opponent. Secondly, to a great extent at least, the work of keeping play well distributed falls upon the center halfback. In the third place, the center halfback must know and be able to execute all types of passes, tackles and dodges and must be constantly on the alert to get into the proper position in relation to the ball and her opponent.

The center halfback will find it difficult to pass to her own center forward because of the tenacity of the opposing center halfback. She will find a push valuable in playing to the inners and a drive often necessary in order to get the ball out to the wings. Probably the most satisfactory method of getting the ball to her own center forward is through a space and ahead of her.

The center halfback must be able to use any method of tackling, for there is no telling on which side of the opposing center forward she will find herself when it is necessary to tackle. Speed and endurance are prerequisites for the position of center halfback.

Frequently, while backing up at the circle, the center halfback finds an opening for a shot at goal. Such opportunities must be taken advantage of as quickly and as often as they occur. (The center forward should rush a shot by the center halfback.) A surprise shot is often a scoring shot. The usual position for the center halfback to assume when her forward line is within the striking circle is close to the edge of the center of the circle.

When the centers bully, the center halfback should be up as close as the rules allow, with the head of the stick on the ground in a position of readiness. She should stand slightly to the left of the ball in order to cover more adequately a pass to her nonstick side should the bully go to the opposite center forward. She should always be ready for a backward pass from her own center forward on the bully. When she receives a ball from the center bully, she should open out the game by sending it out to one of the wings. When the inners bully, the center halfback must assist in backing it up.

The center halfback is responsible for free hits which occur in her section of the field. She should quickly get into position to mark her opposing center forward when that team has a free hit. She should back up her forward line at the circle on a corner hit and should get into a position opposite the opposing center forward when that team has a corner hit.

THE RIGHT AND LEFT HALFBACKS

The work of the right and left halfbacks is practically the same as that of the center halfback. There is less call for the use of a variety of tackles because they play one side of the field, but they should both be familiar with all tackles because during interchange they are often forced to shift position. These halfbacks are responsible for roll-ins and for free hits occurring in their section of the field. The roll-in and free hit should be taken quickly and with a definite idea of "what to do with the ball" in mind.

When on the attacking team, the halfbacks should back up the forward line and at the circle they should be in position to intercept clearing passes from the opposing goalie and to center the ball again. The halfbacks of the defending team should mark closely in the circle.

The right halfback is responsible for the opposing left wing. If the halfback will learn to stay on the stick side of her opponent when attempting to overtake her or when coming forward to tackle, she will have little trouble in preventing the wing from cutting toward the circle. In this position she will be between the wing and the goal she is attacking and, further, will be in position for a left-hand lunge. The right halfback should have little difficulty in placing herself in an excellent position to intercept passes to the left wing, because in order for a pass to reach the wing it must cross to the stick side of the halfback.

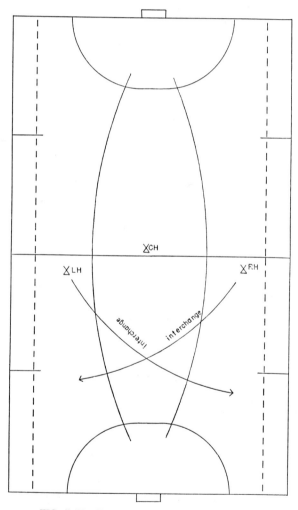

FIG. 5–56. Territory covered by the halfbacks.

CHAPTER 5. HOCKEY

The left halfback is responsible for the opposing right wing. Her duties are the same as those of the right halfback but more difficult to fulfill. She must keep close to the side line and not allow herself to be passed on that side or she will find herself in an awkward position for tackling, and she will also find that the wing has a free path toward the striking circle. The left halfback must be master of the circular tackle, the right cut, the left job and the right-hand lunge.

THE FULLBACKS

The right fullback is responsible for the opposing left inner and the left fullback for the opposing right inner.

Fullbacks should be able to drive well, to push, to tackle and should develop the ability to anticipate.

Fullbacks cover the field from their own goal line up to or slightly beyond the far 25-yard line. They should shift up and down the field so that one is always playing up and one back, except when the ball is within their own striking circle. In that case, both fullbacks should mark closely. The side of the field on which the ball is determines which fullback should play up. The rule for fullbacks to follow is "up when the ball is on your side of the field, cover when it isn't."

Fullbacks should never be caught standing opposite one another, for in that position through passes can be easily and successfully executed by the opposing team.

Fullbacks are responsible for initiating interchange. This requires a thorough knowledge of when to change and in what part of the field interchange should take place.

Fullbacks should learn to control the ball before clearing it out from goal, except when especially hard pressed. Hitting the ball on the fly is apt to be dangerous and should be used only in an emergency. A fullback should learn to get rid of the ball quickly and not to play with it. Get the ball to the forwards as soon as possible! In passing to the forwards, remember that the inner on the far side of the field is apt to be unmarked. This type of cross-field pass should not be attempted near the fullback's own goal. A pass by either fullback, aimed at the corner of the field, will stay on the field of play. This is especially good in passing to a wing.

When following the opposing forwards into the striking circle, care should be taken not to back up in front of the goal and obscure the goalie's view. Remember, if the goalie is expected to stop any shots she must be able to see them before it is too late.

Fullbacks should be prepared to take free hits, especially those which occur in or near the striking circle. It is there that long, diagonal through passes can do so much toward getting the team started on the attack.

The right fullback, like the right halfback, has the easier side of the field on which to play as far as tackling goes. Right fullbacks are often inclined to pass across their own goal because this is the easier

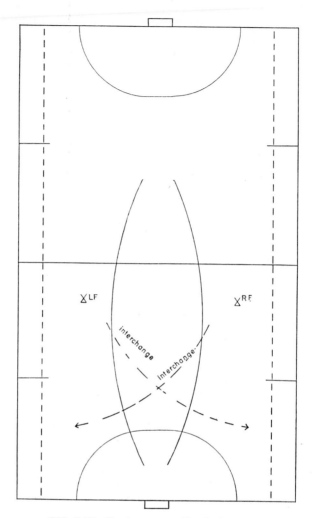

FIG. 5-57. Territory covered by the fullbacks.

direction in which to hit. They are also inclined to hit the ball backward while running toward their own goal. The right fullback must learn to get herself turned around facing the direction in which she wishes to hit the ball. She should develop a good right drive and a good push in order to be able to clear the ball toward the right side line. She should be well versed in all types of tackles.

The left fullback has many of the problems of the left halfback. She too must be especially skilled in tackling from the left of her opponent. The circular tackle is her strongest tackling stroke. The left fullback is responsible for the center forward should that player elude the center halfback. Her tackling stroke in that case should be a left-hand lunge.

CHAPTER 5. HOCKEY

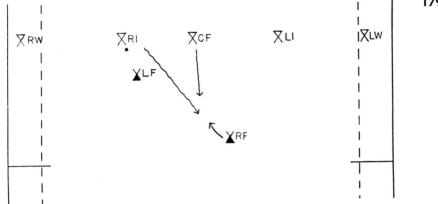

FIG. 5–58. Through pass blocked by fullbacks standing diagonally.

The right fullback should play farther up the field than the left fullback on a center bully.

The backs and halfbacks both need stickwork adequate for any situation which might arise. They should possess the ability to anticipate in order to intercept. They need both endurance and stamina. Sense of timing in tackling is vital. They must be able to press the attack. They must have such highly developed teamwork that they feel themselves so closely connected with other players that they are constantly adjusting their positions to those of their teammates.

THE GOALIE

The last resort of the defending team is the goalie. The problems of her position are many, and not the least of these is having her view obscured by her own backs.

The goalie must learn that shots from certain angles on the field can enter only certain parts of the cage, and so she must be quick to adjust her position to cover these parts (p. 141).

A goalie should come out to meet a forward approaching alone with the ball. It is far less ignominious to have the ball flicked into goal while attempting a tackle than while standing waiting for a shot. Once the goalie has made up her mind to come out, she should not hesitate. The goalie should always come out if she can reach the ball before an opponent. The only time a goalie should *never* come out is when two forwards are free in the circle.

The goalie must have courage to face hard shots from close in. She must be able to stand up under repeated shots and must not lose her head as forwards rush. If a goalie is expected to do her part well, she should be properly protected with adequate equipment.

Summary of Field Hockey Rules

WHEN TAKEN	REGULATIONS	WHAT HAPPENS IF REGULATIONS ARE NOT FULFILLED
	Free Hit	
1. Foul in the field of play outside of the striking circle Advancing the ball Dangerous hitting Delaying the game Interfering with opponent's stick Kicking the ball Obstruction Offside Picking up or throwing the ball Playing ball between own feet Playing without a stick Pushing, charging or personal contact Sticks Stopping the ball with any part of the body except the hand Tripping Undercutting Using round side of stick	a. Hit for opponents on spot where foul occurred b. All other players 5 yds. away c. Ball must be motionless d. Player taking hit may not replay the ball	Repeat Repeat unless for purpose of delay Repeat Free hit opponents
2. Foul by attacking team within opponent's striking circle	a. Hit for opponents from anywhere within the striking circle b., c., d. Same as above	Same as above
	Roll-in	
Out of bounds over the side line off the stick of one or more players of the same team	a. Roller stands with feet and stick outside of side line b. Ball must be rolled, not thrown, bounced or spun c. Roll-in taken opposite spot where ball went out d. Ball must touch ground within 1 yd. of where it left the field e. Player taking roll-in may not replay the ball f. All other players outside of alley and in field of play. g. Roller must have stick in hand h. Ball must enter field of play	Roll-in opponents Roll-in opponents Repeat Roll-in opponents Free hit opponents Repeat unless for the purpose of delay Free hit opponents Repeat

CHAPTER 5. HOCKEY

Summary of Field Hockey Rules — *Continued*

WHEN TAKEN	REGULATIONS	WHAT HAPPENS IF REGULATIONS ARE NOT FULFILLED
	The Bully*	

Center bully

1. At beginning of game	a. Ball on center of 50-yd. line	Repeat
2. At beginning of 2nd half	b. All players except centers on own side of center line	Repeat
3. After each goal and penalty goal	c. No other player closer than 5 yds. to ball	Repeat
	d. Bully must be complete	Repeat
	e. Bulliers must stand squarely, feet must not move	Repeat

25-yd.-line bully (all regulations for center bully valid except *a*)†

1. Out of bounds off sticks of opponents over goal line	a. Opposite spot where ball went out	Repeat
2. Ball over goal line off stick of attack (not in goal)	b. Opposite spot where ball went out	Repeat
3. Ball over goal line off stick of defending team from beyond the nearer 25-yard line (unintentional)	c. Opposite spot where ball went out	Repeat
4. After penalty bully with no score	d. Center of 25-yd. line	Repeat
5. Defense sends ball out of circle into field of play during penalty bully	e. Center of 25-yd. line	Repeat
6. Foul by attack on penalty bully	f. Center of 25-yd. line	Repeat
7. Attack sends ball over goal line	g. Center of 25-yd. line	Repeat

Bully-on-the-spot (Center bully regulations hold, except *a*)

1. Simultaneous foul by both teams		
2. After time out if no previous penalty called		
3. Interference with progress of game		Spot chosen by umpire
4. Illegal substitution by both teams simultaneously		Spot chosen by umpire

Bully-on-alley-line (Center regulations hold, except *a*)

1. Opponents send ball over side line		

*No bully may be taken closer than 5 yds. to the goal line or the side line.
†A 15-yard hit out *may* be substituted for the 25-yard-line bully.

CHAPTER 5. HOCKEY

SUMMARY OF FIELD HOCKEY RULES—*Continued*

WHEN TAKEN	REGULATIONS	WHAT HAPPENS IF REGULATIONS ARE NOT FULFILLED
	Corner Hit	
	a. Hit from a point no farther than 5 yds. from the corner on the goal line or side line on side of goal where ball went out	Repeat
	b. Six of defending team, feet and sticks behind the goal until the ball is hit	Repeat
	c. Rest of defending team back of nearer 25-yd. line until ball goes out of circle or has been touched by another player	Repeat
Defending team player, from between her own goal line and nearer 25-yd. line, unintentionally sends ball over her own goal line	d. Attacking team, feet and sticks outside the striking circle, except wing taking hit	Repeat
	e. Players 5 yds. from ball	Repeat unless for purpose of delay
	f. Attack must stop ball before shooting unless first touched by a defending team player	Free hit opponents
	g. Player taking hit may not replay the ball	Free hit opponents anywhere in circle
	h. Striker may not make sticks	Free hit opponents anywhere in circle
	Penalty Corner	
1. Foul by defending team within own striking circle	a. Hit taken from the goal line no nearer than 10 yds. from the nearer goal post, on either side of goal	Repeat
2. Ball sent over goal line intentionally by defending team from between goal line and nearer 25-yd. line	b., c., d., e., f., g., h. Same as under Corner Hit	
3. Illegal substitution		

CHAPTER 5. HOCKEY

WHEN TAKEN	REGULATIONS	WHAT HAPPENS IF REGULATIONS ARE NOT FULFILLED
	Penalty Bully	
	a. Bully taken 5 yds. in front of goal	Repeat
	b. All players except those taking bully beyond nearer 25-yd. line	Repeat
1. Willful foul by defending team in own striking circle	c. Bully must be complete	Repeat
2. Foul by defending team in own striking circle which prevents goal from being scored	d. Players taking bully must stand squarely	Repeat
	e. Attack or defense sends ball between goal posts	Goal
	f. Attack sends ball over goal line, not between posts	Center bully on 25-yd. line
	g. Defense sends ball out of circle into field of play	Center bully on 25-yd. line
	h. Ball goes over goal line not between goal posts off both players	Repeat
	i. Defense sends ball over goal line not between posts	Repeat
	j. Foul by attack	Center bully on 25-yd. line

CHAPTER 5. HOCKEY

SOCCER

SECTION I. INTRODUCTION

HISTORY

There is much doubt as to the actual time and place of origin of soccer. Certainly football – any game played by kicking a ball – can be traced back to early Greek and Roman civilizations. Historians say that football came to England with the Romans, but the Irish claim that kicking games were played in their land a thousand years before the advent of the Romans.

Be that as it may, football games suffered many vicissitudes of fortune before coming into their own. They were played by the soldiers in camp and they were played in the streets of England, where they were forbidden in 1314 and made a penal offense under Henry VIII in 1504. It was not until 1603, during the reign of James I, that sports in England were again revived, although during the time of Puritan dominance they were once more temporarily discouraged.

The famous old English public schools began to develop football games after the ban was lifted, and from the same common stock were developed the three kicking games of football, rugby and association football or soccer.

Soccer in the United States failed to gain much of a foothold until after World War I. Even now, although it is an international game, it fails to rank high as an intercollegiate game in this country. It is, however, gaining in popularity and is being included in physical education programs in many schools.

Soccer for women is a modification of the men's game. The rougher elements of play have been eliminated and a few of the regulations have been changed to make it a more suitable game for girls and women. The first record of soccer being played in a women's college in the United States is in 1919 at Bryn Mawr.

In the United States, at the present time, soccer is a popular activity for high school girls. Many colleges and high schools include it in their programs and many junior high schools play modified games of soccer. Simple games and relays involving the fundamentals of the game can be and have been successfully introduced into programs in elementary schools.

EQUIPMENT AND ITS CARE

Personal Equipment. A player should equip herself with a pair of cleated tennis shoes with a rubber or leather covering on the toe and on the inside of the ankle. The covering adds protection where needed.

Any suitable gymnasium costume can be used. A shorts and shirt combination or a tunic is suggested.

Additional Equipment. A set of pinnies for distinguishing the teams is most desirable. If possible, the pinnies should be numbered in order to make it easier to spot players who are roaming out of position.

If desired, players may use shin guards. They need not be required and should not be regarded as a permanent piece of equipment. Players using guards for an entire season tend to become careless in personal contact, and this should be discouraged. On the other hand, guards sometimes give the timid player courage to tackle or to use the shins against the ball.

Glasses guards should be provided for those players who need them. The goalie requires no additional equipment.

Playing Equipment. The only playing equipment needed is a field and a regulation soccer ball. This fact alone makes soccer a very acceptable game in schools where the budget fails to provide for more expensive sports equipment.

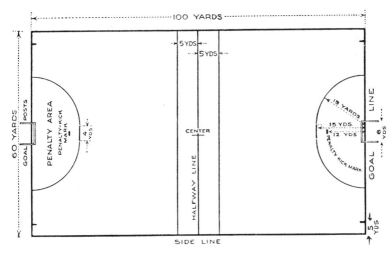

FIG. 6-1. Soccer field (Williams and Brownell).

CHAPTER 6. SOCCER

Care of Equipment. A soccer ball should be kept well inflated during the playing season. Since the ball is frequently used in wet weather, it is wise to apply a coat of protective wax or saddle soap at the beginning of the season and at frequent intervals throughout. This prevents the leather from becoming water soaked. If the ball is subjected to frequent soakings, the leather stiffens and cracks or rots.

At the end of the season the ball should be partially deflated and stored in a cool dry place.

The Field. The field should be a level space measuring no more than 40 to 60 yards in width and 80 to 100 yards in length. The surface should be covered with even turf. While the surface of a soccer field should be as smooth as possible, this is not as essential to the playing of the game as it is to the playing of a game of hockey. The field should be marked as indicated in Figure 6–1.

OFFICIALS

In order to conduct a match game of soccer efficiently it is advisable to have two umpires, a scorer and a timer. As in hockey, each umpire is responsible for half of the field and for the entire side line of her side of the field (see Fig. 5–1). Each umpire is responsible for the following:

1. Calling fouls and imposing penalties in her half of the field.

2. Calling out of bounds in her half of the field and along the entire side line on her side.

3. Indicating when a goal or penalty kick has been scored.

4. Starting the center kickoff according to previous agreement with the other umpire.

5. Calling time out when necessary.

6. Seeing that all penalties are properly taken.

The umpire on the side of the field with the scorer and timer should recognize substitutes and should blow the whistle for half time and for the end of the game.

Umpires should use arm signals, as in hockey, whenever possible. Each umpire should follow play up and down the field in her own half, staying on a line with or slightly ahead of the ball. Umpires should stay off the field of play and out of the players' way as much as possible. There are times when it is necessary for the umpire to go on the field in order to see more clearly close play near the goal area. In such cases she should return as quickly as possible to her proper position.

The umpires should refrain from awarding any penalty if, in so doing, the offending team would gain advantage by stopping play for the penalty.

THE GAME

Soccer is played with eleven players on a team, lined up as in hockey, five forwards, three halfbacks, two fullbacks and a goalie. The game

CHAPTER 6. SOCCER

is started with a kickoff at the center, after which the ball is in play. The ball continues in play until a goal has been scored, when it is again kicked off from the center by the team which did not score. The playing time is divided into four quarters of 8 minutes each. A field goal scores 2 points; a penalty kick scores 1 point.

SAFEGUARDS IN TEACHING SOCCER

COMMON TYPES OF INJURIES

Injuries include:
Sprained ankles or knees due to slipping.
Sprained toes caused by kicking with inadequate protection to the foot or by lack of skill in kicking.
Face and body injuries caused by being hit with a kicked ball. This includes bloody nose, black eyes, body bruises and similar injuries.
Charley horse, muscle strain and the like caused by lack of warm-up periods.

SUGGESTIONS TO THE TEACHER FOR HELPING TO PREVENT INJURIES

Select proper playing equipment.
Provide balls in good condition and blown up to the proper circumference, 27 to 28 inches.

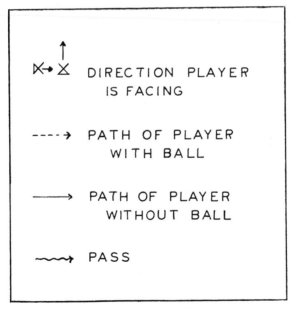

FIG. 6-2. Key to soccer diagrams.

CHAPTER 6. SOCCER

Provide for care of the field. See that is is properly lined and well drained. The surface should be smooth and trimmed, well sodded and free of sticks, stones, glass and other debris.

Check costume and personal equipment. All players should have proper clothing, including rubber-cleated shoes with toe and inside of ankle protected. Glasses guards should be given to players who must wear glasses. Shin guards may be worn as added protection if desired.

Stress thorough knowledge of skills. Players should have thorough grounding in the fundamental skills of ball handling and body control.

Provide for a warm-up period before playing.

Place players as to position and ability.

SECTION II. INDIVIDUAL SKILLS AND TACTICS

DRIBBLING THE BALL

DRIBBLING WITH THE INSIDE OF THE FOOT

BODY MECHANICS

Starting Position. The leg should be rotated outward so that the inside of the foot is in position to meet the ball.

Both feet should be used in dribbling, and the ball should be touched every two or three steps.

The ball should be 10 to 12 inches in front of the dribbler.

The arms should be free at the sides.

The eyes should be on the ball most of the time, but the dribbler should look up occasionally.

Application of Force. The ball should be tapped lightly below its center.

The inside of the foot should come in contact with the ball.

Follow Through. The body weight should follow through onto the foot which last tapped the ball or with a hop onto the other foot.

USE

Used to maintain possession of the ball and to carry it while running.

COACHING SUGGESTIONS

Tap the ball with both feet; using one foot only sacrifices speed.

Keep the ball close while dribbling; it is then under control.

Turn the foot well out before tapping the ball, a zigzag dribble will result.

Rotate the foot inward immediately after contacting the ball if the

FIG. 6–3. Dribbling with the inside of the foot.

follow through is to be on that foot. The foot should be in its normal position when receiving the body weight.

Don't *kick* at the ball. A slight tap is sufficient.

Keep the ball constantly under control.

DRIBBLING WITH THE OUTSIDE OF THE FOOT

BODY MECHANICS

Starting Position. The foot should be rotated inward so that the outside of the foot is in position to meet the ball.

The ball should be 10 to 12 inches ahead of the dribbler.

The toe of the foot contacting the ball should be pointed diagonally toward the ground.

The arms should be free at the sides.

The eyes should be on the ball.

Application of Force. Running normally, the foot should be turned inward to meet the ball with the outside of the instep.

Follow Through. The body weight should follow through onto the foot which last contacted the ball or with a hop on the other foot.

USES

Used to carry the ball while running. Especially usable when combined with use of the inside of the foot for dribbling in a circular direction. Dribbling with the inside of one foot and the outside of the other foot makes it possibe to turn more quickly.

Used as the beginning of a dodge.

COACHING SUGGESTIONS

Generally used in combination with dribbling with the inside of one foot.

Should be used in such combination for a circular or diagonal dribble rather than a straight-forward dribble.

Often used with one foot only contacting the ball and the player moving toward that foot.

The foot must swing back to its normal position before taking the body weight.

Dribbling with the Toe

This is not recommended except for skilled players.

BODY MECHANICS

Starting Position. The feet should point in the direction in which the player is progressing.

The ball should be 10 to 12 inches in front of the dribbler.

The arms should be free at the sides.

The eyes should be on the ball at the moment of contacting it.

Application of Force. The foot should contact the ball every two or three steps.

The toe should be directed slightly under the ball in order to impart the backspin necessary to keep the ball close to the dribbler.

Follow Through. The body weight should follow through onto the foot which last contacted the ball or with a hop onto the other foot.

USE

Used to carry the ball while running. This method of dribbling is difficult and should be taught to advanced players only.

COACHING SUGGESTIONS

Use each foot in the dribble.

This is a difficult dribble to master. Beginners tend to use the toe against the ball rather than getting under it and thus lose control of the ball through failure to impart sufficient backspin to keep it close.

Players should be coached to take the dribble as a part of the running stride. A broken stride does not make for speed. Beginners have a favorite foot for dribbling which necessitates a hopping adjustment resulting in a broken stride.

TEACHING PROGRESSION

Dribble with the inside of the foot, with the outside of the foot, combination inside and outside, and with the toe.
1. Demonstrate and explain.
2. Practice dribbling slowly, then at full speed.
3. Dribble and pass.

CHAPTER 6. SOCCER

4. Dribble and shoot.
5. Dribble, pass, receive.
6. Dribble and dodge.

Single Column Formation (see Fig. 2–1).   1. Five to ten players form a column, each column with a ball. Opposite each column place a marker 30 feet from the first player. X¹s dribble to the marker, dribble around it and back to X²s. X¹s go to the end of the column. *Variation:* Dribble to the marker, stop the ball with the heel and dribble back.

2. Six to eight players in a column, 12 feet between players. X¹ dribbles in and out between players, around the end of the column and back to place. X² takes the ball and X¹ takes her place above X⁶. As the players become more skillful, the distance between the players should be decreased. *Variation:* Indian clubs can be used instead of players as obstacles. If a club is knocked over it must be replaced before the player can continue. This is excellent practice for controlled dribbling and is a good preliminary to dodging.

Circle Formation. (see Fig. 2–13).   Six to eight players 10 feet apart in each circle. X¹ dribbles clockwise or counterclockwise around the circle, returns to place and passes the ball to her left or right.

Shuttle Formation (see Fig. 2–7).   Columns 30 feet apart. X¹ dribbles across to X² and goes to the end of that column. X² dribbles back.

Couple Formation.   Dribbling and passing.

KICKING THE BALL*

KICKING WITH THE INSIDE OF THE FOOT (Fig. 6–4)

BODY MECHANICS

Starting Position.   The right leg should be raised diagonally outward and backward.

The right knee should be slightly bent.

The toe should be pointed toward the ground.

The weight should be supported on the left leg.

The eyes should be on the ball.

The ball should be in front of the player.

The arms should be free at the sides.

Application of Force.   The right leg should be swung diagonally across the body to meet the ball with the inside of the foot.

The knee should be straightened at contact.

Follow Through.   There should be a short follow through of the

---

*All kicks are analyzed for one foot only.

FIG. 6-4. Kicking with the inside of the right foot.

leg in the direction of the kick. The length of the follow through is limited by contact of body parts.

The trunk should lean slightly to the right.

USES

Used for a diagonally forward pass or shot. (The right foot should be used for a pass to the left, and the left foot for a pass to the right.)

Used as the beginning of a dodge.

Used for place kicks which include free kicks, penalty kicks, kickoffs and defense kicks.

COACHING SUGGESTIONS

For a sharp diagonal pass, the toe should be turned well out from the midline of the body.

For a square pass the toe should be turned slightly out.

Coach to use this as a deceptive pass following a dribble.

Contact the ball below its center.

Keep the eyes on the ball, especially when kicking a moving ball.

For a quick kick shorten the backswing.

The backswing should be in line with the direction of the pass.

Learn to kick with either foot.

KICKING WITH THE OUTSIDE OF THE FOOT (Fig. 6-5)

BODY MECHANICS

Starting Position. The left leg should be raised diagonally forward toward the right.

The knees should be bent.

FIG. 6–5. Kicking with the outside of the left foot.

The toe should be pointed toward the ground.

The arms should be free at the sides.

The ball should be in front of and outside of the left foot.

The body weight should be supported on the right foot.

The eyes should be on the ball.

Application of Force. The leg should be swung sharply toward the left.

The outside of the foot should meet the ball just below the center.

Follow Through. There should be a slight follow through of the left leg in the direction of the kick.

The body should lean slightly to the right to aid in balance.

USES

Used as a short pass diagonally ahead.

Used as a shot at goal.

Used as a place kick.

Used as the beginning of a dodge.

COACHING SUGGESTIONS

Be sure that the ball is within reach before attempting to kick it.

Don't just poke at the ball, get a good leg swing.

To direct the ball ahead, the toe should be turned well in.

For a square pass, the toe should be pointed ahead in its normal position.

The backswing of the leg is limited, therefore this cannot be a very powerful pass.

Only the fore part of the foot should come in contact with the ball.

Players should be coached to use this pass as a push, that is, a pass to a nearby teammate or a short shot at goal.

Learn to kick with either foot.

BODY MECHANICS

Starting Position. The right leg should be swung back with the knee bent.

The toe should be pointed toward the ground.

The body weight should be supported on the left leg.

The arms should be free at the sides for balance.

The eyes should be on the ball.

The ball should be in front of the player and slightly toward the right foot.

Application of Force. The entire leg, with the knee slightly bent, should be swung forward to meet the ball below the center.

The top of the instep should come in contact with the ball.

Additional force can be added if the kick is preceded with a step or two.

Follow Through. If a horizontal kick is desired, the knee should remain bent and the leg should follow through in the direction of the kick.

If a raised kick is desired, the knee should be straightened at the moment of contact with the ball and the follow through should be high.

The trunk should be bent forward to maintain balance.

USES

Used for a long pass in the direction in which the player is facing.

Used for a long shot at goal.

Used for place kicks of any sort.

COACHING SUGGESTIONS

Keep the toe pointing toward the ground so that the top of the instep comes in contact with the ball.

FIG. 6–6.   Kicking with the top of the instep of the right foot.

CHAPTER 6.   SOCCER

Keep the eyes on the ball.

Meet the ball squarely; if not, a kick diagonally to right or left will result.

Meet the ball below the center or the ball will be topped and much of the force of the kick will be lost.

Advanced players can learn to play the ball off one side or the other of the instep and so get a deceptive diagonal direction to the kick.

Learn to kick with either foot.

KICKING WITH THE HEEL

BODY MECHANICS

Starting Position. The right leg should be raised forward with the knee slightly bent.

The heel should be toward the ground.

The body weight should be supported on the left leg.

The arms should be free at the sides.

The ball should be 4 to 8 inches behind the right foot.

Application of Force. The right leg should be swung backward so that the heel meets the ball below the center.

The knee should be straightened just before contact with the ball.

Follow Through. There should be a slight follow through in the direction of the kick.

The knee should bend on the follow through.

The trunk should incline slightly forward to aid in maintaining balance.

USES

Used to pass the ball backward.

Used to save the ball from going out of bounds.

COACHING SUGGESTIONS

When executed following a run, the player should jump over the ball and make the kick in her stride. In this case there is no follow through.

At best this is a very doubtful kick because the player cannot see the ball. It should be reserved for advanced players.

Watch to see that a player does not step on the ball when attempting to clear it.

Learn to kick with either foot.

KICKING WITH THE TOE

This is not highly recommended, except for skilled players.

CHAPTER 6. SOCCER

Starting Position. The right leg should be swung straight back. The toe should be pointed slightly toward the ground.

The knee should be slightly bent.

The arms should be free at the sides for balance.

The body weight should be supported on the left leg.

The eyes should be on the ball.

The ball should be directly in front of the right foot.

Application of Force. The right leg should be swung forcibly forward.

The knee should be straightened at the moment of contact with the ball.

The ankle should be flexed from the starting position so that the toe is pointing straight ahead at the moment of contact with the ball.

Follow Through. The leg should follow through in an upward direction.

The force of this kick should lift the player onto her toes or even off the ground.

The trunk should be bent forward from the waist to aid in maintaining balance.

USES

Used for place kicks, especially for penalty kicks and free kicks near the player's own goal.

Used for volleying the ball.

Used for meeting the ball at the top of a high bounce.

COACHING SUGGESTIONS

This is a difficult kick to execute properly without using a box-toed shoe. Injury to the kicking foot is apt to result. It should never be given to beginners because of the possiblity of toe injury.

If a raised kick is desired, the ball should be kicked well below the center.

Watch kicking under the ball and so wasting force by putting backspin on the ball.

Learn to kick with either foot.

CHART OF KICKS

DIRECTION OF BALL	TYPE OF KICK TO USE
Elevated kick	Toe or top of instep with knee straight and ball well forward Inside or outside of foot for short lifted pass
Forward kick	Top of instep or tow with knee bent
Backward kick	Heel
Sideways kick	Inside or outside of foot

CHAPTER 6. SOCCER

Inside of foot, outside of foot, top of instep, heel, toe.
1. Demonstrate and explain.
2. Practice from stationary position.
3. Dribble and pass.
4. Dribble and shoot.

SQUAD PRACTICE

Double Line Formation (see Fig. 2–13).   Five to six players in a line can practice various types of kicks from a stationary position. Lines should be facing each other for kicks with the top of the instep and the toe, and one line should be behind the other for kicks with the heel. Players should be in double column formation (see Fig. 2–8) for kicks with the inside or outside of the foot.

Circle Formation (see Fig. 2–13).   Players stand 10 feet apart in a circle. X^1 starts the ball and passes to X^2. The ball continues around the circle until it is returned to the starter.

1. If passing clockwise, use the inside of the right foot or the outside of the left foot.
2. If passing counterclockwise, use the inside of the left foot or the outside of the right foot.

Diagonal Line Formation (Fig. 6–7).   Players are 15 feet apart. X^1 starts the ball, passes to X^2, who stops the ball and passes to X^3. When the ball reaches the last player, all face in the opposite direction and the ball is passed back again. This can be used as a relay with lines of equal numbers.

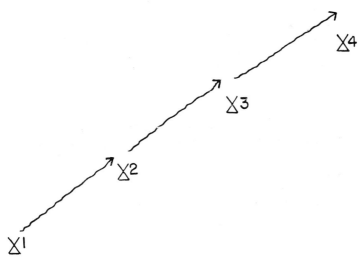

FIG. 6–7.   Kicking, squad practice, diagonal line formation.

CHAPTER 6.   SOCCER

Kicking Through. Eight to fifteen players on a team. Two goal lines marked 50 yards apart. One team starts the play with a place kick from its own goal line. The opposite team *stops* the ball and kicks it back. This is continued until one team crosses the opposite goal line. This scores two points. Touching the ball with the hands scores 1 point for the opposite team. After a score across the goal line, the team scored against kicks off. No opponent may stand closer than 5 yards to a player kicking. This game develops kicking, blocking and trapping.

Kick for Accuracy. A circle 4 feet in diameter or a 5-foot square is marked 20 to 25 feet from the starting line. Players use any specified type of kick in trying for a score. Ball scores 2 points if it lands wholly within the marked area and 1 point if it lands on a line. This can be used as a self-testing activity. If a lifted kick is used, score from the first point of contact with the ground.

TRAPPING THE BALL

TRAPPING WITH THE INSIDE OF THE LOWER LEG (Fig. 6–8)

BODY MECHANICS

Starting Position. The right leg, with the knee bent and the foot in contact with the ground, should form a 45-degree angle with the ground.

The weight should be on the left foot which should be obliquely ahead of the right.

The left knee should be bent.

The trunk should be inclined forward.

The arms should be free at the sides.

The player should be in line with the ball.

Application of Force. The ball should be caught in the pocket formed by the inside of the leg and the ground.

Follow Through. There should be no follow through.

USES

Used to stop a fast moving ball coming toward the player.

Used to stop a ball moving toward the player from the side.

COACHING SUGGESTIONS

Get the pocket formed just as the ball moves into it.

Avoid pressing down on the ball or it will shoot out from under the leg.

Keep the eyes on the ball!

Get your body directly in line with the ball.

CHAPTER 6.   SOCCER

FIG. 6–8. Trapping with the inside of the lower leg.

Come up quickly after trapping the ball in order to be in position to play it.

Keep the weight well over the left leg. If the right leg takes the weight, quick recovery is not possible and quick adjustment of the size of the pocket is not possible.

Learn to trap with either leg.

TRAPPING WITH THE INSIDE OF BOTH LEGS

BODY MECHANICS

Starting Position. The feet should be in a narrow side stride position, the toes pointing slightly outward.

The knees should be bent forward and inward.

The trunk should be inclined forward.

The weight should be evenly distributed on the inner part of both feet.

The body should be directly in line with the oncoming ball.

The arms should be free at the sides.

Application of Force. As the ball rolls to the player, the knees should bend deeply until the ball is trapped between the inside of both legs and the ground.

Follow Through. There should be no follow through.

USES

Used to stop a fast-moving ground ball.

Used to stop a ball as it starts to rise from the ground.

COACHING SUGGESTIONS

Keep the eyes on the ball until it has been stopped. An unevenness in the surface of the ground may cause the ball to rise suddenly, necessitating an adjustment.

Get the body directly in line with the ball.

Come back quickly to the normal position after stopping the ball.

The ball should be pushed forward into the playing position as the player comes up. This is best done by using the inside of one foot while recovering.

This method can best be used when no opponent is close because the recovery is comparatively slow.

TRAPPING WITH THE FRONT OF BOTH LEGS

BODY MECHANICS

Starting Position. The player should be directly in line with the oncoming ball.

The feet should be together, toes pointing forward.

Both knees should be bent, heels off the ground.

The trunk should be inclined forward.

The weight should be carried evenly on the balls of the feet.

The eyes should be on the ball.

The arms should be free at the sides.

Application of Force. As the ball rolls toward the player, the knees should be deeply bent until the ball is caught in the pocket formed by the front of the legs and the ground.

Follow Through. There is no direct follow through.

USE

Used to stop a rolling or bouncing ball.

COACHING SUGGESTIONS

This is more difficult for most players than either of the preceding methods of trapping. Many players find it difficult to bend the knees deeply enough to actually trap the ball.

Can be coached as a method of trapping in which the ball bounces forward from the shins of the player into an excellent position to be played immediately by the trapper.

Players should be coached to recover the normal position quickly.

TRAPPING WITH THE SOLE OF THE FOOT

BODY MECHANICS

Starting Position. The body should be directly in line with the oncoming ball.

The right leg should be raised forward with the knee bent and the heel low.

The body weight should be supported on the left leg.

CHAPTER 6. SOCCER

The trunk should be inclined slightly forward.

The eyes should be on the ball.

Application of Force. As the ball rolls toward the player, the sole of the foot should be pushed down diagonally against the ball.

Follow Through. There should be *no* follow through.

USES

Used to stop a slowly moving ball.

Used to stop a ball starting to rise.

Used to stop a ball just as it drops from a height.

COACHING SUGGESTIONS

Do not put the weight on the ball; it will roll out from under foot if this is done.

Do not step on the ball.

Keep the heel low so that the ball cannot roll under the foot.

In recovering, play the ball with the foot which was used in trapping.

In stopping a ball as it drops from a height, the foot should be placed on the ball just as it strikes the ground. If the ball has started to rise, some other method of trapping must be used.

TRAPPING WITH THE HEEL

In stopping the ball with the heel, the principles of the backward kick are used except that the backswing of the leg is reduced to a minimum. This method of trapping can be used when opponents are running for a ball moving in the same direction, or for preventing a ball from going out of bounds.

TEACHING PROGRESSION

With the inside of one leg, with the inside of both legs, with the front of both legs, with the sole of the foot, with the heel.

1. Demonstrate and explain.
2. Trap a slowly moving ball.
3. Trap and kick immediately.
4. Trap and dribble.
5. Trap a fast-moving ball.

SQUAD PRACTICE

Double Line Formation (see Fig. 2–10). Lines face each other, about 10 feet apart for zigzag passing and trapping. The ball should be passed slowly at first.

Shuttle Formation (see Fig. 2–6). Columns face each other, 15 feet apart. X^1 passes to X^2 and immediately steps to the end of the column. X^2 traps, passes to X^3 and steps to the end of the column.

Circle Formation (see Fig. 2–15). 1. Eight to ten players form a circle with one player in the center. Center player passes to X^1, who traps and passes back. The ball is played around the circle in this way to all players. This can be used as a relay which emphasizes getting rid of the ball quickly after trapping it.

2. Players stand 4 feet apart in circle with one player in center. Center player attempts to kick the ball out of the circle. Others attempt to prevent it by trapping or blocking the ball. When the ball goes through the circle, the player on whose right it passed must take the center position. All kicks must be below shoulder level to be legal.

"Teacher and Class" Formation (see Fig. 2–5). "Teacher" passes to X^1, who traps and passes back. When the ball reaches X^5, that player dribbles to the teacher's place. Teacher moves to the head of the line and play continues. Player in teacher's position calls for type of pass and type of trap to be used.

Single Column Formation (see Fig. 2–1). Squad leader is ahead of and to the left of the column. Squad leader rolls the ball out. X^1 runs out to trap the ball and sends it back to the squad leader. X^1 returns to the end of the column. This is excellent for teaching players to get in line with a moving ball.

Line Soccer (Fig. 6–9). The group is divided into two equal teams, preferably no more than twelve on a team. The teams are lined up along the base lines, facing one another and about 30 feet apart. (Distance varies with age and skill.) The right-hand player from each team comes into the center, and the ball is put in play by rolling it between the two players. The object of the game is for one of the center players to kick the ball through the opposing line.

SCORING: Two points for the kicker's team if the ball goes through

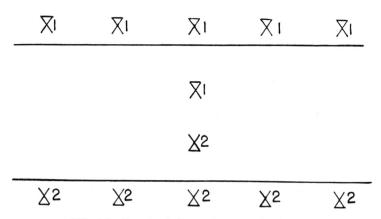

FIG. 6–9. Trapping ball, squad practice, line soccer.

CHAPTER 6. SOCCER

the line below the waist level, and 1 point if it goes through between waist and shoulder height. A line player sending the ball through her own line scores for the other team.

FOULS: Touching the ball with the hands, pushing, shoving an opponent.

PENALTIES: Free kick for the other team from the spot where the foul occurred.

MISCELLANEOUS: When the ball goes over the base line without score, or beyond the side boundaries, it is a kick-in for the opposite team. When center players have played 2 minutes without score, both teams rotate. When a score is made, the scoring team rotates clockwise. When three successive scores have been made against the same center player, that team must rotate.

VOLLEYING THE BALL

VOLLEYING WITH THE KNEE

BODY MECHANICS

Starting Position. The body should be in line with the descending ball.

The weight of the body should be supported on one foot.

The other leg should be raised forward, the knee slightly bent.

The trunk should be inclined slightly forward, unless the ball is dropping perpendicularly, in which case it should be inclined backward.

The arms should be free at the sides for balance.

The eyes should be on the ball.

Application of Force. As the ball drops, the knee should be raised to meet it.

Follow Through. There should be a slight follow through of the leg in the direction of the volley.

USE

Used to play a descending ball. Correctly speaking, the volley should be used only on a ball which has not touched the ground, but this type of play can also be used on a ball which bounces high.

COACHING SUGGESTIONS

Meet the ball as high in the air as possible, but not so high that there is no force in the volley.

Meet the ball with the top of the knee.

Meet the ball well out from the body.

The volley with the knee can be preceded by a jump into the air.

CHAPTER 6. SOCCER

The knee volley can be used to advantage on balls which are too far away or too low for heading.

Learn to volley with either knee.

Volleying with the Foot

BODY MECHANICS

Starting Position. The weight should be carried on the left foot.

The right leg should be extended backward, in line with the oncoming ball.

The right knee should be slightly bent and the toe should be pointed toward the ground.

The trunk should be inclined slightly forward.

The arms should be free at the sides.

The eyes should be on the ball.

Application of Force. As the ball comes within reach of the player, the right leg should be swung forward to meet it.

The *top of the instep* should contact the ball.

Follow Through. The right leg should follow through in the direction of the kick.

If the kick is hard, the body should rise on the toe of the left foot.

The trunk should incline forward from the hips.

In this volley, the inside or the outside of the foot may also be used. The mechanics are essentially the same as those for kicking.

USES

Used to play a descending ball.

COACHING SUGGESTIONS

The height from the ground at which the ball is kicked will determine its trajectory.

Keep the eyes on the ball; timing is especially important.

The kick can be made at the end of a run, the player leaping into the air as it is made.

Learn to volley with either foot.

This may also be used in playing a bouncing ball, but it is not a true volley.

Volleying with the Shoulder

BODY MECHANICS

Starting Position. The weight should be on both feet.

The arms should be free or folded across the chest.

The eyes should be on the ball.

Application of Force. As the ball comes toward the player the entire body should be extended toward the ball.

Follow Through. The entire body should follow through with a jump in the direction of the volley.

USE

Used to play a descending ball which is too low to head and too high for a knee or foot volley.

COACHING SUGGESTIONS

Keep the eyes on the ball.

Moving the shoulder forward or backward at the moment of contact with the ball gives direction to the volley.

Learn to volley with either shoulder.

Avoid letting the ball touch the arms; this is a foul unless the arms are folded across the chest.

The angle at which the jump is made helps to determine the direction of the volley.

TEACHING PROGRESSION

Volley with the foot, volley with the knee, volley with the shoulder.
1. Demonstrate and explain.
2. Toss ball for self and volley.
3. Volley a thrown ball.
4. Volley a ball kicked up from the ground.

SQUAD PRACTICE

Double Line Formation (see Fig. 2–9). Lines of six to eight players are 5 yards apart and facing. X^1 tosses the ball to X^2, who volleys it to X^3. X^3 catches it and tosses it to X^4 to volley and so on down the line. X^6 volleys the ball back to X^5, and the ball is then returned to X^6 and the opposite line volleys.

Relay with Leader Formation (see Fig. 2–2). Ten players are in each column, with the squad leader 4 yards in front of the first player. Squad leader kicks the ball up from the ground to X^1, who returns it with a volley – foot, knee, or shoulder – depending upon the height of the ball. Leader traps and repeats for X^2. Each player goes to the end of the column after volleying.

Circle Formation (see Fig. 2–15). Eight to ten players stand in a circle, with the squad leader in the center. Squad leader tosses the ball to the circle players, who attempt to keep it in the air as long as possible using the knee volley.

Single Practice. Practice tossing and volleying individually. Inside, toss ball to self and volley at target.

CHAPTER 6. SOCCER

BLOCKING WITH THE CHEST

BODY MECHANICS

Starting Position. The feet should be in a slight forward stride position.

The knees should be easy.

The arms should be folded across the chest.

The eyes should be on the ball.

The body should be directly in line with the oncoming ball.

Receiving the Force. As the ball strikes the arms, the body should give. This is done by caving in and jumping slightly backward. As the player jumps back the trunk should bend forward.

Follow Through. There should be *no* follow through.

USE

Used to stop a ball in order to gain better control of it. A blocked ball need not be stopped dead.

COACHING SUGGESTIONS

Keep the arms folded across the chest. This is most important for girls.

Check any tendency to raise the arms to meet the ball.

The body must give *just* as the ball comes in contact with it. If it gives too soon, the entire force of the moving ball will be felt. If it gives too late, the force will be expended in a rebound from the body.

Bending the trunk helps to keep the ball in contact with the body longer, and so it is better controlled.

The bending and give cause the ball to fall almost perpendicularly to the ground so that it lands in a good spot to be played again by the blocker.

Check any tendency to go into the ball. This imparts force to the ball but does not block it.

BLOCKING WITH THE THIGHS OR ABDOMEN

The same principles of blocking apply to these methods as apply to blocking with the chest. The arms need not be crossed over the chest.

TEACHING PROGRESSION

Block with the chest, block with the thighs or abdomen.

1. Demonstrate and explain.
2. Practice blocking a ball thrown for a definite type of block.
3. Intercept a thrown ball by blocking.

CHAPTER 6. SOCCER

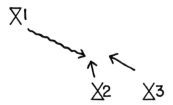

FIG. 6–10. Block ball with thighs and abdomen, squad practice, groups of three.

SQUAD PRACTICE

Shuttle Formation (see Fig. 2–6). Columns should be 10 feet apart. X^1 tosses the ball for X^2 to block. X^1 goes to the end of the column. X^2 tosses the ball for X^3 to block and then goes to the end of the column. The toss can be made for a special type of block — chest, thigh, abdomen — or it can be made for any type of block.

Groups of Three (Fig. 6–10). X^1 is 10 feet ahead of X^2 and X^3. X^1 tosses the ball to X^3, and X^2 comes in and attempts to block it. Repeat the same formation several times and then rotate positions.

HEADING THE BALL (Fig. 6–11)

This is essentially a type of volley.

BODY MECHANICS

Starting Position. The feet should be in a slight stride position, forward preferably.

The arms should be free at the sides.

The body should be inclined slightly forward.

The eyes should be on the ball.

Application of Force. A jump into the air should precede contact with the ball. This adds force and gives additional height.

The neck muscles should be firm and the body in complete extension as the ball is touched.

The ball should be met with the part of the head just above the forehead.

A forward arm swing as the player leaves the ground will add height to the jump.

Follow Through. The body should follow on upward in the direction of the jump (Fig. 6–11).

USE

Used to play a ball descending from a height or bouncing high.

FIG. 6–11. Heading.

COACHING SUGGESTIONS

Keep the eyes open and on the ball as long as possible.

Meet the ball with the part of the head just above the forehead, not the top.

The first heading practice should be very short and if possible, volleyballs should be used.

Jump into the ball, don't wait for the ball to fall on your head.

The side of the head can be used for directing the ball sideways.

The angle of the jump and the part of the head which contacts the ball determine the trajectory of the ball.

Don't head a low ball; another player may kick at it at the same time.

Keep the neck rigid at the moment of contact.

Direction can be attained by a twist of the neck and a swing of the head in the direction in which the ball is to go.

TEACHING PROGRESSION

    1. Demonstrate and explain.
    2. Practice heading a tossed ball. (Use a volleyball at first.)
    3. Practice directing a headed ball.

SQUAD PRACTICE

"Teacher and Class" Formation (see Fig. 2–5). "Teacher" tosses successively to X^1, X^2, X^3, X^4 and X^5. Each in turn heads the ball back to the

CHAPTER 6. SOCCER

and is in position to begin again.

Circle Formation (see Fig. 2–15). Circle consists of from eight to ten players with the squad leader in the center. Squad leader tosses the ball to the players in the circle, who volley it back. This can be used as a relay with circles of equal size.

Shuttle Formation (see Fig. 2–6). Two columns stand 15 feet apart, with the squad leader between the columns, 10 feet to one side. Leader tosses the ball to X^1, who heads it to X^5. X^5 blocks or traps the ball and passes it back to the squad leader. X^1 and X^5 each go to the end of the column. When X^5 again comes to the head of the column, that group heads the ball and the other column blocks and traps. *Variation:* Player blocking the ball dribbles to the end of the column and passes to the squad leader from there.

TACKLING

THE FRONT TACKLE

BODY MECHANICS

Starting Position. The tackler should be directly in front of the oncoming opponent.

The feet should be in a slight forward stride position.

The knees should be easy.

The weight should be evenly divided on both feet.

The trunk should be inclined forward.

The arms should be free at the sides.

The eyes should be on the ball.

Application of Force. One foot should be placed on the ball.

The knee of the rear leg should bend.

The weight should be shifted to the rear foot.

The tackler should reach forward as far as possible to contact the ball.

Follow Through. There should be *no* follow through.

USES

Used as a head-on tackle against a player dribbling the ball.

Used to block the ball as a player starts to kick.

COACHING SUGGESTIONS

Tackle with a reach. Don't run in close to the opponent to tackle, as bodily contact is apt to result.

Keep your eye on the ball and play it rather than the opponent.

Keep the body weight back; block the ball, don't push into it.
Pass or body block (p. 222) immediately after the tackle.

THE SIDE TACKLE

The side tackle is similar to the circular tackle in hockey, but since there is no obstruction in soccer it may be done from either side. The tackler should run parallel with her opponent and attempt the tackle in either of the following ways:

1. By getting ahead of her opponent and dribbling around in front of her, using a combination of dribble with the inside of the foot and dribble with the outside of the foot.

2. By tapping the ball to the opponent's side, using the outside of the nearer foot.

USE

Used to tackle a player while running parallel with her.

COACHING SUGGESTIONS

Don't attempt to dribble around an opponent unless it is possible to outrun her.

When tapping the ball out of reach, be careful to avoid tripping.

Attempt to reach the ball when it is not in contact with the opponent's foot.

THE HOOK TACKLE

BODY MECHANICS

Starting Position. The tackler should face the oncoming opponent, ahead of her and slightly to one side.

The feet should be in a side stride position.

The knees should be easy.

The weight should be evenly divided on both feet.

The trunk should be inclined slightly forward.

The arms should be free at the sides.

The eyes should be on the ball.

Application of Force. The leg near the opponent should be extended sideways with the inside of the foot toward the ground.

The weight should be transferred to the stationary foot.

The knee of the stationary leg should bend deeply.

The trunk should bend to the side of the stationary leg.

The moving leg, after contact with the ball, should pull toward the tackler.

Follow Through. There should be *no* follow through.

Used to tackle a player when slightly to one side of her and facing her.

Used only to hook the ball away from an opponent.

COACHING SUGGESTIONS

Reach for the ball. Play it from a safe distance.

Keep your body out of the way. Tackle only with the foot.

Avoid body contact.

Time the tackle so that it is made at a time when the opponent does not have contact with the ball.

Pull the ball away quickly. Don't give the opponent a chance to recover it.

A pass is the safest play after a hook tackle, because the tackler herself is not in a good position to play it.

THE SPLIT TACKLE

BODY MECHANICS

Starting Position. The tackler should be in front of or to the side of her opponent.

The feet should be apart in an easy stride position, the weight evenly divided.

The knees should be relaxed.

The trunk should be inclined slightly forward.

The arms should be free at the sides.

The eyes should be on the ball.

Application of Force. The tackler should drop on one knee while extending the other leg in the direction of the ball.

The toe should be toward the ball and the knee should be straight.

The weight should be on the bent knee.

The tackler should lean away from the ball.

Follow Through. There should be *no* follow through.

USE

Used to tackle a player when the ball cannot be reached by any other method.

COACHING SUGGESTIONS

If possible, send the ball to a teammate on this tackle. If this is not possible, pass the ball immediately upon recovery.

This is more of a spoiling tackle than one in which the tackler gains possession of the ball.

CHAPTER 6.   SOCCER

Play the ball, not the opponent.

Keep the arms down in order to avoid any tendency to push.

CHART OF TACKLES

POSITION OF TACKLER	TYPE OF TACKLE	DISPOSITION OF BALL
In front of opponent	Front tackle	Pass or retain
	Split tackle	Pass
Facing opponent, but to one side of her	Hook tackle	Pass or retain
	Split tackle	Pass
Running parallel with opponent	Side tackle	Pass or retain

TEACHING PROGRESSION FOR TACKLING

Front tackle, side tackle, hook tackle, split tackle.
1. Demonstrate and explain.
2. Practice on a rolling ball.
3. Practice on a player dribbling slowly.
4. Practice on a player dribbling at full speed.

SQUAD PRACTICE FOR TACKLING

Double Line Formation (see Fig. 2–9). Opposite lines should be 15 feet apart. If a sufficient number of balls is available, each X^1 player should have one. The balls should be kicked slowly to X^2s, who advance to tackle an imaginary opponent. X^2s return the balls with a slow kick and X^1s advance to tackle. If only one ball is available for each squad, pass and tackle in zigzag formation.

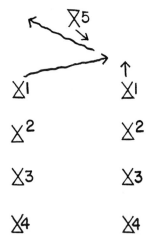

FIG. 6–12. Split tackle, squad practice, double column formation.

Shuttle Formation (see Fig. 2–6). X¹ dribbles the ball and X² advances to tackle. If X² tackles successfully, she passes immediately to X³ and goes to the end of that column. If X¹ carries the ball through, she passes it back to X³ and goes to the end of the opposite column.

Double Column Formation (Fig. 6–12). One couple at a time advances, dribbling and passing the ball. X⁵ advances to tackle. This teaches timing both for tackling and for passing to avoid being tackled. Rotate positions after several attempted tackles by the same player.

THE PUNT (Fig. 6–13)

BODY MECHANICS

Starting Position. The ball should be held in front of the body, about waist level and at arm's distance.

The fingers should be spread and the hands opposite on the ball.

The elbows should be slightly bent.

The feet should be together.

The trunk should be inclined slightly forward.

The eyes should be on the ball.

Application of Force. The ball should be dropped from the above position as a step is taken on the left foot. The right leg should be swung forward to contact the ball just before it touches the ground.

As the leg is swung forward, the knee should straighten and the toe should point so that the top of the instep contacts the ball.

Two or three steps may precede the kick, during which time the ball is carried in the hands.

Follow Through. The right leg should follow through in a continuation of the kicking movement.

The trunk should be inclined forward.

In a very forceful kick the heel of the left foot, or the entire foot, may leave the ground.

FIG. 6–13. Punting.

CHAPTER 6. SOCCER

Used by the goalkeeper as a long clearing kick.

COACHING SUGGESTIONS

Keep the eyes on the ball!

A ball kicked just before it touches the ground is best for a distance kick.

Beginners tend to kick the ball too high from the ground and consequently they get more height than distance.

Keep the ball well away from the body when carrying it.

Timing is most important. The rhythmic pattern is even. *Drop* the ball, *step* on the left foot, *kick* with the right foot.

TEACHING PROGRESSION

1. Demonstrate and explain.
2. Punt from a stationary position.
3. Punt for accuracy and distance.
4. Punt from a moving base.

SQUAD PRACTICE

Line Formation. With lines facing about 25 yards apart, punt back and forth.

Relay with Leader Formation (see Fig. 2–2). Leader stands 30 yards in front of and facing the column. A line is drawn midway between the leader and X^1. X^1 is in possession of the ball. She dribbles to the line and passes to the leader, who picks up the ball and punts back to X^2. X^2 starts to dribble. X^1 takes the place of the leader who goes to the end of the column.

Puntover. Group divides into even teams with 10 to 20 players to a team. Two goal lines are set up 50 to 75 yards apart, depending upon the skill of the group. The ball is put in play by one team with a punt from its own goal line. A player on the opposite team catching a punt may advance three steps and punt from there. A ball not caught must be blocked or trapped without the use of hands and punted from there. The team which can advance to the opponents' goal line wins.

Column Formation (Fig. 6–14). Each squad is in two columns: one column parallel to the side line and 35 yards from the goal line, the other column parallel to the goal line and to the left of the goal. X^1 dribbles the ball in a semicircle toward the goal and shoots against X^6, who steps into the goal cage. X^6 catches or recovers the ball and punts out to X^2, who repeats what X^1 did, this time shooting against X^7. X^1 continues on around after shooting and goes to the end of the other column. X^6 goes to the end of the dribbling column.

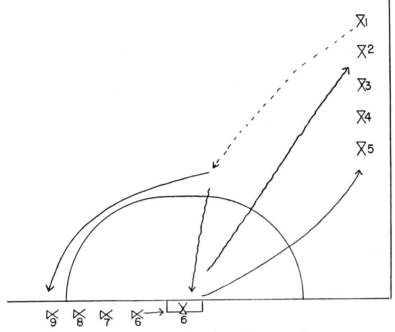

FIG. 6–14. Punt, squad practice, column formation.

Double Line Formation (see Fig. 2–9). Opposite lines 70 to 80 feet apart, depending upon the skill of the players. Zigzag punting and trapping. X¹ takes two steps, right–left (if a right-footed kicker), and punts across to the opposite player, who traps the ball, picks it up and returns it in the same way to the next player. *Variation:* Two steps, followed by a bounce, followed by the punt from a moving base as described above.

THE DROP KICK

BODY MECHANICS

Starting Position. The ball should be held in front of the body, about waist level and at arm's distance.

The fingers should be spread, hands on opposite sides of the ball.

The elbows should be easy.

The feet should be together.

The trunk should be inclined slightly forward.

The eyes should be on the ball.

Application of Force. The ball should be dropped from the above position.

CHAPTER 6.   SOCCER

One step forward should be taken on the left foot as the ball drops.

The right leg should be swung forward, knee straightening as the top of the instep contacts the ball (just as the ball bounces up from the ground).

Follow Through. The right leg should follow through in the direction of the kick.

The trunk should incline forward.

USE

Used by goalkeeper as a clearing kick.

COACHING SUGGESTIONS

Keep the eyes on the ball.

Kick the ball with the top of the instep *just* as it rebounds from the ground.

The rhythm for the drop kick is uneven—long, short, long: step, drop, kick.

Keep the ball away from the body while holding it.

Beginners tend to wait too long before kicking and consequently get more height than distance.

It sometimes helps to have beginners bend forward, bringing the body and the ball closer to the ground.

SQUAD PRACTICE

Double Line Formation (see Fig. 2–9). With lines 15 feet apart, drop kick the ball back and forth, using proper technic. Gradually increase distance.

Column Formation. (Fig. 6–15). Two columns are 20 feet apart and facing in the same direction. A third column is midway between the two and 15 yards from the first player. X^1 punts or drop kicks to X^9, who punts or drop kicks to X^5. X^5 kicks to X^{10} who plays to X^2. Players rotate to the end of own line.

Progressive Punt or Drop Kick (Fig. 6–16). Teams line up in column formation. X^1 from each team kicks the ball from behind the starting

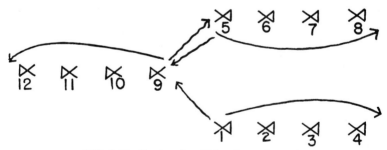

FIG. 6–15.   Punt or drop kick, column formation.

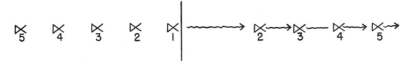

FIG. 6–16.   Progressive punt or drop kick.

line, X^2 from each team starts her kick from where the previous kick first touched the ground, and so on through the five players. Team gaining the greatest total distance of the five kicks wins.

GOALKEEPING

BODY MECHANICS

Position.   The goalkeeper should stand about 3 feet in front of the goal line and in the center of the goal.

The feet should be slightly apart in an easy stride position.

The knees should be easy.

The weight should be evenly carried on the balls of the feet.

The eyes should follow the play on the field.

The position of the goalkeeper should be one of readiness.

Application of Force.   There is no special method for the application of force.

The ball may be caught and punted or drop-kicked; caught and thrown, batted, fisted or slapped out of goal; or kicked on the fly.

Follow Through.   The follow through depends upon the type of clearing method used.

USE

Used by the goalkeeper to prevent the ball from going into the goal.

COACHING SUGGESTIONS

Keep the eyes on the ball as attack begins to approach the goal.

Use whatever method seems safest in securing the ball.

Don't kick on the fly except as a last resort.

Goalkeeping is a specialized job on the team; don't feel punished or neglected if asked to play it.

Look alive in the position. The goalkeeper who leans against the goal post gives a feeling of confidence to the opposing team.

Clear the ball toward the nearer side line!

TEACHING PROGRESSION

1. Catching and clearing with a throw.
2. Catching and clearing with a punt or drop kick.

CHAPTER 6.   SOCCER

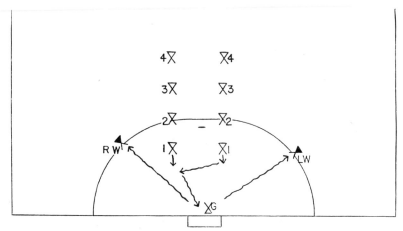

FIG. 6–17.   Goalkeeping, squad practice, couple formation.

3. Scooping a ground ball and clearing with a throw or punt.
4. Batting, fisting or slapping a high ball.
5. Kicking on the fly.

SQUAD PRACTICE

Column Formation.   Players line up in front of the goal, one player in the goal. One at a time players dribble and shoot at goal. Use easy shots at first, and place the ball where the goalkeeper can get it. Work up to more difficult shots, both from the point of view of placement and saving. Change players in the goal frequently.

Couple Formation (Fig. 6–17).   Couples line up in front of the goal, each couple with a ball. One at a time the couples start for goal, dribbling, passing and shooting. One player in goal attempts to prevent score. *Variation:* One player stationed in wing position on either side of the goal to receive a clearing pass from the goalkeeper.

Single Team Practice.   Using one half of the field, place a full forward line against a full defense. Place one extra defense player back of the center line. Attack scores when the ball goes into goal. Defense scores when the ball goes to the extra player. Rotate positions after each score or after 3 minutes of play.

Use a goalkeeper in the goal against any scoring practice.

DEFENSE TACTICS (INDIVIDUAL)

TACKLES

USE

Used to secure the ball from an opponent.

Front tackle: facing the opponent, stop the ball with the sole of the foot.

Side tackle: running parallel with the opponent, tap the ball sideways with the outside of the nearer foot and pick it up with a dribble.

Hook tackle: facing opponent, but to one side, hook the ball away with the top of the instep.

Split tackle: facing the opponent, or to one side, block the ball with the sole of the foot. (Advanced tackle.)

COACHING SUGGESTIONS

Advance to tackle as soon as your opponent has the ball.

If actual possession of the ball is not gained, at least the opponent's shot or pass will be hurried.

Play the ball, not the opponent.

Don't charge at your opponent. There should be no body contact on a tackle.

After a tackle it is best to play the ball away at once in order to prevent tackling back.

Watch for a dodge as you advance to tackle.

Proper timing of the tackle is important. Try to reach the ball when the opponent is not in contact with it.

TACKLING BACK

USE

Used as a means of recovering the ball immediately after being tackled.

METHODS

The same methods which are used for tackling are used for tackling back.

COACHING SUGGESTIONS

Tackle back as soon as the ball is lost to an opponent.

A quick tackle back often catches the opponent off balance from the first tackle.

Always pass immediately after successfully tackling back.

Avoid following an opponent far out of position.

CHAPTER 6. SOCCER

USE

Used to prevent a goal from being scored.

METHODS

Catching the ball, followed by a kick or a throw.
Kicking the ball on the fly.
Scooping the ball.
Batting, slapping or fisting the ball.

COACHING SUGGESTIONS

Catching the ball is the safest, for it can then be cleared with a punt, a throw or a drop kick.
Get the body directly in line with the oncoming attack.
Watch for shots played to the corners, especially high ones.
High balls which cannot be caught should be batted.
Clear to the side. Clearing passes diagonally to the right or left are best. Never clear across the goal.
Stand near the nearer goal post if a shot comes in from the wing. This gives a clear vision of the whole field.
The privilege of handling the ball is accorded the goalkeeper only within her own penalty area. Within this area she may bounce the ball once or take two steps with the ball in her hands preceding a kick or a throw. This may not be combined with a bounce.

GENERAL COACHING SUGGESTIONS FOR INDIVIDUAL DEFENSE TACTICS

Play the ball, not the opponent.
Cover all possible passing angles.
Use the tackle most suited to the position in which you find yourself.
Don't waste time running around an opponent in order to get into a better position for tackling.
If you can't intercept or tackle, at least you can hurry or spoil your opponent's pass or shot.
Tackle back when you lose the ball.

OFFENSE TACTICS (INDIVIDUAL)

PASSING

USE
Used to send the ball to another player.

CHAPTER 6. SOCCER

Any legal method of playing the ball (kicking, volleying, heading, *etc.*) can be used as a pass.

COACHING SUGGESTIONS

Pass ahead of a moving player.

Pass into a space rather than directly at a player.

Learn to pass equally well from either foot. A one-footed soccer player is at a decided disadvantage.

Pass just before being tackled.

If you are deep in your own defensive territory, pass quickly without waiting to draw a defense player.

Defense players should pass quickly rather than carry the ball.

It is generally best to pass immediately after securing the ball from a tackle.

Don't follow in the direction of your pass.

SHOOTING

USE

Used as a method of scoring points.

METHOD

Any legal method of playing the ball (kicking, volleying, heading, *etc.*) can be used in shooting.

COACHING SUGGESTIONS

Shoot immediately, once you are within scoring distance of the goal, unless definitely marked by an opponent.

Always shoot with the idea of scoring a goal. Don't kick the ball in the general direction of the goal and hope that it will go through.

Look up to locate the goal and the position of the goalkeeper before shooting. (See Fig. 5–23, p. 141.)

Follow-up shots often score, especially if the goalkeeper is rushed and forced to clear quickly or on the fly.

Play for the corners of the goal; the high corners are particularly vulnerable.

DODGING

USE

Used to avoid an opponent while dribbling the ball.

Draw opponent to the right and dodge to the left.

Draw the opponent to the left and dodge to the right.

Use body block until opponent is off balance, and then go around her.

COACHING SUGGESTIONS

Soccer is a team game. If there is any opportunity to pass, do so; if not, use a dodge.

Dodge when ahead of the rest of the forward line and in possession of the ball.

Dodging is a matter of throwing the opponent off balance and then going through. A dodge should be made to the side on which the opponent is carrying her weight.

It is frequently necessary to maneuver in front of an opponent before finding opportunity to dodge.

Don't approach close enough for the opponent to tackle. It will be too late to dodge then.

If a dodge fails, try at once to go into a body block.

BODY BLOCKING

USES

To prevent an opponent from reaching the ball in your possession.

To prevent an opponent from reaching the ball in possession of a teammate.

METHOD

Protecting the ball with the body by getting between the opponent and the ball.

COACHING SUGGESTIONS

No personal contact or pushing while blocking.

Don't attempt to block too long or another opponent may come up to tackle from the other side.

Blocking is effective if properly used.

PICKING UP PASSES

USES

Used to receive the ball from a teammate.

Used to intercept a pass to an opponent.

CHAPTER 6.   SOCCER

METHOD

Any legal method of contacting the ball may be used.

COACHING SUGGESTIONS

Pick up the pass facing in the direction in which you wish to continue.

A pass coming from the right can be tipped forward with the outside of the right foot or the inside of the left foot. The latter is preferable, if time permits, because no shift in body position will be needed in order to go on with the ball.

A pass coming from the left can be tipped forward with the outside of the left foot or the inside of the right foot, preferably the latter.

Whenever possible, avoid stopping the ball before going on in a dribble.

If a pass goes behind you and is moving with sufficient force to reach a player farther to the side, let it go.

DRAWING

USE

Used to move an opponent away from the direction in which a pass or shot is to be made.

METHOD

While dribbling the ball, veer away from the direction in which the pass is to be made, drawing the opponent in that direction.

COACHING SUGGESTIONS

Move toward the right if the pass is toward the left and vice versa.

A forward with the ball should continue in possession of it until she has drawn an opponent, unless she is behind the rest of the forward line at the time. In that case the ball should be passed at once.

Beginners often tend to get rid of the ball as soon as they get it.

Don't wait to draw an opponent if you are deep in defensive territory.

Defense players should not wait to draw an opponent before passing. If they wait the opposing defense will have time to cover the forwards.

CENTERING

USE

Used to send the ball across from the wing position to the scoring area.

CHAPTER 6. SOCCER

A hard pass, generally with the inside of the foot, is used for centering.

COACHING SUGGESTIONS

When centering from the right to the left, the inside of the right foot should be used; when from the left, the inside of the left foot. This type of pass can be made more quickly than any other because it requires no shift of body position on the part of the dribbler.

A centering pass should be diagonally forward if started well back from the scoring area. If the pass is started level with the scoring area, it should be a flat pass across the goal.

If the fullback on the side from which the pass is coming is playing up, the pass should go behind her; if she is playing back, the pass should go in front of her.

A wing should be coached in the technic of lifting the ball on a centering pass. This type of pass is valuable when the defense is crowding to the wing side of the penalty area.

GENERAL COACHING SUGGESTIONS FOR INDIVIDUAL OFFENSE TACTICS

Draw an opponent and pass or shoot.

Pass diagonally.

Shoot as soon as possible and follow up your shots.

If you are behind the rest of the forward line and in possession of the ball, pass at once.

Don't use the dodge excessively.

Be quick to body block for a teammate with the ball.

Centering and clearing passes should be long diagonals.

Don't give up the attack until a goal has been scored.

Be constantly on the alert, shifting your position so that it will be most advantageous to the team as a whole.

SECTION III. TEAM TACTICS AND FORMATION PLAYS

Team tactics mean those tactics which are used by the team as a whole or by any combination of players, in contrast to those tactics used only by an individual player.

CHAPTER 6. SOCCER

MARKING

Marking means playing close enough to an opponent to intercept a pass to her or to tackle her immediately, should she be in possession of the ball (see Fig. 5–31).

When any forward line player is in possession of the ball, the defense players responsible for the forwards next to her should be in a marking position, that is, within 2 or 3 feet of their respective opponents. If the right inner has the ball, the left halfback and the center halfback should be marking, with the left fullback tackling or coming in to tackle. This position of the two halfbacks makes it difficult or impossible to get a pass through to either the center forward or the right wing. The marking position is a strong defense position, but strong only insofar as the proper players mark and the remaining defense players cover.

COVERING (BY BACKS)

Covering means playing in such a position as to fill the spaces through which long through passes might be sent. One fullback, the one on whose side of the field the ball does not happen to be at a particular moment, plays the covering position (see Fig. 5–31).

If the right inner of one team has the ball, the right fullback of the opposite team should be in a covering position and the right halfback should have dropped back. Such positions enable the above two players to intercept long through passes by the opposing right inner. Here again, defense is strengthened by proper combination of backs.

INTERCHANGING (BY BACKS)

Interchanging means shifting the defense so that it is concentrated on the side of the field where the ball happens to be at a particular moment. Interchange is always initiated by the covering fullback (see Figs. 5–32 and 5–33).

If the right inner should succeed in getting around the left fullback and find herself free with the ball, some other defense player must take her on. Obviously, if either the left fullback or the center halfback should attempt this their opponents would be left in an excellent position to receive a pass as the shift was made. The right fullback, in the covering position, should shift or interchange to take the right inner. At the same time, the right halfback should shift back into the covering position vacated by the fullback.

COVERING SPACES (BY FORWARDS)

Covering spaces means covering all possible angles of pass. This tactic is performed primarily by the forwards of the defending team.

CHAPTER 6.   SOCCER

226 This is particularly important on free kicks, roll-ins, defense kicks and corner kicks. Should the forwards fail to cover spaces on these penalties, the defense of their team will be decidedly weakened (see Fig. 5–35). Many times forwards fail to understand this, their contribution to defense work.

GENERAL COACHING SUGGESTIONS ON
DEFENSE TEAM TACTICS

The defending team should work as a unit and not leave all the defense work to the backs.

A thorough understanding of defense tactics requires practice.

Playing different positions gives the individual a better understanding of the whole organization of defense play.

Beginners should be taught marking and covering before being introduced to interchange.

OFFENSE TEAM TACTICS

RUSHING

Rushing means following up a shot at the goal. This is important because the second shot often catches the goalkeeper off balance and results in a score.

Once the ball is in scoring position, the forwards should concentrate on getting it into the goal. If the first shot is stopped, the forwards should rush in to attempt a second shot or to block the goalkeeper's clearing pass. Rushing should follow the first shot immediately. Forwards should not wait to see whether or not it scores. The two inners and the center forward should consider rushing one of their special duties.

Generally speaking, a forward should rush her own shot and be supported by one other forward. If the shot comes from the left, the right side should rush and vice versa. If the shot comes from the center, the inner in the position toward which the shot was directed should support the center.

PASSING

Triangular passing is a quick exchange of short diagonal or square and diagonal passes between adjacent forwards. Any type of pass can be used in executing a triangular pass.

In addition to the triangular or short diagonal pass, the long diagonal pass is important in offense tactics. The long diagonal pass is used most frequently by the backs in passing the ball to the forwards. A wing should center with a long diagonal pass toward the center of the field. If the attack has succeeded in concentrating the opposite defense on

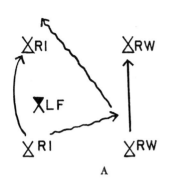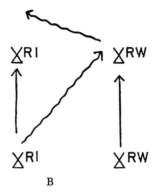

FIG. 6–18. Triangular passes. *A*, Square pass followed by diagonal pass. *B*, Diagonal pass followed by square pass.

one side of the field, a long diagonal pass to the opposite side will open up new attack possibilities.

Square passes should be cut to a minimum. A game built on square passes is apt to be a slow one because often a player must slow down in order to receive such a pass. A square pass can, however, often be used to advantage at the beginning or end of a triangular pass, depending upon the position of the opposing defense players.

BACKING UP

Backing up is the tactic employed by the backs to strengthen the attack when their forwards are in possession of the ball. The backs should follow the forward line down the field, giving them support in the attack. The fullback on the side of the field where the ball is should assist in backing up. This means a constant shift for the fullbacks, from covering position to backing-up position, as the ball shifts back and forth across the field.

GENERAL COACHING SUGGESTIONS ON OFFENSE TEAM TACTICS

Attack is more difficult to initiate than defense. Immediate advantage must be taken of any break in the game.

Triangular passing is the strongest offense tactic.

Long diagonal passes which reverse the field from left to right or right to left confuse the opponents and tend to disrupt the defense.

Attack should vary the tactics used.

Combination between forwards and forwards and backs makes for a strong offense.

Dribbling is the slowest method of advancing the ball.

CHAPTER 6. SOCCER

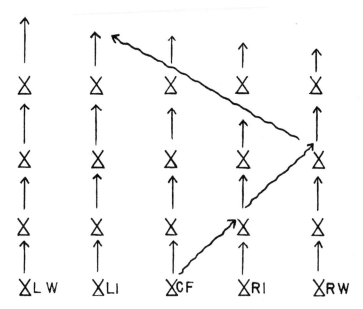

FIG. 6–19.   Diagonal pass, squad practice, line formation.

SECTION IV. FORMATION PLAYS

THE KICKOFF

The kickoff is a place kick from the center of the halfway line. It is used at the start of the game (Fig. 6–20), at the start of the quarters and after a score has been made. (NOTE: Attacking team is in possession of the ball, defending team is not.) For rules and regulations concerning formation plays, see summary of soccer rules, page 246.

After a goal, the team scored against kicks off.

THE ATTACKING TEAM

The members of the attacking team may be in any position they desire in their own half of the field. They may not cross the center line until the ball has been kicked. The ball must be kicked forward from the center of the center line and must roll a distance equal to its circumference. Figure 6–20 shows some of the kickoff possibilities:

The ball can be played directly from the center forward to the right wing or the left wing. In the same way it can be sent to either inner. The inner can either play the ball herself or send it on out to one of the wings. An especially good play is a pass from the right inner to

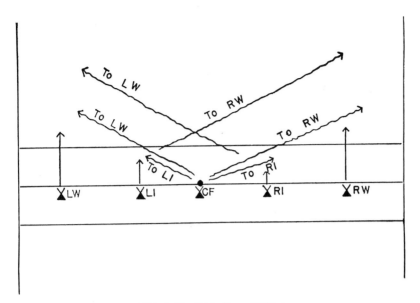

FIG. 6–20.   Kickoff possibilities.

the left wing or vice versa. This works well if the pass can be placed behind the opposing center forward and in front of the center halfback.

As soon as the kickoff has been taken, all members of the attacking team except the goalkeeper should move forward in the direction of the goal which they are attacking. A field goal may not be scored directly from a kickoff. The object of the kickoff is for a team to keep possession of the ball rather than send it deep into the opponents' territory.

THE DEFENDING TEAM

The players of the defending team must be on their own side of the restraining line. They may not cross this line until the ball has been kicked. The forward line players should attempt to intercept the kickoff. The halfbacks and fullbacks should be ready to intercept but at the same time in position and ready to advance to tackle should the forwards fail to intercept.

THE KICK-IN

The kick-in is awarded when the ball goes over the side line, having last been touched by one or more players of the same team. The kick-in is a place kick from the side line directly opposite the spot where the ball went out.

The player, generally a halfback but occasionally a wing, taking the kick-in must be quick to do so or her teammates will be marked and she will lose much of the advantage to be gained from the penalty.

The forward line players on the attacking team should place themselves ahead of the player taking the kick-in, endeavoring to make spaces through which the ball can be passed. The wing and the inner near the kicker should play out toward that side of the field.

The attacking halfback and fullback on the side where the ball is

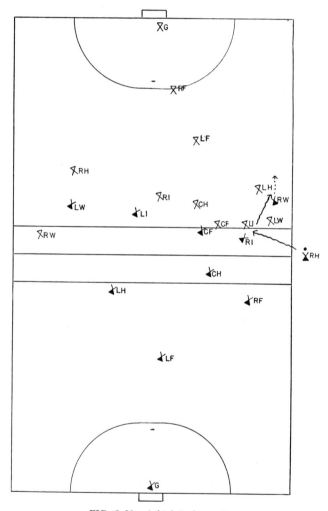

FIG. 6–21. A kick-in formation.

CHAPTER 6. SOCCER

should back up the forward line and shift somewhat nearer to the side line than usual. The other halfbacks and fullback should cover spaces through which a pass might be sent should the opposite team intercept the kick. No goal may be scored directly from a kick-in.

THE DEFENDING TEAM

The forwards of the defending team on the side of the field where the kick-in is being taken should block spaces through which a pass might be made. It is well for the forwards on the opposite side of the field to play up, ready for a pass from their teammates should one intercept the kick. In that way the ball can be quickly moved from the area of concentration of players to a freer space.

The halfbacks and fullback near the kicker should each carefully mark her opposing forward. The other halfback and fullback should be in a covering position. No member of the defending team may be closer than 5 yards to the ball.

THE FREE KICK

A free kick is a place kick most commonly awarded for a foul committed on the field of play, except when committed by a member of the defending team within her own penalty area. (For additional free kick penalties see the rules chart.) The free kick is taken on the spot where the foul occurred.

THE ATTACKING TEAM

A free kick is generally taken by one of the halfbacks, although it may occasionally be taken by a wing or a fullback. The player taking the free kick must be quick to do so in order to gain the greatest possible advantage from the penalty.

The forwards on the attacking team should space themselves to receive a pass. The halfbacks and fullbacks should back up the forwards and be ready to tackle or intercept should the opponents get possession of the ball.

THE DEFENDING TEAM

The placement of the members of the defending team is very similar to that of the kick-in, the forwards blocking spaces and the defense marking and covering. No member of the defending team may be closer than 5 yards to the ball.

Members of the defending team must be quick to assume their places if they are to prevent the attacking team from gaining a decided advantage from the penalty.

A free kick formation is shown in Figure 6–22.

CHAPTER 6.   SOCCER

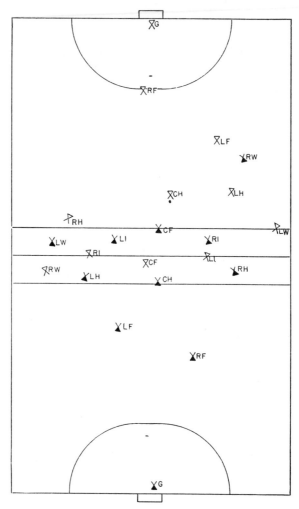

FIG. 6–22. A free kick formation.

THE DEFENSE KICK

The defense kick is a place kick awarded when a member of the attacking team sends the ball behind the opponents' goal line without scoring or over the goal bar. The ball may be placed anywhere on the quarter circles marking the penalty area.

THE ATTACKING TEAM

Any player of the attacking team may take the defense kick, although it is generally taken by a fullback. In playing such a kick the

CHAPTER 6. SOCCER

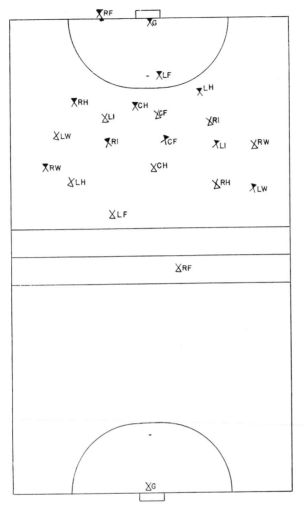

FIG. 6–23. A defense kick formation.

object should be to get the ball well down the field, away from scoring possibilities, and, at the same time, to start the forwards off on attack. The ball should be played out toward the wing, and at no time should it be sent across the goal.

If the situation warrants it, the fullback may raise the ball to the goalkeeper, who should be within the penalty area, and the goalkeeper may punt or throw the ball out. This should not be attempted when opponents are in the penalty area.

The forwards of the attacking team should be down field, ready to receive the ball and go on with it. The backs should carefully mark the opposing forwards, for, should the latter intercept the kick, they

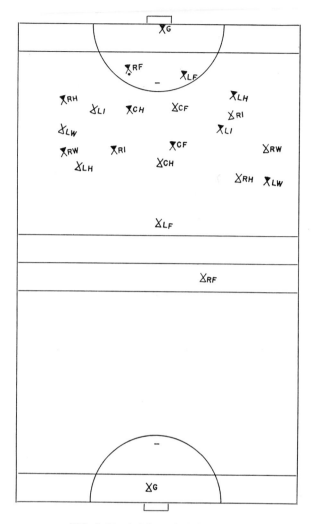

FIG. 6–24. A defense kick formation.

would be in excellent scoring position. A goal may not be scored directly from a defense kick.

THE DEFENDING TEAM

No member of the defending team may be closer than 5 yards to the ball. The forwards should place themselves in position to intercept; the halfbacks and fullbacks should be in marking and covering positions.

CHAPTER 6. SOCCER

This penalty is a place kick, awarded when a player sends the ball over her own goal line not between the goal posts or over the goal bar. The ball is placed on the goal line 5 yards from the nearer corner of the field on the side of the goal on which it went out of bounds.

THE ATTACKING TEAM

The corner kick is generally taken by the wing on the side of the field where the ball went out. The kick should be made diagonally infield from the corner.

The attacking team should shift its strength to the side of the field from which the kick is to come. The forwards must be ready to

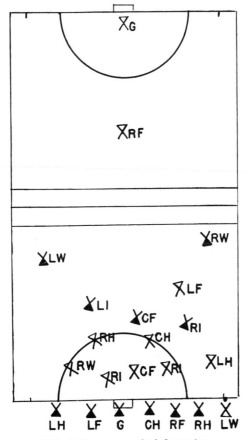

FIG. 6–25. A corner kick formation.

try a quick shot at goal, and the backs ready to cover up any slip on their part. The attacking players may take any position on the field. There is no offside from a corner kick. A goal may be scored from a corner kick.

THE DEFENDING TEAM

No member of the defending team may be within 5 yards of the ball. The halfbacks, fullbacks and goalkeeper must stand on or behind the goal line until the ball has been kicked. The forwards should be somewhat down the field, waiting for a clearing kick.

THE PENALTY KICK

A penalty kick is a place kick most commonly awarded for the fouls of tripping, kicking, striking, holding, pushing, charging, jumping at an opponent and handling the ball, committed by a member of the defending team within her own penalty area. For additional instances when the penalty kick is awarded consult the rules chart. For a penalty kick, the ball is placed on the penalty kick mark in front of the goal.

THE ATTACKING TEAM

The player, any member of the attacking team, taking the penalty kick should stand near the penalty mark ready to play the ball at the umpire's whistle. All other members of the attacking team should be outside of the penalty area but in the field of play, and ready to partici-pate as soon as the kick is taken. A bona fide attempt to shoot a goal must be made.

THE DEFENDING TEAM

All members of the defending team, except the goalkeeper, should be outside of the penalty area and in the field of play. The goalkeeper may stand on the goal line but must not advance until the ball has been kicked. The halfbacks and fullbacks should be as near as possible to their opponents on the opposite forward line. The forward line should be down the field ready for a clearing kick.

THE ROLL-IN

The roll-in is awarded when the ball goes over the side line or the goal line off players of opposite teams, after a double foul, and after a temporary suspension of the game if no previous penalty has been awarded.

When the roll-in is taken for out of bounds, it shall be taken at a

CHAPTER 6. SOCCER

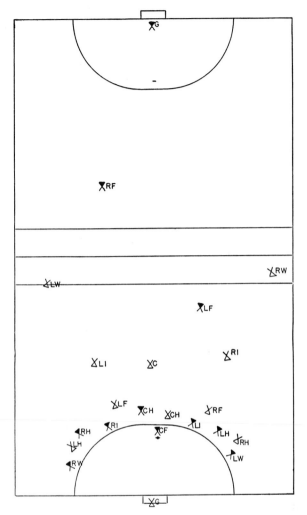

FIG. 6–26. Penalty kick formation.

point 5 yards in from where the ball left the field of play. If this occurs within 5 yards of the goal, the roll-in shall be taken at the penalty kick mark.

There is no attacking or defending team on the roll-in. The ball is rolled by the umpire between two opponents, who stand backs toward their own goals and 5 yards apart. The umpire should blow her whistle as soon as the ball leaves her hands, and the two players taking part in the roll-in may move forward to play the ball. All other players must remain 5 yards away until the ball has been played.

Players should be taught to be tricky when playing a roll-in. Too

CHAPTER 6.   SOCCER

often hard kicking is the only play attempted, frequently resulting in bruised shins. The subtle player who can play the ball carefully and strategically is the one who generally gains possession of the ball or passes it to a teammate. Practice stopping the ball with the sole of the foot and reversing the roll by tapping it in the direction from which it came, or tapping it on in the direction in which it is rolling.

SECTION V. POSITION PLAY

A soccer team, like a hockey team, consists of eleven players, divided into five forwards, three halfbacks, two fullbacks and a goalkeeper. The forwards are the primary attacking and scoring players, the halfbacks are defense and attack players, the fullbacks primarily defense, and the goalkeeper is purely defense.

THE FORWARD LINE

The forwards are named as follows: right wing, right inner, center forward, left inner, and left wing or left outer forward. These five players cover the entire field laterally, and the distance which they travel up and down the field is indicated in Figure 6–28.

Forward line players must be speedy and capable of good control of the ball. This includes the technics of dribbling, accurate passing and shooting. They must be able to maintain a steady attack, passing, shooting and rushing until the ball is in the goal.

THE CENTER FORWARD

The center forward is the general of the forward line. She must be able to direct the play to the advantage of her team and must be able to keep it well distributed, using both sides equally.

She must be an aggressive player and a good shot, because to her come many opportunities to score.

She must be able to combine with other forwards when advancing the ball by triangular passes.

She must be able to dribble and draw effectively before passing or shooting.

The center forward is considered to be the most dangerous player on the forward line, and as such she should never be left unmarked by the opposing center halfback. Because of this, it is necessary that she be well versed in the fundamentals of ball control and she must be able to use these fundamentals to the best possible advantage.

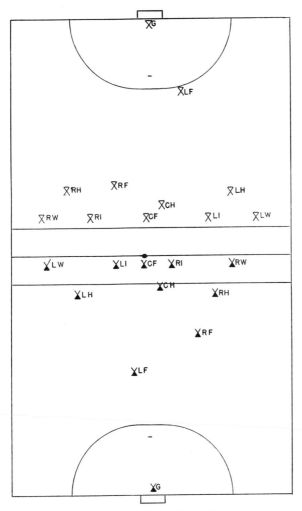

FIG. 6–27.   A kickoff formation.

THE INNERS

The inners should have the same general abilities as the center forward. They must be able to combine with the center forward or the wings or each other when advancing the ball.

They must know when to stop a pass and when to let it go on through to another player, remembering that every pass which crosses their territory is not meant for them.

The inners are important in scoring. They must be able to shoot

CHAPTER 6.   SOCCER

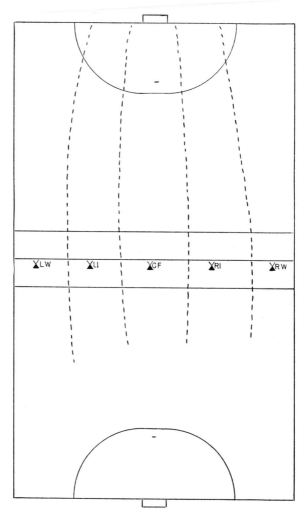

FIG. 6–28. Territory covered by forward line.

quickly, especially with the inside of the foot in order to avoid the necessity of shifting the body to face the goal.

Frequently, especially when on the defensive, the inners play well back of the rest of the forward line.

THE WINGS

The prime requisite of a wing is ability to control the ball while traveling at top speed.

CHAPTER 6.   SOCCER

A wing must possess speed and be master of the arts of dribbling and centering.

She must be able to combine with the inner on her side of the field.

A wing who dribbles fast and furiously down the field, but who keeps control of the ball until she is tackled or until the opportunity to center has passed, is no asset to any team. Worse than that, she is a source of annoyance, because other players expect so much from her and get so little.

Wings seldom have an opportunity to shoot, but should a wing find herself in possession of the ball and ahead of the rest of the forward line, she should cut in toward the goal for a shot.

Wings should be ready to take corner kicks when they occur and may take the kick-in when it occurs near the opponents' goal line.

THE HALFBACK LINE

The halfbacks have the most grueling positions on the team. They must be ready to back up their own forward line and quick to shift to a defense position. There is little or no rest for the halfbacks.

THE CENTER HALFBACK

The center halfback marks the most dangerous player on the opposite forward line, namely the center forward.

She must be a speedy, heady player, and the leader of the halfback line.

She must be able to make quick decisions, to tackle well, to anticipate and intercept and to distribute play.

The center halfback must back up her own center forward when the forward line is in possession of the ball, and she must be ready to assist in backing up either inner.

She must quickly take free kicks in her territory.

The center halfback is probably the hardest-worked player on the team.

THE RIGHT AND LEFT HALFBACKS

The right halfback marks the opposing left wing, and the left halfback the right wing. Since they mark speedy players, they themselves must possess speed.

These two halfbacks must be sure tacklers and good passers.

The halfbacks take kick-ins and free kicks which occur in their section of the field.

They must know the regulations concerning such penalties, must be ready to take them quickly, and must be able to play the ball to the best possible advantage on such occasions.

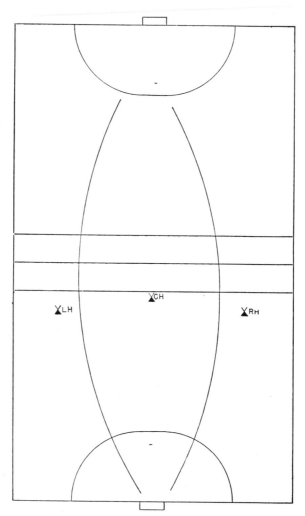

FIG. 6–29.   Territory covered by the halfbacks.

When their own forward line has the ball, the halfbacks back up the line rather closely and play slightly infield toward the inners.

When the attack shifts to the opposite direction, the halfbacks must be quick to get back to marking and covering positions.

THE FULLBACKS

The former picture of two rather solid-looking individuals playing side by side not far in front of the goalkeeper, ready to give a mighty

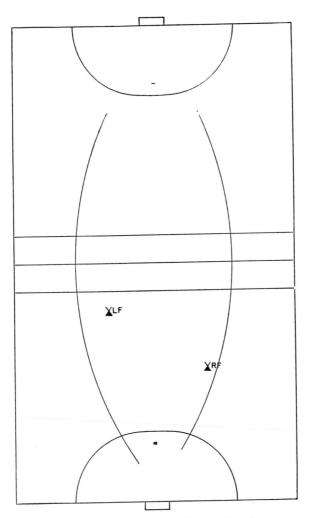

FIG. 6–30. Territory covered by the fullbacks.

kick to the approaching ball, no longer represents the fullback in soccer.

The modern fullback plays her part in attack as well as defense and covers a fair portion of the field.

The right fullback is responsible for the opposing left inner, and the left fullback for the right inner.

Fullbacks may play in either a tandem position or in a straight line position.

In the *tandem position* (Fig. 6–31), the fullback, on the side of the field where the ball is, plays up the field, both when her team is attacking and defending. At the same time, the other fullback plays

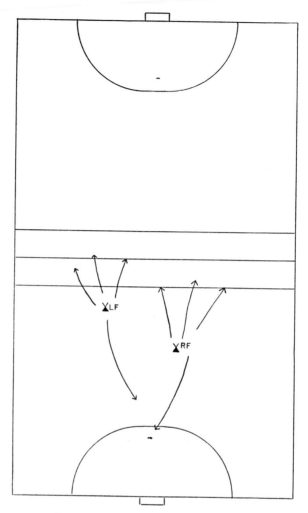

FIG. 6–31. Fullbacks in tandem position.

down the field in a covering position. This type of formation makes it possible for the backs to take part in the attacking game as well as the defending game. The back playing up assists in backing up the forward line when on the attack. This formation calls for a constant shift in the positions of the backs, the shift depending upon the position of the ball at any given time.

The *straight line position* (Fig. 6–32) leaves one fullback up the field and the other back. The first fullback should be the speedier of the two. This fullback is responsible for the primary tackle or attempt to break up the attack of the opposing forward line, and the second fullback is a reserve, should the first one fail. This type of play makes the fullback position entirely defensive.

CHAPTER 6. SOCCER

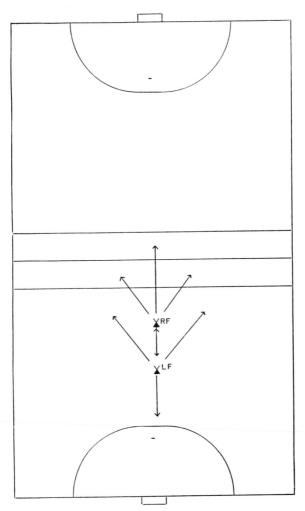

FIG. 6-32. Fullbacks in straight line position.

THE GOALKEEPER

The goalkeeper is the last line of defense. An accurately aimed ball which passes her is a score of 2 points for the opponents. The goalkeeper must be a cool, level-headed player, quick to size up situations and quick to respond to them. Height is a decided asset to a goalkeeper.

The goalkeeper should be able to punt, to drop kick, to throw and to kick on the fly. She must be able to catch and handle a fast-moving ball. Her special privileges include handling the ball while within the penalty area. She may catch the ball, throw the ball or take one bounce. She may not take more than two steps with the ball in her hands. She may combine a bounce with a punt, with a drop kick or with a throw.

Summary of Soccer Rules

WHEN TAKEN	REGULATIONS	WHAT HAPPENS IF REGULATIONS ARE NOT FULFILLED

Free Kick

WHEN TAKEN	REGULATIONS	WHAT HAPPENS IF REGULATIONS ARE NOT FULFILLED
1. Foul by either team outside penalty area	a. Place kick from spot where foul committed	Repeat
2. Foul by attack inside penalty area Carrying Charging Handling Holding Jumping at opponent Offside Kicking opponent Pushing Striking an opponent Tripping an opponent	b. Ball must roll distance of circumference c. Kicker may not replay own ball d. Opponents 5 yds. away (Exception: for free kick awarded attackers within 5 yds. of the goal, goalkeeper may stand on the goal line)	Free kick opponents (no goal) Free kick opponents (no goal) Repeat if advantage gained
3. Infringement of goalkeeper's privileges 4. Illegal defense kick inside penalty area 5. Infringement of substitution rules except 30 sec. regulation	e. Goal may be scored from free kick awarded for pushing, tripping, holding, striking, jumping at opponent or handling (except by goalkeeper in own penalty area)	

Kickoff

WHEN TAKEN	REGULATIONS	WHAT HAPPENS IF REGULATIONS ARE NOT FULFILLED
1. At beginning of game	a. Ball must go forward distance of circumference	Free kick opponents (no goal)
2. After each score	b. Kicker may not replay own ball	Free kick opponents (no goal)
	c. No opponent may cross restraining line until ball is kicked	Free kick opponents
3. At beginning of each quarter	d. No teammate may cross halfway line until ball is kicked	Free kick opponents (no goal)

Kick-in

WHEN TAKEN	REGULATIONS	WHAT HAPPENS IF REGULATIONS ARE NOT FULFILLED
1. Out of bounds over the side line off one or more players of the same team (No goal may be scored from a kick-in)	a. Ball kicked in from side line at point where it left field	Repeat
	b. Ball must roll distance of its circumference	Free kick opponents
	c. Kicker must stand off field of play	Repeat
	d. Kicker may not replay her own ball	Free kick opponents (no goal)
	e. Opponents 5 yds. away	Repeat if advantage gained

CHAPTER 6. SOCCER

Summary of Soccer Rules — Continued

WHEN TAKEN	REGULATIONS	WHAT HAPPENS IF REGULATIONS ARE NOT FULFILLED
	Penalty Kick	
1. Foul by defending team inside own penalty area (Only the fouls of tripping, kicking, striking, jumping at, holding, pushing an opponent and handling the ball) 2. Taking time out more than twice 3. Failure to report change of goalkeeper; goalkeeper handles ball in penalty area	a. Place kick from penalty kick mark b. Ball must be kicked forward and goal attempted c. All defending players except goalkeeper outside penalty area and in field of play d. All attacking players except kicker outside penalty area and in field of play e. Kicker may not replay	Repeat Free kick opponents Repeat, if advantage gained Free kick, if advantage gained (no goal) Free kick opponents (no goal)
	Defense Kick	
1. Out of bounds over goal line by attacking team or over cross bar	a. Place kick from any point on penalty area quarter circle b. Ball must be kicked forward distance of circumference c. Kicker may not replay ball d. Opponents 5 yds. away	Repeat Free kick opponents (no goal) Free kick opponents (no goal) Repeat if advantage gained
	Corner Kick	
1. Out of bounds over goal line or over goal bar off defending team	a. Place kick from goal line 5 yds. from nearer corner b. Defending halfbacks, fullbacks, goalkeeper on or behind goal line c. Opponents 5 yds. away d. Ball must be kicked distance of circumference e. Kicker may not replay ball	Repeat Repeat if advantage gained Repeat Free kick opponents (no goal) Free kick opponents (no goal)
	Roll-in	
1. Out of bounds over goal line or side line off opponents 2. After time out with ball in play 3. After double foul	a. Ball may be played after it leaves umpire's hand b. Kickers 5 yds. apart c. All other players 5 yds. away d. Ball must be played by kickers e. If within 5 yds. of goal, roll-in at penalty kick mark	 Repeat Repeat Repeat Repeat

SECTION I. INTRODUCTION

HISTORY

Ball throwing as a sport has been enjoyed since the time of the early Greeks. Softball, like many of the highly technical sports which we enjoy today, developed from games of early origin.

Baseball, the parent of softball, has been officially declared to be the invention of Colonel Abner Doubleday, who devised the diagram of bases and positions in 1839. Preceding baseball, the games of "rounders," an English game, "cat" and "town ball" were the more popular ball games.

The game of softball has no individual inventor. It has grown from a group of games, variously known as kitten ball, playground ball, diamond ball, indoor baseball and others. A committee of men, meeting at the National Recreation Congress in 1923, published playground rules which helped to standardize the game. It was not until 1932, however, that the name "softball" was officially adopted.

Women played baseball for years, using the playground, indoor and professional rules. In 1926, Miss Gladys Palmer compiled outdoor rules for women that were adopted by the American Physical Education Association in 1927.

The official rules are in the *Softball Guide*, prepared and revised at two-year intervals by the Division for Girls and Women's Sports of the American Association for Health, Physical Education and Recreation, a department of the National Education Association.

EQUIPMENT AND ITS CARE

Bats. Softball rules require that the bat be no more than $2\frac{1}{8}$ inches in diameter at its largest part and no more than 34 inches long. The bat must have a safety grip of cork, tape or composition material of not more than 15 inches and not less than 10 inches from the small end of the bat.

Balls. Balls of good quality should be purchased, as they long outlast those of inferior grade. The official rules require a smooth-seam ball with concealed stitch not more than 12⅛ inches nor less than 11⅞ inches in circumference. The ball must weight not more than 6¾ ounces nor less than 6 ounces. Other requirements are given in the official softball rules guide.

Personal Equipment. Softball rules provide that gloves may be worn by any player, but mitts may be used only by the catcher and first baseman. In addition, the catcher must be provided with mask and body protector (Fig. 7–1). It is recommended that the appropriate mitts and gloves be provided for all defensive players.

In purchasing equipment, it would be well to investigate boys' masks and gloves, as they are better fitted to the physique of girls and women than men's equipment.

Slacks are the preferred costume.

Diamond. Dimensions of the diamond are shown in Figure 7–2. The playing field should have an unobstructed area with a radius of

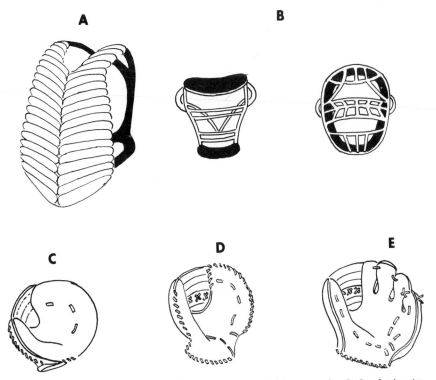

FIG. 7–1. Protective equipment. A, Body protector. B, Catcher's masks. C, Catcher's mitt. D, First baseman's mitt. E, Fielder's glove.

CHAPTER 7. SOFTBALL

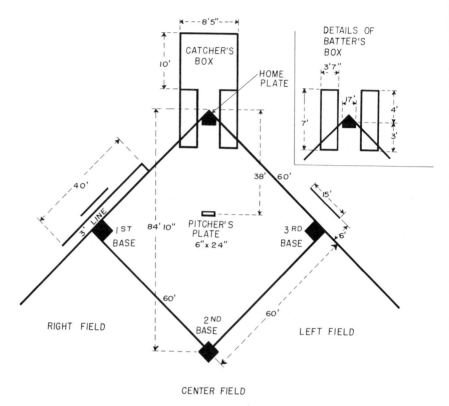

FIG. 7-2. Softball diamond.

200 feet from home plate between the foul lines. Between home plate and the backstop outside the foul lines, the unobstructed area should be not less than 25 feet.

OFFICIALS

For match games, it is desirable that there be two umpires and two scorers. When two umpires are used, one should be designated as the plate umpire. Her position is directly behind the catcher. The second umpire is the base umpire. She should shift her position on the diamond as the base runners progress.

If there is one umpire only, her best position is behind the catcher when no runners are on base or when runners are on second and third bases. When there is a runner on first, and second and third bases are unoccupied, the umpire's best position is behind the pitcher.

The Plate Umpire. The duties of the plate umpire are listed in the official rules. In general, she is responsible for the proper conduct of the game. Her principal duties are to:

Start the game.

Call all decisions concerning pitcher, catcher and batter, such as balls and strikes, fair or foul batted balls, and infield or outfield fly balls.

Determine whether a pitched ball touches the clothing of the batter.

Make decisions at the plate and at third if the other bases are occupied.

Use appropriate signals in calling the balls and strikes.

Give decisions on appeal plays at third base.

Call "game" to announce the end of a game.

Declare game forfeited.

The Base Umpire. The base umpire's duties are:

Decisions at first, second and third bases except those at third base assigned to the plate umpire.

Assisting the plate umpire where necessary.

When there are no base runners, the base umpire should stand outside the first base line, in line with first base. When there is to be play at a base, the base umpire should move to a position on the diamond near that base, but care should be taken to avoid interference with the play.

Signs. Both umpires should use the following signs for indicating "safe" and "out":

"Safe"—arms obliquely outward, palms facing downward.

"Out"—fist closed, thumb upward, elbow bent and hand opposite the shoulder.

All decisions should be given quickly and clearly. Keenness of observation and sureness of judgment are essential to eliminate disputes.

THE GAME

Softball is played in seven innings by two teams of nine players each. An inning consists of a turn at bat (three outs) for each team, during which period at bat the other team plays in the field. A game will be terminated in six and one-half innings if at that time the team last at bat has scored more runs than the team first at bat.

The location of players on the diamond is shown, in a general way, in Figure 7–32, page 288.

SAFEGUARDS IN TEACHING SOFTBALL

Softball injuries can be reduced to a minimum if the teacher will observe certain rules of safety and take the necessary precautions in preparing class work.

Common injuries in softball are:

Sprained and broken fingers from thrown or batted balls.

Sprained ankles and knees.

Bruises and abrasions from falls, attempts to slide or collisions.

"Glass arm" and muscle soreness from throwing without warming-up periods.

Less common injuries in softball are:

Cuts from illegal spikes and broken eyeglasses.

Nose and chest injuries to the catcher if she is improperly outfitted.

Injury from bats carelessly thrown.

Bone bruises to the hands from holding them too rigidly while receiving the ball.

Suggestions to the Teacher for Helping to Prevent Injuries

Select proper playing equipment:

Mitt, mask and chest protector for the catcher.

Gloves for the first baseman and other players who may want them.

Smooth-seam, concealed-stitch or flat-seam ball.

Softened balls for beginners.

Bats with safety grip of cork, tape or composition material.

Provide for proper care of the playing field:

Well-rolled diamond and field, with gravel or cinders removed.

No obstructions on the playing area.

Bases fastened with stakes driven into the ground. Buckles or fasteners should be on the under side of the bases.

Check costume and personal equipment of players:

Glasses guards for those who must wear glasses.

Slacks, knickers or full-length trousers.

Proper shoes, well laced. Narrow skirts and shoes with heels should be banned entirely.

Ankle supports for players with weak ankles.

If cleats are worn, the rules require that they be of hard rubber, or they may be of metal, provided the spikes have blunt edges all around and do not extend more than $3/4$ inch from the sole or heel. Track spikes are barred.

Stress thorough knowledge of the skills used in softball, with emphasis upon body control and footwork as well as upon position of the hands in receiving the ball.

Develop speed in throwing gradually in each practice period and from the beginning of the season. A warm-up period should start each practice session or game.

Avoid collisions and interference by:

Placing the catcher far enough behind the batter.

Developing an understanding of base running and sliding.

CHAPTER 7. SOFTBALL

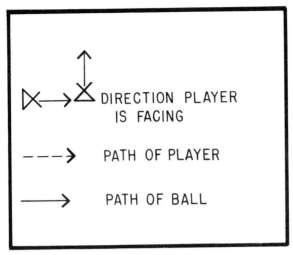

FIG. 7–3. Key to softball diagrams.

SECTION II. INDIVIDUAL SKILLS AND TACTICS

BALL HANDLING

Three general principles should be considered in handling a batted or thrown ball:

Keep the eyes on the ball. The player must watch the ball carefully to judge whether to move to either side, forward or backward, or to follow a bad bounce.

Be relaxed, not tense. The body must be relaxed, but at the same time the player must be alert and always "on her toes."

Get in line with the ball at once. The player's first thought should be to get in front of the ball, then she can move to field it as quickly as possible.

BODY MECHANICS

The fingers should be curved and relaxed until the instant of contact with the ball. The ball should be gripped firmly and drawn toward the body.

The angle of the hands must vary with the type of ball received, depending upon whether it is a ground ball, line drive, fly ball or thrown ball.

For a ball that reaches the player above the waist, the thumbs should be together, palms outward, fingers curved and pointed upward. The wrists should be bent backward (Fig. 7–4).

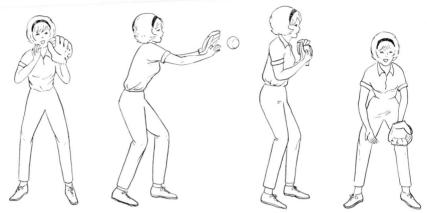

FIG. 7–4. Fielding the ball above and below the waist.

For drives and ground balls below the waist, the fingers should be curved, pointing downward, little fingers toward the inside (Fig. 7–4).

Whenever possible, fly balls should be taken in front of the body, fingers pointing upward and palms facing away from the player (Fig. 7–5).

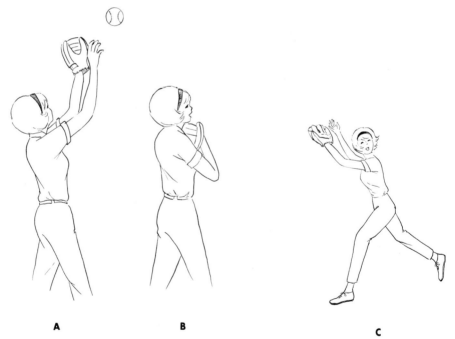

A   B   C

FIG. 7–5. Fielding a fly ball. A, Reaching up to meet ball, fingers curved. B, "Giving" with the ball as it enters the glove. C, Ball farther out than fielder: back turned to ball to run deeper into field; reaching with glove, palms up.

CHAPTER 7.   SOFTBALL

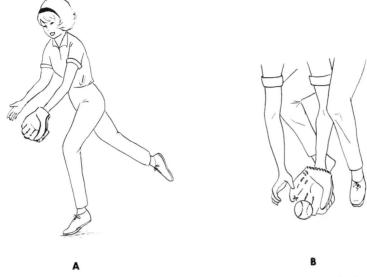

A   **B**

FIG. 7–6.   Fielding a ground ball. A, Running toward the ball. B, Knees bent; back of glove
on ground, palm up; ball rolls into glove and is trapped with ungloved hand.

The arms should be extended forward easily, with elbows bent.

With the catch the ball should be drawn into throwing position, the whole body relaxing to absorb the jar.

In fielding grounders, the feet should be slightly apart, one foot forward. This position is used because balance for the succeeding throw is assured. The body should bend forward from the hips and only slightly in the knees (Fig. 7–6).

COACHING SUGGESTIONS

The arms and hands must not be rigid. Many balls are fumbled because the ball rebounds from tense fingers.

Get in front of the ball.

If possible, catch with hands in front of the chest or above.

The easiest place for a beginner to field a bounding ball is at the height of the first bounce. The ball is more easily handled at this stage. However, the player should not wait for the long bounce if the ball can be fielded sooner.

Advanced players should field grounders by smothering the bounce. This lessens chances for a bad hop on the rebound.

Move forward to meet a ground ball, don't wait for it.

CHAPTER 7.   SOFTBALL

1. Explain and demonstrate catching position for balls above the waist.

2. Check hand positions for balls above waist before a ball is thrown, then practice catching.

3. Check hand positions for low balls, then practice catching.

4. Catch flies and grounders.

5. Practice catching balls thrown to the right and left and overhead.

SQUAD PRACTICE

Double Line Formation (see Fig. 2–9).   Lines about 30 feet apart. Toss the ball underhand to each player in turn and back to the original player.

Competition Between Squads, Same Formation. Establish lines behind which the ball must be thrown. Following the same course as in the preceding formation, have the squads complete three circuits. The ball must be returned to the first player at the end of the third circuit before a squad is finished.

Relay Formation with Leader (see Fig. 2–2). The leader should throw to the first player, who should return the ball immediately to the leader and sit down. When all players are seated except the leader with the ball in her hands, a team is finished.

THROWING

The type of throw to be used varies with the kind of play, the place where the ball is recovered in relation to the body, and the distance of the next throw. After fielding a hit, getting the ball to the infield and the proper base is the important consideration. After fielding a ground ball, the fielder will often use an underhand whip or side-arm throw. In fielding a fly ball, the fielder is erect and can use the faster overhand throw.

Throwing also includes the various types of pitches.

THE OVERHAND THROW

BODY MECHANICS

Starting Position.   The ball is held in a tripod grip, first and second fingers on top of the ball, slightly separated, the thumb under the ball, and the third and fourth fingers on the side of the ball. The ball should be held by the fingers, not palmed. The wrist should be bent backward (Fig. 7–7).

The ball should be raised about ear level, well behind the head. The elbow should be back and level with the shoulder.

For a right-hand throw, the left foot should be forward, the left

A

B

C

D

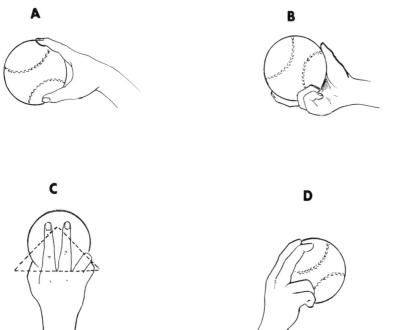

FIG. 7-7. Grip for overhand throw. A, Ball held in tips of fingers. B, Reverse view, showing last two fingers at side of ball. C, First and second fingers straight and close. D, Side view showing last two fingers.

shoulder pointing in the direction the ball is to go. The weight should be on the right foot.

The trunk should rotate toward the throwing arm.

Application of Force. The throwing motion is a full arm swing forward and downward with extension of the elbow as the hand comes forward.

The trunk rotates forward.

The wrist snap of the throw is very important, and the final movement of the wrist from hyperextension to flexion supplies much of the power of the throw.

Follow Through. The arm should swing forward and downward across the body, but in the direction of the throw.

The weight should be well forward on the left foot when the ball is thrown with the right hand (Fig. 7-8).

USES

This throw is used by outfielders for long throws to the infield.

For any throw that requires distance or speed, this throw should be used.

FIG. 7–8. Overhand throw.

COACHING SUGGESTIONS

If the teacher understands the fundamentals of throwing, she will recognize the following factors.

To increase the speed of the throw, it is necessary to increase the movement in the parts of the body which will affect the arm swing and get the body behind the throw. This may be done by:

Flexing of the ankle, knee and hip followed by extension of these joints.

Increasing the length of the backswing by bringing the weight well back on the right foot and raising the left leg.

Increasing the speed of contraction of all muscles.

To improve the accuracy of the throw, the arc of the arm swing must be flattened. This may be accomplished by:

Flexing of the ankle, knee and hip.

Taking a step in the direction of the throw.

Dropping the shoulder of the throwing arm.

The so-called "girl's throw" is the result of rigidity in the shoulder joint and faulty elbow position.

Watch for tenseness not only in the throwing arm but in the entire body.

Beginners tend to bring the elbow in close to the body rather than keeping it well out and at shoulder level.

TEACHING PROGRESSION

1. Explain and demonstrate the full arm throw.
2. Emphasize the easy, full arm swing.
3. Practice throwing and catching from a stationary position.
4. Practice running in to field the ball, following with a throw to a definite spot immediately.
5. Increase the distance the ball is to be thrown.

CHAPTER 7. SOFTBALL

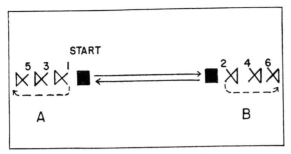

FIG. 7-9. Overhand throw, squad practice.

SQUAD PRACTICE

"Teacher and Class" Formation (see Fig. 2-2).   Use when the number of balls is limited.

Establish two bases 35 or more feet apart. (Six to eight players in a squad as indicated in Fig. 7-9.) X^1 throws to X^2, then goes to the end of the line. X^3 should replace X^1 at once. X^2 must touch the base in front of her squad as she catches or after she has caught the ball, then throw to X^3. X^3 must touch the base in front of her squad and throw immediately to X^4, now at the head of line B. Players should move fast enough to be waiting to receive the ball on the base.

This formation may be used for squad relay competition to improve speed of handling the ball. Each base should be watched to make sure it is touched when or immediately after the ball is caught.

Throwing Practice on a Regulation Diamond (Fig. 7-10).   Three or

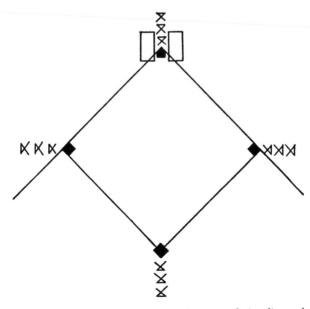

FIG. 7-10. Overhand throw practice on regulation diamond.

CHAPTER 7.   SOFTBALL

four players stand in line behind each base. Many variations in directions of throwing can be derived from this formation:

1. Around the diamond: plate to first, first to second, second to third, third to the plate.

2. Third to first, first to second, second to plate.

3. Plate to second, second to first, first to third, third to plate.

After each complete circuit, each player should go to the end of her line, and the second in line should move up to base.

THE SNAP OR SHORT-ARM THROW

BODY MECHANICS

Starting Position. The grip is similar to that of the overhand throw. The ball is raised about even with the ear, elbow well back.

Because this is a throw that is taken very quickly, time is not taken to get the body into position for maximum efficiency. The shoulder should rotate toward the throwing arm.

Application of Force. The force of the throw comes almost entirely from extension of the elbow and the wrist snap. The radius of the throwing arc is the elbow.

Follow Through. The arm should swing forward in line with the body.

USES

The uses for this throw are usually limited.

It is a good throw for infielders when the throw is short and must be hurried.

Catchers may use it to good advantage when throwing to second base on a steal if they have a strong throwing arm.

COACHING SUGGESTIONS

(See The Overhand Throw.)

TEACHING PROGRESSION

Teach the snap throw *after* players have developed a good overhand throw.

SQUAD PRACTICE

Target Practice. Six to eight on a squad about 60 feet from a target (Fig. 7–11) plotted on the wall with the center 36 inches from the floor. The circles should have the following dimensions:

I—radius 9 inches
II—radius 21 inches
III—radius 33 inches

CHAPTER 7. SOFTBALL

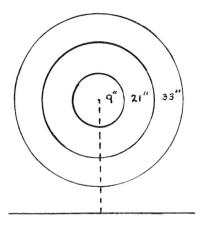

FIG. 7–11. Snap throw, target practice.

Have each player throw three or four times, then go to the end of the line. Each circle may be assigned a value and the individuals or squads compete to see which has the best score with each girl throwing three or more times.

THE UNDERHAND WHIP THROW

BODY MECHANICS

Starting Position. The ball is held with the thumb on top, the first two fingers under the ball, the third and fourth fingers resting easily on the side of the ball.

The body position is similar to the overhand throw, but the ball is held low, usually below the shoulder but well behind the body for a long throw.

Application of Force. The arm should move in a full arm swing which supplies most of the force with the wrist snap.

The swing is practically parallel to the ground, below the shoulder, making possible little extension of the elbow.

Rotation of the trunk and transference of the weight to the forward foot adds force to the throw.

Follow Through. The arm swings well away from the body and should finish straight out about waist high.

USES

This throw is often used when the ball is picked up from the ground and there is not time to straighten the trunk for a full arm throw.

It is often used in fielding bunts.

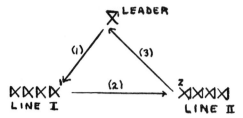

FIG. 7–12.   Underhand whip throw, squad practice.

TEACHING PROGRESSION

    1. Explain and demonstrate the throw.
    2. Practice the arm action a few times without the ball.
    3. Throw from stationary position.
    4. Throw after receiving a low ball or grounder.

SQUAD PRACTICE

Triangular Formation (Fig. 7–12).   The sides of the triangle should be 30 to 35 feet long; six to eight players in a squad, plus a leader. The leader throws a grounder to X^1 in line I. X^1 should field it and throw with an underhand whip to X^2. X^1 should go to the end of line II. X^2, after receiving the throw, should return the ball to the leader with a snap throw, then go to the end of line I.

PITCHING

    Fundamentally, pitching is a matter of control of the ball. It means that the pitcher can throw a fast ball from a given pitching distance to a target about 24 inches from the ground, 3 feet in height and 17 inches in width with at least 70 per cent accuracy. Control means that the pitcher can not only hit the target but that she can deliberately place the ball high or low or to either side within the target.

    The fast ball can be thrown in diagonals, either lateral or vertical. These are called slants. The slant is the result of throwing from a particular position on the pitcher's place or of a high or low release.

    The next step in pitching involves spins on the ball. These spins together with forms of delivery result in drops, rises and curves. The majority of pitchers, however, depend largely upon a straight, fast ball or slants.

    As a general principle, it may be said that a ball rotating on its vertical axis (all thrown balls do to a greater or lesser degree) will break in the direction in which the front or nose of the ball is rotating as it leaves the pitcher's hand. The break must come as the ball approaches the plate, otherwise a "ball" will be called.

    The various paths and spins of the ball are shown in Figure 7–13.

CHAPTER 7.   SOFTBALL

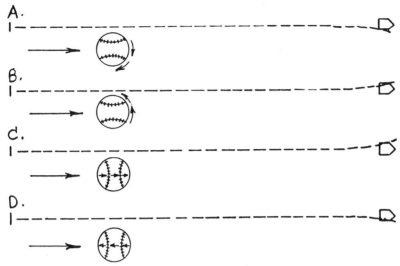

FIG. 7–13. Various paths and spins of ball from pitcher's plate to home plate. A, Nose rotates downward; ball drops. B, Nose rotates upward; ball rises. C, Nose rotates to left; outcurve to right-handed batter. D, Nose rotates left to right; incurve to right-handed batter.

THE CURVE

Once the pitcher is able to deliver the fast ball with accuracy, she should learn to give the ball a definite spin which will cause the ball to curve as it approaches the plate. The manner in which the ball is held and the amount and direction of the spin determine the path of the curve, either up or down, to or away from the batter.

Sinker. Hold the ball with the thumb on top of the ball and the first three fingers underneath the ball. The ball is pitched with the palm facing the batter. As the ball is released, the first three fingers come up over the ball, giving it a forward spin.

Hop. Hold the ball with the thumb underneath, the first two fingers on top, and the third and fourth fingers on the side. The ball is pitched with the palm facing the ground. As the ball is released, the wrist snaps up and the top fingers pull on the ball, giving it a definite backspin. The ball must be delivered at top speed if the ball is to "hop" as it approaches the plate.

Fadeaway. Hold the ball with the thumb near the body and the first three fingers on the opposite side of the ball. As the ball is released, the wrist snaps to the left, bringing the outside fingers around the ball and spinning it from right to left.

Hook. Hold the ball with the thumb in front and the first three fingers in back of the ball. As the ball is released, the wrist snaps outward, spinning the ball from left to right and causing it to curve toward a right-handed batter.

Master the straight fast ball before attempting curves and drops.

Emphasize an easy arm swing not only for warming-up but for control as well.

Before using the full wind-up, make sure that the players have mastered the style of pitch.

Control is the most important requirement in pitching. When the form has been perfected control should be the main objective.

Watch for mechanical errors in the throwing arm and body position, then study the length of pitching step and follow through.

WIND-UPS

There are a number of variations in wind-ups. The pitcher may use any she desires provided that, in the final delivery of the pitch to the batter, the hand is below the hip and the wrist not farther from the body than the elbow. In other words, the delivery must be underhand rather than outward.

More experienced players sometimes use a full circle of the arm in the wind-up. This wind-up is known as the windmill.

FIGURE-EIGHT OR SHORT WIND-UP

BODY MECHANICS

Starting Position. The pitcher should stand with feet parallel and slightly separated on the plate. The rules require a pitcher to come to a full stop and face the batter squarely with both feet on the plate for not less than one second.

The hands should be brought to the chest, the left hand covering the back of the right hand. A pitcher must hold the ball in both hands and the entire body, feet, arms and hands come to a full stop of at least 1 second and not more than 20 seconds before any wind-up is attempted. The pitcher grips the ball firmly in tripod fashion or with all fingers of the right hand. The finger tips are just over a seam.

The trunk should rotate toward the right as the right hand swings slightly outward and downward across the body and backward.

The weight should be on the right foot with the left toe on the plate for balance.

The throwing arm should, as part of the back swing, reach well behind the body, elbow slightly bent.

The backswing should be in line with the direction of the pitch and the forward swing must be parallel with the body, completing the figure eight. To start the forward swing, the pitcher rotates the trunk forward until she is again facing the batter.

Position of the Body Following the Pitch. The step with the forward swing and the release of the ball should be in the direction of the pitch,

CHAPTER 7. SOFTBALL

and should be a long step. One step only is permitted in delivering the pitch. This pitching step should always be the same length, as variations will cause high or low balls. For a right-handed pitch, it should always be a step with the left foot.

Following the step on the left foot, the right foot should immediately be brought up parallel with the left in a fairly wide side stride position. This brings the pitcher definitely facing the batter with her whole body. The reason for this position is to bring the pitcher in fielding position for a hit through the pitcher's box (Fig. 7–14).

When the pitcher, her weight well under control, faces the batter, she is in position for any fielding duties that might arise. She can field a drive through the box or move forward to field a bunt, or she can run to cover first base if the first baseman has been drawn away from the bag.

The Underhand Fast-Ball Pitch (Fig. 7–14)

BODY MECHANICS

Starting Position. The ball may be held with all of the fingers or with the tripod grip. It is suggested that the five-fingered grip be used if the hand is small, as the size of the ball makes control with any other grip difficult.

The tip of the middle finger should be just over the seams at the narrowest point.

Application of Force. The chief source of power is the full arm swing parallel with the body and extension of the elbow. The elbow must not be locked.

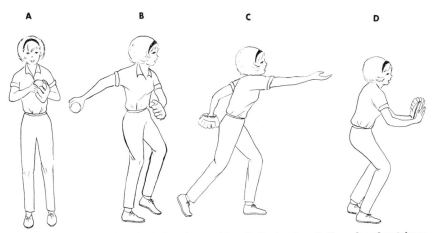

FIG. 7–14.   Underhand pitch. A, Starting position. B, Backswing. C, Transfer of weight to left foot and follow through of pitching hand. D, Fielding position immediately after pitch.

The final wrist snap as the ball rolls off the finger tips adds further power.

Rotation of the trunk and the one step forward result in the full use of the body for power.

Follow Through.   To increase the accuracy of the pitch, the throwing arm should follow through in the direction of the pitch.

The elbow should be straight at the end of the pitch.

USE

The straight fast ball without spins or curves is the basic softball pitch. More advanced players progress to the curves, drop balls and others by changes of grip. But mastery of the fast ball is every pitcher's concern.

COACHING SUGGESTIONS

The ball must be held in the fingers, not palmed.

Balls which are pitched too high to the batter are often the result of a late release.

Balls which are low to the batter are usually the result of an early release.

The forward step will flatten the arc of the arm swing and add accuracy to the pitch.

Emphasize the straight back swing and the straight follow through.

SQUAD PRACTICE

Target Practice (Fig. 7–15). Diagram a target of the following dimensions on the wall: 36 by 18 inches with the lower line 20 inches from the floor. Place squad 35 feet from the target. Score as a strike each placement on the target. Have each player pitch 3 strikes with the fewest number of pitches.

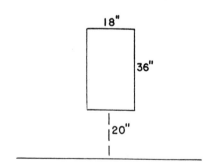

FIG. 7–15.   Underhand fast ball, target practice.

CHAPTER 7.   SOFTBALL

Have one player act as umpire to call the balls and strikes and indicate to the pitcher balls that are "inside" and "outside." The catcher can be a valuable aid to the pitcher by placing her hands as a target.

UNDERHAND CURVES

Curves, slants and slow balls should be delivered with the same motions as the fast ball to confuse the batter. The differences lie in the spins produced by different grips and rotations of the arm.

In pitching the outcurve, the fingers should grip the ball toward the right side (right-handed pitching). As the ball is released, the arm and hand should be rotated inward, causing the ball to spin away from the batter as it approaches the plate. The follow through should be straight as in the fast ball, but the palm should face downward at the completion of the pitch.

The incurve is the result of rotation of the arm outward. This pitch is more difficult to execute than the outcurve.

UNDERHAND SLANTS

The lateral slants are the result of the position of the pitcher on the pitcher's plate (Fig. 7–16).

If the pitcher stands to the extreme right of the pitcher's plate, she will find it possible to pitch a straight ball to the outside corner of the home plate for a right-handed batter. Similarly, if she stands to the extreme left of the pitcher's plate, she can pitch a slant to the inside corner of home plate.

An upward slant can be thrown by holding the ball in the fingers, palm upward, and releasing the ball at the lowest possible point. On the forward step, the knees should be well bent, and the throw must be fast from this point. The ball should be rising as it crosses the plate.

An upward slant with spin can also be thrown, but it need not be a fast ball. This type is gripped with the palm facing backward and downward, the back of the hand toward the batter. The wrist is in a flexed position and, as the ball is released, the final spin comes from a movement from flexion of the wrist to hyperextension across the top of the ball. The release should be fairly low.

PITCHER'S
PLATE

HOME
PLATE

FIG. 7–16. Lateral slants.

CHAPTER 7. SOFTBALL

With a target as previously given, pitch slants toward the various sections. Have each player pitch 12 times, three at each section in the following order: high outside, high inside, low outside, low inside. A simple scoring system may be arranged in which a player receives 3 points for hitting the designated section, 1 point for hitting the target not in the designated section, and 0 for missing the target. Score a ball that touches a line as within the section bounded by the line.

GENERAL COACHING SUGGESTIONS FOR
THROWING AND PITCHING

Catch and throw with the same movement when fielding.

Players should know several types of throws to meet situations demanding quick fielding and return throws.

Watch the shoulder and elbow positions of beginners to eliminate errors which restrict movements in those joints.

Do not attempt to teach several types of pitches until pitchers have control of the fast ball.

Wildness in pitching may be due to variations in the length of the step the pitcher is taking.

Watch the timing of the release. Early and late releases of the pitch often cause "balls."

BATTING

Batting is the foundation of the offense in softball, and for that reason, it is a skill which must be developed immediately and practiced often by every player on the team.

BODY MECHANICS

Starting Position (right-handed batter). Several grips on the bat are possible, but for beginners the most successful is the standard grip. From the standpoint of maximum force to be gained, the grip with the longest lever, *i.e.*, the end grip, should be the most effective. The average player will sacrifice accuracy with this grip and should, therefore, use the standard grip (Fig. 7–17).

The right hand should always be placed above the left and close to it.

The lower hand, the left, should be several inches from the end.

The bat should be gripped firmly but not tensely.

A natural position should be assumed at the plate. The distance of the batter from the plate will vary because of the differences in length of the arms and length of grip.

The distance from the plate must be gauged individually so that

CHAPTER 7.   SOFTBALL

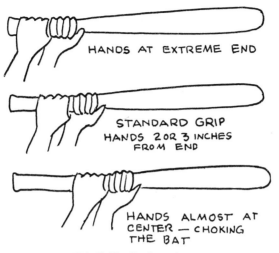

HANDS AT EXTREME END

STANDARD GRIP
HANDS 2 OR 3 INCHES
FROM END

HANDS ALMOST AT
CENTER — CHOKING
THE BAT

FIG. 7–17. Batting grip.

the end of the bat is above the far edge of the plate in the middle of the swing.

The body should be bent slightly at the waist with the shoulders over the toes. The knees should be slightly bent. The left shoulder should be a little closer to the plate than the right.

The left foot should be 8 or 10 inches ahead of the right. The left toe may be pointed toward the pitcher while the right is at a right angle to the plate, or the feet may be parallel at right angles to the plate (Fig. 7–18).

The right foot should be about opposite the back corner of the plate.

The stroke should start back and on a line with the right shoulder, elbows and right wrist flexed. The bat should be back only as far as the left arm can reach easily across the chest. The elbows should be well out from the body, left elbow in line with the hand.

Application of Force. The bat should move in a smooth, level swing, parallel to the ground. The swing should be forceful but comfortable. The batter should concentrate on "meeting the ball," rather than on "swinging for the grandstands." The eye must remain on the ball at all times.

The shoulders, elbows and wrists must get into the swing. As the bat meets the ball, the elbows should be extended, well out from the body.

A definite step forward and toward the plate should be taken to be completed as the ball is hit. The batter must be careful to avoid "stepping in the bucket" (*i.e.,* stepping away from, rather than into, the ball: Fig. 7–18). Such a tendency will impair the accuracy of the swing and result in weakly hit balls. The ball should be met just in front of the plate.

Follow Through. The bat should be allowed to swing forward easily with the ball.

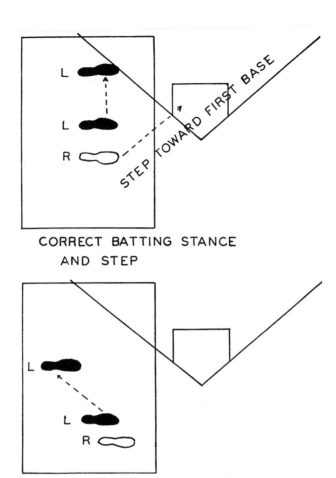

CORRECT BATTING STANCE
AND STEP

INCORRECT BATTING STANCE
AND STEP

FIG. 7–18.   Position of the feet for batting.

From the farthermost point of the backswing to the end of the forward swing, the bat ought not to travel more than 220 degrees. The short swing will increase accuracy in batting because the eye is distracted less from the ball.

The right hand should finish with the palm downward.

The weight should be on the left foot. At the completion of the swing, the bat should be dropped with the left hand, the right foot should cross the plate and take the first step toward first base (Fig. 7–19).

COACHING SUGGESTIONS

The waiting position should be an easy, relaxed one with the bat held firmly but not tensely.

The batter should not crouch at the plate.

CHAPTER 7.   SOFTBALL

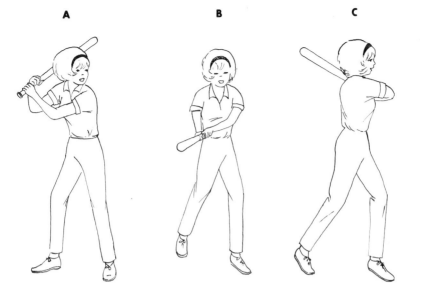

A **B** **C**

FIG. 7–19. Batting positions. A, Feet apart, square stance, bat back and above right shoulder ready to swing. B, Weight forward as ball is hit. C, Follow through over left shoulder.

The ball should be watched all the way to the plate.

The bat should not be pointed at the pitcher while the batter is waiting for her to wind up. It should be kept back of the shoulder with locked wrists.

Standing with the bat on the shoulder delays the swing and makes it choppy.

Only good balls should be hit.

A swing completely around should be avoided.

The feet must not be too wide apart or the step too long because the batter will then tend to strike under the ball.

Stress the level swing, as many batters tend to chop at the ball.

Against a fast-ball pitcher and especially on a small diamond, the batter should move farther back in the box to give a little more time for the swing.

Only if the batter prepares to hit every pitch will she be in a position to connect solidly with the good pitches. On each pitch, the left foot should step forward and the bat should descend partway toward the plate. The batter should check her swing if the pitch is bad or continue to follow through if the pitch is good.

TEACHING PROGRESSION

1. Have the players stand in the box and watch several pitched balls without striking at them. Emphasize watching the ball and choosing good ones.

2. Feet in stationary position, use short swing making sure that each ball is met squarely with the bat level. (Pitching should not be fast.)

3. Add the short step and three-quarter swing.

4. Practice swinging and starting for first base immediately.

Form squads with a pitcher, catcher, 3 or 4 fielders and several batters. Establish a pitching plate and home plate or use the diamond (Fig. 7–20). Five rather easy strokes should be pitched to each batter, then rotate. Emphasize position at the plate, eyes on the ball, square hit.

Increase the speed of the pitch. Emphasize stepping with the hit.

Fungo Hitting (batter and 5 or 6 fielders). The batter hits the ball either on the ground or on the fly to provide fielding practice. A regular rotation may be established or a player who catches a fly or fields two grounders perfectly may become the batter.

In fungo hitting, the bat is held with the right hand fairly high and the ball is tossed into the air directly in front of the batter with the left hand. The left hand is placed upon the bat as soon as the ball is tossed. The bat should be back as the toss is made.

The value in fungo hitting lies in training to watch the ball and in placing hits. It offers good practice for fielding.

Errors (a game for batting and fielding practice). On a regulation diamond, place all of the infield and outfield players. There may be 4 to 6 batters. This is a form of work-up or scrub in which a player, when she is put out, goes to the right field position and all players move up one position. The order of rotation of fielding positions is right to center,

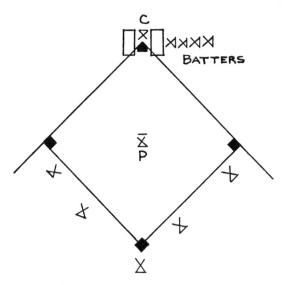

FIG. 7–20. Batting, squad practice.

CHAPTER 7. SOFTBALL

to left, to shortstop, to third, to second, to first, to pitcher, to catcher, to batter. Thus when a batter is put out, all players rotate one position. When a fielder makes an error (let the players decide the errors) all fielders should rotate one position up to the position held by the player making the error. The player making the error must go to right field. Thus rotation takes place after each out or error.

Batting and Fielding Game. Form two squads. A pitcher and a catcher are the only fixed positions, the other players on the squad are placed anywhere in the field. The second squad is at bat. A player at bat is entitled to the usual 3 strikes. On a fair hit, she must run to first base and *return to the plate.* If a fly is caught, she may still run to the base and return. An out is made by the fielder when the ball is returned to the plate ahead of the runner and when a batter strikes out. Score 1 point for each player who gets to first base and back before the ball is returned to the plate. Rotate squads after 3 outs.

PLACE HITTING

The average right-handed batter hits to left field, but for some purposes it may be desirable to change the direction of the hit. With the shortstop in left infield, a ball placed between the first and second baseman will often be successful, whereas the same ball to the left might be fielded by the shortstop.

To place a ball accurately at all times is impossible, but a batter who is able to place a fair number of hits will be a decided asset to a team.

For a right-handed batter to place a hit to right field, it is necessary to shorten the grip an inch or two from the standard grip and to shorten the swing. Place hitting with a full swing is next to impossible.

With the shortened swing, the wrists must be held rigid, as an inward rotation common to batting will pull the ball to the left. The step on the left foot should be more toward the plate than for the free-swinging hit.

A second method of placing the ball to right field is to hit the ball as it passes the plate and fairly early in the forward swing. The timing for this type of place hitting is so difficult that it is not worth spending time trying to develop it.

TEACHING PROGRESSION

1. Natural hitting should be emphasized first.
2. Practice against slow-ball pitching.
3. Bat against fast-ball pitching.

SQUAD PRACTICE

Form squads with a catcher, pitcher and batter, and with fielders in a semicircle 8 or 10 feet behind the pitcher. (Fig. 7–21.) The pitcher

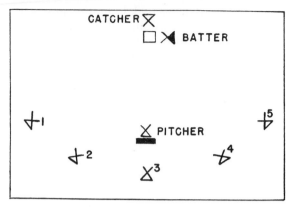

FIG. 7–21.   Place hitting, squad practice.

should pitch easily to the batter, who attempts to place the hits to the fielders in order: 1, 2, 3 and so on.

The hits should be easy but not bunts. The batter should replace X^5 and X^1 should become the batter.

BUNTING

Bunting is a form of place hitting which may serve one of several purposes. The bunt may be used as a sacrifice, or by a fast runner it may be used for base hitting. A bunt is a tap rather than a free-swinging hit (Fig. 7–22).

The bunt must not be attempted on bad pitches, nor is it wise to bunt high balls. The ball must be hit on top or above the center, otherwise it will go into the air and be easily fielded. The bunt should be *along the base line*, either first or third, depending upon the type of play for which it is used, but never directly forward. A bunt forward is too easily fielded by the pitcher (Fig. 7–23).

BODY MECHANICS

Starting Position (right-handed batter).   The position before the pitch and during the pitcher's wind-up should be the same as for a full swing in order to deceive the infielders.

As the pitcher delivers the ball, the batter should turn to face the pitcher, feet set firmly apart.

The right hand should slide to the middle of the bat for greater accuracy. The bat should be held loosely with the palm of the right thumb behind the bat and the fingers under or behind it.

Application of Force.   The ball is tapped with the section between the tip and the right hand.

The bat should be pushed in a plane horizontal with the ground by using only extension of the elbows.

CHAPTER 7.   SOFTBALL

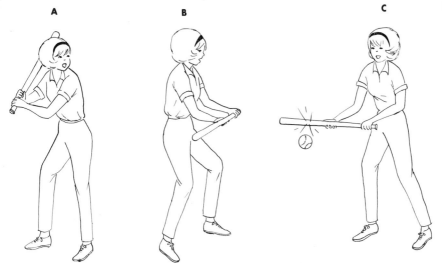

FIG. 7–22. Bunting position. A, Side view: normal stance and position for batting. B, Side view as ball approaches: right foot forward to face pitcher; right hand in bunting grip. C, Front view: fingers and thumb behind bat as ball is tapped.

The arms should be relaxed as the ball is met over the forward foot.

The step on the left foot should be short, followed immediately by the step toward first base on the right foot, making practically a running start.

Follow Through. As there is no swing involved in the bunt, there is no follow through. Once the ball is contacted, the batter should immediately run toward first base.

In most cases, the bat should finish well away from the body.

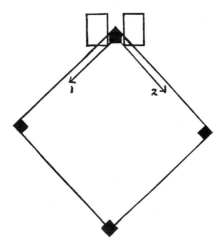

FIG. 7–23. Placing the bunt.

CHAPTER 7. SOFTBALL

If the bunt is down the first base line, the body should rotate to the right and the top of the bat should be turned toward first base.

For a bunt down the third base line, the tip of the bat should be turned toward third base.

USES

The bunt was originated as a sacrifice to advance a runner, but it may also be used as a hit by a fast runner.

COACHING SUGGESTIONS

The form of bunting must be learned before attention is given to direction of the ball.

The ball must be watched carefully and only good pitches bunted.

Relaxation must be stressed or the ball will be bunted too hard and, as a result, easily fielded.

The tendency of beginners is to flex the arms too much and to pull the elbows in too close to the sides.

If a long step is taken, the ball will probably be hit below the center, causing a pop-up.

The weight must be kept well forward on the toes.

TEACHING PROGRESSION

1. Explain and demonstrate a bunt.
2. Practice the change of grip without striking the ball.
3. Practice the bunt from a stationary position with the feet 10 to 12 inches apart.
4. Step into the bunt.
5. Work for placements along the base lines.

SQUAD PRACTICE

Squads of Six to Eight. Use a catcher, pitcher, shortstop, first, second and third basemen. Each player bunts five or six times, then changes position with one of the other squad members. Vary the direction of the bunt.

Same Formation. Draw a semicircle with 6-foot radius around the plate. Place infielders in position. Have the players try to have the bunt strike the ground within that radius along the base line. Change batters after five or six bunts.

Same Formation with a Runner on First Base. The batter should bunt down the third base line and run out the bunt to first base. The fielders should attempt to make a double play as the runner at first base advances.

Same Formation with Added Runner on Second Base. The batter should bunt down the first base line and run out the hit. The fielders should try to make the out at third or first base. Third base is preferable.

CHAPTER 7. SOFTBALL

Base running is an important aspect of softball offense which should not be neglected in the practice of softball skills. A speedy and clever base runner can often score runs which would not be scored by mediocre base running.

Skillful base running involves not only speed in running out hits but also taking advantage of pitches and lead-off.

Base running begins from the batter's box as the ball is hit. The right-handed batter must keep in mind that the first step toward first base is on the right foot. The step on the right foot will maintain body balance and save the runner one step.

From the Plate

Starting Position. Following the hit, the body is tilted forward in a semicrouch position with the weight well forward on the balls of the feet.

The start should be made quickly with vigorous arm and knee action. Too many batters stand to watch where the ball is going before starting for first base.

The first strides should be short ones, and the trunk should be gradually raised during the early strides.

To reach a full stride, the knees should be lifted and extended forward.

A high kick in back with the heels should be avoided.

SQUAD PRACTICE

Squad Formation. (Fig. 7–24). Line up the squad opposite the box. The first one in the squad takes her position in the box for batting, bat

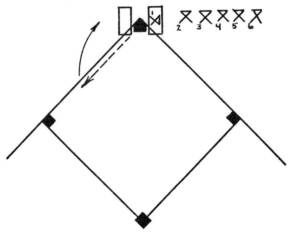

FIG. 7–24. Base running, squad formation.

278 in hand. She swings, drops the bat and starts toward first. The run is only about halfway down the base line. Emphasize the step on the right foot, speedy start and lengthening of stride after the first few steps. The runners should replace each other in the box.

RUNNING TO FIRST BASE

The batter should run out every hit to first base at top speed, regardless of whether the ball is a pop-up or any other contact most certain to be fielded. Fielders do make errors.

The head should not be turned to watch the ball until the runner is well on the way to the base. When about 20 feet from the plate, the batter should take a quick glance at the outfield to see if her hit warrants an attempt at second base.

If the hit is short and for one base only, the runner should follow a straight course on the base line or a little to the inside. The base should be crossed in stride without a leap or jump. The runner should run beyond the base, slowing only after the base is crossed.

If the hit is deep in the outfield, the runner will try for extra bases. Many steps will be saved if the bases are circled properly (Fig. 7–25). When about 10 or 15 feet from the base, the runner should swing out of the base line to the right. The swing should be 6 or 8 feet out of the line.

The runner should try to touch the inside corner of the base with the left foot on the inside of the bag and pivot toward second or the next base.

SQUAD PRACTICE

Team Formation. Hit, run through to first base, overrunning the base (Fig. 7–26).

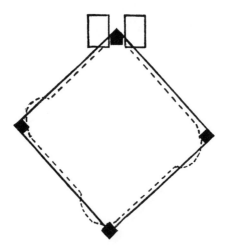

FIG. 7–25. Circling the bases.

CHAPTER 7. SOFTBALL

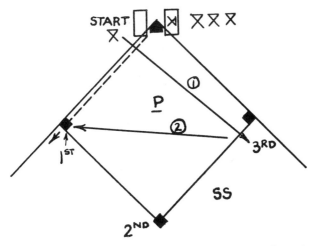

FIG. 7–26.   Running to first base, squad practice, team formation.

Place the infielders except a catcher. The leader standing opposite the left-hand batting box should toss up the ball and bat easy infield hits. The runner should stand in the box in batting position and run to first base as the ball is hit. The runner must try to beat out the hit to first base while the ball is fielded and thrown to first base. A new runner should be ready in the box as soon as a runner has left. The leader should change the direction of the hit on each toss. This drill gives practice in: base running, fielding and throwing.

Running Bases Beyond First Base

After first base has been reached, cleverness in base running plays as important a role as speed. The softball rules provide that a base runner may not leave her base while the pitcher, standing on the plate, holds the ball ready to deliver a pitch.

The runner should be a threat to the catcher and pitcher at all times. She should maintain enough activity around the base so that she is ready for immediate take-off with the pitch.

LEAD-OFF AS PITCHER RELEASES BALL

The distance which a runner can lead off depends upon her skill, her ability to analyze the play, and the position of the first baseman.

While the pitcher is standing in the box with the ball in her hand, the runner may not leave the base.

As the pitcher releases the ball, the runner should move down the base line 10 or 12 feet with short, quick side steps or slides. The runner should beware when the first baseman is playing close to the base, as a throw from the catcher may pick off the runner with too great a lead.

CHAPTER 7.   SOFTBALL

As the ball passes the batter, the runner should be facing the diamond, eyes on the catcher. The trunk should be inclined forward, knees easy, arms hanging freely from the sides. The weight should be more on the right foot than on the left, but the runner must be ready to return quickly to the base she has just left.

If the catcher drops the ball, or if there is a wild pitch, the runner should break toward the next base at once.

If a ground ball is hit, the runner should break for second with the hit. A good lead will often save a force-out.

When the ball is returned to the pitcher, the runner again returns to the base.

SQUAD PRACTICE

Have the base runners start, one following the other from the batter's position, side to the pitcher, and complete a circuit of the bases.

Repeat, but time each runner for the complete circuit.

Squad Formation. One squad is in the field in regular positions and one squad is at bat (Fig. 7–27). The leader should devise certain situations, such as:

Runners on first and second bases.

Runners on second and third bases.

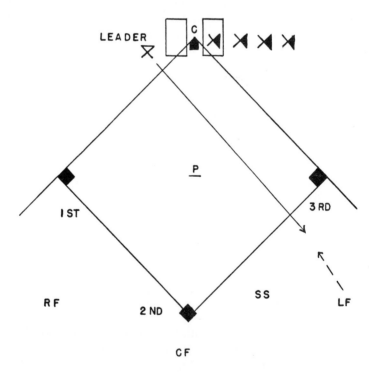

FIG. 7–27.   Running bases beyond first base, practice formation.

CHAPTER 7.   SOFTBALL

Bases loaded.

Runner starting from the plate with other runners on bases.

Runners should be placed on bases and the fielders' attention drawn to the situation. The leader should throw the ball, varying between a high fly, short or long ground ball and in different directions. As she releases the ball, the runners should hold bases or advance accordingly. The base runners should be changed within the squad at bat, then the whole squad sent to the field.

TEACHING PROGRESSION

1. Explain and demonstrate the fundamentals of running.
2. Practice from the box, starting with the right foot.
3. Run through first base without attempting second.
4. A few steps from first base and with an easy trot, touch first base preferably with the left foot and pivot toward second base.
5. At a slow pace, circle all bases.
6. Circle the bases at top speed.
7. Practice sliding.

GENERAL COACHING SUGGESTIONS FOR BASE RUNNING

It is well to keep in mind in coaching that the base runner may not run more than 3 feet out of the base line to avoid being tagged by a fielder with the ball.

In running the bases, the feet should track straight ahead.

The head should be held naturally, not back.

Emphasize the quick start from the batter's box without waiting to see where the ball is going.

SLIDING

The question as to whether girls should be taught sliding is debatable. There is no doubt that there is a possibility of injury in sliding, and without protection for the thighs, bruises and scratches often result. The head-first slide should not be taught to girls, and sliding should not be allowed if the players are in shorts. As the slide is a tricky and potentially dangerous tactic, it should be employed only where the infield turf has been properly prepared. Sliding on a sun-baked or uneven field is dangerous.

The purpose of sliding is to avoid being tagged and to make certain that the base is not overrun. For those reasons sliding to first base is never done, except when returning to first base after a lead-off. Sliding, when done to avoid being tagged, means that the runner touches the base with the most elusive part of her body, usually a foot or hand.

The slide should be done from a full stride without slackening of speed.

As the runner approaches the base, she will descend to the ground by bending her left knee as she places her left foot on the ground.

In the slide position, the right leg will be extended with the left foot under the right knee. The weight of the body will rest on the thigh, knee and foot of the left leg.

The right toe should touch the base first.

THE HOOK SLIDE

This slide is used to elude a baseman who is waiting on the base with the ball.

It is called the hook slide because the base is hooked with the front part of the foot and the toe.

The leg which carries the weight may be folded under or straight; injury is less apt to happen if the under leg is out. The body should be inclined away from the base.

THE FALLAWAY SLIDE

The fallaway is a hook slide, a little wide of the base and away from the ball.

As the dirt is hit, the runner should roll over in a prone position and reach out to tag the base with the hand.

This slide may be confusing to the baseman, as it brings the runner behind her.

TEACHING PROGRESSION

1. Explain and demonstrate the straight-in slide.
2. Practice short slides in a jumping pit, on a mat or on the grass.
3. Increase the speed.
4. Demonstrate the hook slide.
5. Have players assume the hook slide position without a run or slide.
6. Practice from a short run in a pit or on a mat.
7. Increase the speed.

SQUAD PRACTICE

On a diamond place a pitcher, catcher, first baseman, second baseman, center and right fielders in their usual positions. Line up the rest of the squad opposite first base with the first player in line as a runner on first base (Fig. 7–28).

The pitcher has the ball and delivers a legal pitch to the catcher.

CHAPTER 7. SOFTBALL

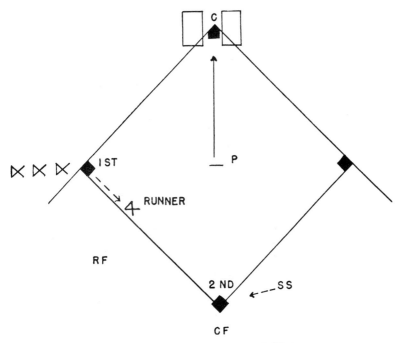

FIG. 7–28. Base running drill.

The runner should leave first base with the pitch and attempt to steal second base. She should exercise good judgment and return to first base if she has no chance to reach second base without being put out. The runner should slide into second base, as it will be necessary for the second baseman to tag her. The drill should continue until all runners have had several trials.

Many types of play are involved in this drill, including: pitching, catcher's throw to second base, tagging a runner, lead-off, base running, sliding and backing up second base.

DEFENSE AND OFFENSE

DEFENSE

FIELDING

The starting position of the outfielder or infielder must be such that she is ready to shift quickly in any direction (Fig. 7–29).

The feet should be in easy side stride position, weight forward and evenly distributed. The knees and hips should be slightly flexed. The hands should be on the knees, and the shoulders should be over the toes.

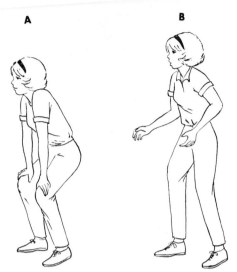

A   **B**

FIG. 7–29.   Fielding positions. A, Waiting for the pitch. B, Ready to move as the pitch is made.

As the pitcher delivers the ball, the body should be tensed and poised to go in any direction, and the hands removed from the knees. The eyes are concentrated solely on the hitter. From this position, the player can move quickly to cover her base, field the ball or move to back up a teammate.

In fielding fly balls, the ball may be taken in one of two ways, although the first is preferred by most experts.

1. Hands cupped, little fingers together about belt high.
2. Hands at the chest, thumbs together forming a V.

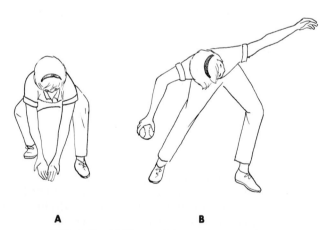

A   **B**

FIG. 7–30.   Fielding and throw of a ground ball.

CHAPTER 7.   SOFTBALL

In fielding a ground ball, it is first necessary to get in line with the ball and directly in front of it (Fig. 7–30). The fielder must move in toward the ball rather than waiting for it. The hands should be close to the ground, little fingers pointing downward. The hips and knees should be flexed.

Circumstances permitting, the feet should be in a stride position, the left foot in front of the right. If the throw is to be made to the side rather than the front, the feet should be set apart to facilitate the throw.

In fielding a line drive or ball moving directly overhead, the thumbs should be together, wrists flexed, fingers cupped. Figure 7–31 shows the fielder catching a drive and an immediate hop and pivot for the following throw.

When fielding a fly ball that is beyond the fielder, the fielder should turn her back to the ball and run back as far as necessary to get under the ball, then turn to face it. Never run backward unless it it just a step or two.

COACHING SUGGESTIONS

When the fly ball is in a territory where several players are likely to get under it, the nearest one should call "mine" and the others should get out of the way to avoid a collision.

The fielder should draw hard-hit balls in toward the body to absorb the jar and prevent fumbles.

On long hits the ball should be relayed in from the outfield.

If a throw to the base will be late, the outfielder should throw to the base ahead of the runner.

The ball should be thrown in immediately from the outfield. It should never be held by an outfielder after it is fielded.

Fielders must remember to back each other up at all times.

FIG. 7–31. Fielding and throw of a fly ball.

CHAPTER 7. SOFTBALL

Fielders must bear in mind that runners may advance after a foul fly is caught.

The fielder, whenever possible, should get set to field a line drive or fly rather than getting it on the run. Get under the ball and wait for it.

Tagging the Runner

The base runner must always be tagged with the ball except on a force-out and a caught fly.

Catching the ball and tagging the runner should be done with one motion.

The ball should be held firmly and low.

If a glove is worn, the gloved hand should be brought in with the bare hand to prevent fumbling.

The ball should not be thrust at the runner or the danger of losing it will be increased. The runner should tag herself by sliding into the ball.

When a runner has been tagged, withdraw the ball. If it is held over her it is likely to be knocked from the hand.

The baseman should follow the runner who comes in at full speed, as she might overrun the base if she has not been tagged before the base is reached.

Backing Up Other Positions

A more complete discussion of backing up is given under position play, but the players in the field must keep in mind at all times that part of their function is helping each other.

When backing up another player stand 10 to 15 feet away. If a player misses the ball, the player backing up will be in better position to see it if she is not too close.

Every fielder of a hit ball, or throw, should be backed up by another player.

On a run-down between bases, the basemen should be backed up.

Offense

Individual offense consists of batting, bunting, base running and sliding. These technics are explained under fundamental skills. However, a word or two about the use of each may be helpful to the teacher.

Straight-away Batting

This means that the batter swings freely to get as long a hit as possible. However, straining for distance can result in frequent strike-outs.

CHAPTER 7. SOFTBALL

With no one on base, the batter should try for a walk or a hit.

With runners on second and third bases, a hit will score both.

Against a weak pitcher, batters should try for long hits.

If a slow runner is on a base, a hit is best. She will be unable to beat out a bunt.

BUNTING FOR A HIT

Only a fast runner should try to bunt for a hit.

BUNTING AS A SACRIFICE

The purpose of this bunt is to advance a runner from first to second, or from second to third base.

A fast runner can often beat out a sacrifice for a hit.

Bunting should be used only under the following conditions:

1. There are less than two outs.

2. There are less than two strikes on the batter. (Foul bunt on the third strike is an out.)

3. The score is close.

BASE RUNNING AND LEAD-OFF

The base runner must keep in mind the following:

1. Where the ball is.

2. Her speed.

3. The speed of the catcher and pitcher in throwing.

4. The out and the score.

When the catcher has the ball, the lead should be shortened. Runners must make sure the baseman has thrown the ball and is not using the hidden ball play.

A slow player should not take too big a lead when the pitcher has released the ball or she will be picked off base.

Against a catcher who throws poorly, the lead may be increased.

If there is none or one out, the base runner should be more cautious.

After the second out, the runner should run as the ball is hit, regardless of whether it is a fly ball.

Base runners should never take chances if their team is behind or the score is close, unless a weak batter is in the box.

SLIDING

The chances for injury in sliding make it dangerous for girls unless slacks are worn.

Slide when the chances of being tagged are certain.

CHAPTER 7. SOFTBALL

SECTION III. TEAM TACTICS AND FORMATION PLAYS

DEFENSE

Team defense is too often thought of in terms of the number of strike-outs a pitcher makes. While pitching, which limits the number of hit is important, the real test of a team's defense is the support given to the pitcher by the basemen and fielders. The successful team has fielders with:

1. Fielding and throwing ability.
2. The ability to "size up" all situations.
3. The speed to back up other fielders and basemen.
4. Knowledge of where base runners are and the number of outs.
5. Alertness to assist in relaying the ball on long throws.

Every play requires the attention of all players to some extent, either in fielding the ball, backing up the fielder, backing up the baseman or assisting the throw. While each baseman and fielder is respon-

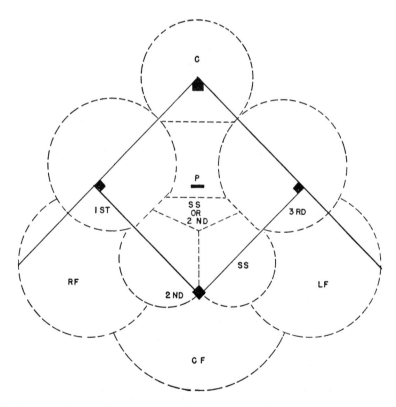

FIG. 7–32. Regular fielding positions and territory for which each player is responsible.

CHAPTER 7. SOFTBALL

sible for fielding in certain territories, many situations require that
the fielder leave these positions for effective defense play. Figure 7–32
shows the regular fielding positions and the territory for which each
fielder is responsible.

The following diagrams represent the play of the defense in specific
situations.

NO ONE ON BASE, HIT TOWARD FIRST BASE (Fig. 7–33)

The Team in the Field.   1. First baseman fields the ball.
2. Right fielder backs up first baseman.
3. Pitcher comes to first base.
4. Catcher backs up the pitcher at first base.
5. Other basemen cover their bases.

NO ONE ON BASE, LONG HIT TO RIGHT FIELD (Fig. 7–34)

The Team in the Field.   1. Right fielder fields the ball.
2. Pitcher should get in line with third base and the ball.
3. Second and third basemen cover their bases.
4. Shortstop backs up second baseman.
5. Left fielder backs up third baseman.
The Team at Bat.   Batter should attempt as many bases as possible
upon advice of coaches at first and third.

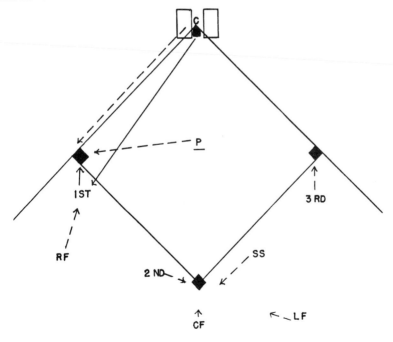

FIG. 7–33. Defense play, no one on base, hit toward first base.

CHAPTER 7.   SOFTBALL

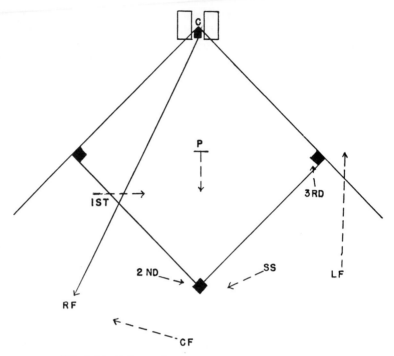

FIG. 7–34. Defense play, no one on base, long hit to right field.

NOTE: The fielders will have to decide where to throw the ball, depending upon whether the runner can make second, third or the plate.

NO ONE ON BASE, LONG HIT TO LEFT FIELD (Fig. 7–35)

The Team in the Field.   1. Left fielder goes after the ball.
2. Shortstop gets in line for relay.
3. Second and third basemen cover their bases.
4. Pitcher backs up third base.
5. First baseman backs up catcher.
The Team at Bat. The batter should attempt as many bases as possible, aided by the coaches.
NOTE: If it is too late to get the runner at second or third, defense should relay the ball to the plate.

RUNNER ON THIRD BASE, WILD PITCH (Fig. 7–36)

The Team in the Field.   1. The catcher fields the ball.
2. The pitcher should cover the plate.

CHAPTER 7. SOFTBALL

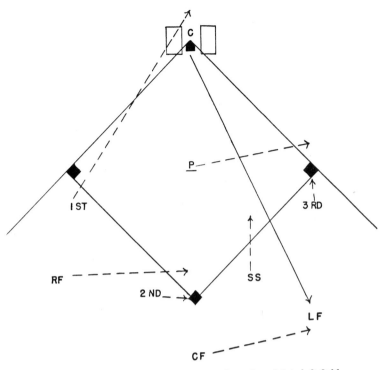

FIG. 7–35. Defense play, no one on base, long hit to left field.

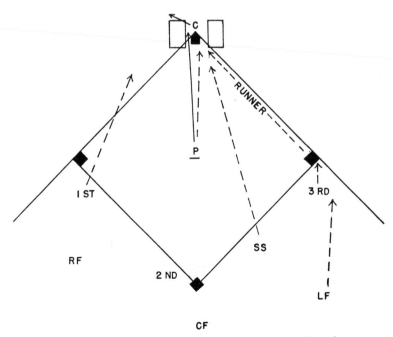

FIG. 7–36. Defense play, runner on third base, wild pitch.

CHAPTER 7. SOFTBALL

3. The shortstop should back up the pitcher.

4. Left fielder backs up third base.

The Team at Bat. The base runner should attempt to reach plate.

RUNNER ON FIRST, HIT TO SHORTSTOP (Fig. 7–37)

The Team in the Field. 1. The shortstop fields the ball and tosses it to the second baseman.

2. The second baseman steps on the base and throws immediately to first baseman. If the second baseman reaches the base with the ball before the base runner, the runner is forced out.

3. The right fielder backs up second base.

4. The third baseman covers third.

5. The left fielder backs up the third baseman.

6. The center fielder backs up the shortstop.

7. The catcher backs up first base.

The Team at Bat. Base runner on first must watch the ball and start with the hit to avoid the force-out.

NOTE: The double play is from second to first base.

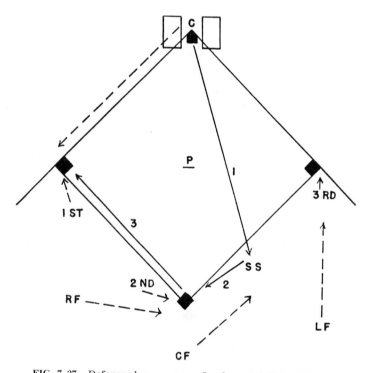

FIG. 7–37. Defense play, runner on first base, infield hit to shortstop.

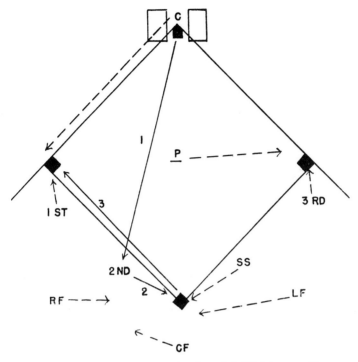

FIG. 7–38. Defense play, runner on first base, infield hit to second baseman.

RUNNER ON FIRST, HIT TO SECOND BASEMAN (Fig. 7–38)

The Team in the Field. The play is second base to first base.

1. The second baseman fields the ball and tosses it to the shortstop covering the base.

2. The shortstop should step on the base and throw at once to first.

3. The left fielder backs up the throw to the shortstop, who is covering second base.

4. The center fielder backs up the second baseman on the hit.

5. The right fielder moves over toward the second baseman on the hit.

6. The catcher backs up first base.

The Team at Bat. Base runner on first must watch the ball and start with the hit to avoid a force-out.

**RUNNERS ON FIRST AND SECOND, GROUND BALL
TO SHORTSTOP, NO OUTS** (Fig. 7–39)

The Team in the Field. 1. The shortstop fields the ball and throws to the third baseman.

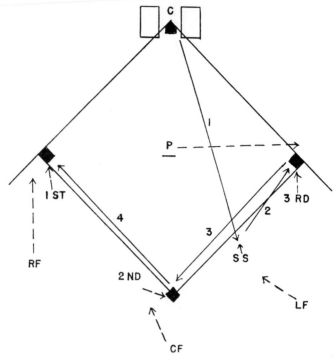

FIG. 7–39. Defense play, runners on first and second bases, no outs, hit to shortstop.

2. The third baseman steps on the base and throws to the second baseman.

3. The second baseman steps on second base and throws to first.

4. The left fielder backs up the shortstop on the hit.

5. The center fielder backs up the second baseman on the throw from third base.

6. The pitcher backs up third base.

The Team at Bat. Base runners must advance immediately to avoid the force-out.

RUNNERS ON SECOND AND THIRD, ONE OUT, GROUND BALL TO SHORTSTOP (Fig. 7–40)

The Team in the Field. The most important consideration is to prevent a run from scoring.

1. If the runner on third base has started for the plate, the throw should be to the catcher.

2. If the runner has held third base, the play should be to first base.

3. The pitcher should back up third base.

4. The left fielder should back up the shortstop on the hit.

CHAPTER 7. SOFTBALL

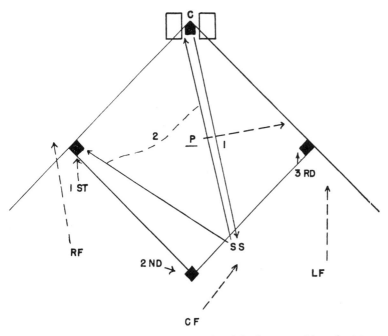

FIG. 7–40. Defense play, runners on second and third, one out, hit to shortstop.

The Team at Bat. The runner on third should try to score on the throw to first base if it is a fairly long throw, or at least try to keep the shortstop from throwing to first base if the hit is short.

NOTE: If there are already two outs, the shortstop should throw to first without delay.

THE "RUN-DOWN" OF A BASE RUNNER CAUGHT OFF BASE
(Fig. 7–41)

Between First and Second Bases. 1. The second baseman has the ball and should pursue the runner back toward the first base at top speed.

2. The shortstop covers second base while the first baseman covers first base.

3. The pitcher backs up first base and the center fielder backs up second base.

4. The runner should be driven back toward first, and when the runner is almost there the second baseman should throw the ball to first.

5. The play should be concluded with one toss of the ball and back toward the base the runner has left.

Between Second and Third Bases. 1. The same number of fielders should be involved.

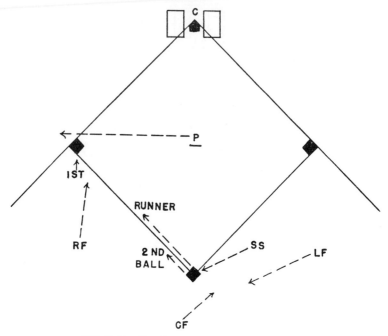

FIG. 7–41. Run-down of runner caught off base.

2. Drive the runner back toward second.

Two Runners on the Same Base. Runner 1 is the first runner on the base, runner 2 steals.

Runner 1 is entitled to the base.

Runner 2 is the runner who must be tagged.

Care must be taken to prevent runner 1 from advancing during the "run-down" of runner 2.

General Coaching Suggestions for Team Defense

Whenever possible, make the out on the runner closest to the plate. If that is doubtful, play for the sure out.

In every case where it is the third out, make the out at the nearest possible base.

Before catching a fly, know where the base runners are. After the fly is caught, see if the base runners have advanced and there is a chance to double the runner off base. If the runner has left the base after the fly is caught, throw the ball to the base toward which she is advancing.

With the runner on third base, the catcher should not throw to second base to trap a runner who is stealing.

The fielders should keep active, moving in and out as the play demands.

CHAPTER 7. SOFTBALL

An intentional walk of a strong batter, when runners are on base,
is often good strategy if a weak hitter follows. The chances are good
that the weak hitter will make an out or hit into a double play.

OFFENSE

Offense tactics in softball are largely individual, but there are
definite forms which the offense may take to build team play.

Careful arrangement of the batting order will often result in bunch-
ing of hits and the scoring of runs. The first player in the batting order
is called the "lead-off." Technically there are nine lead-off players, and
all should keep in mind the qualities of the original "lead-off" who is
the head of the batting order.

"LEAD-OFF" PLAYER

She must get on base either by a bunt, walk or hit.

She must be a fair hitter.

It is a good plan to have a short player who is difficult to pitch to
and may therefore draw a walk.

The "lead-off" should be able to beat out a bunt for a hit.

Get on base!

"CLEAN-UP" POSITION

This position is fourth in the batting order. The batter must be able
to get a base hit.

The strongest hitter on the team is usually placed here, as she
will more often come to bat with runners on bases.

THE BATTING ORDER

The batting order should be related to hitting as follows:

1. "Lead-off," one who will get on base.
2. Fair hitter, good bunter and one who can hit to right.
3. Consistent field hitter.
4. "Clean-up" batter, longest and strongest hitter.
5. Strong hitter.
6. Strong hitter.
7. Weak hitter.
8. Weak hitter.
9. Pitcher, unless the pitcher is an unusually strong batter.

Determining the Batting Order. By keeping the following statistics,
the coach can determine the arrangement of the batting order:

Batting average: (hits divided by the times at bat).

Runs batted in.

The number of times a player gets to first base.

The purpose of the sacrifice bunt is to advance a runner from first base or advance runners on first and second bases.

It is employed only when there are less than two outs, and it should be used only when the score is close.

It makes little difference to which base line the bunt is directed, but some coaches prefer third base, since the throw to first base may not be in time to put out the batter.

With runners on first and second bases, the bunt down the third base line may draw the third baseman from the base.

THE HIT-AND-RUN PLAY

The purpose of the hit-and-run play is to advance a runner two or more bases.

The first base coach should signal both the runner and the batter that the next pitch is to be hit.

The runner should start for second base with the pitch as though for a plain steal.

The second baseman will draw toward her base to cover the steal, and the batter should hit the ball behind the runner between first and second base.

The hit-and-run should not be used very often by a team a little behind in score, as the chance for a double play is great.

The hit-and-run play may be used with a runner on first only or with runners on first and third. If used with runners on first and third, both should start with the pitch.

PINCH HITTER

This is a psychological play when a team is a little behind or the score is very close: a new batter is put in to bat for a regular member of the batting order.

The pinch hitter's chances for a hit must be as good or better than that of the batter replaced.

When a pitcher is to be removed, a "pinch hitter" is often put in to bat for the pitcher.

The batter replaced may not participate in the game again. The team should not be weakened defensively by the replacement.

COACHING BASE RUNNERS

The lines of the coach's box should be drawn 6 feet from and parallel to the lines between home and first and home and third bases. Lines should extend 15 feet toward home plate from the intersection of the base lines.

There may be two coaches only, one at first and one at third base.

CHAPTER 7. SOFTBALL

For the best offense, coaches should be on duty throughout a team's term at bat.

The coach at first base should watch the play and give the following advice:

1. The baseman is close!
2. Take a long (or short) lead!
3. After flies—Run now!
4. After two outs—Run when the ball is hit!
5. Let's have a hit-and-run play.

The coach on third base should watch the play closely, keep track of the outs, and tell the runner when to advance. She should also:

1. Hold the runner on base if a fly is hit unless it will be the third out.
2. Watch for passed balls.

General Coaching Suggestions for Team Offense

Base runners must know the number of outs and where other runners are on the bases. It is inexcusable to run another base runner off a base.

The runners should attempt to lead off as the rules permit, forcing the catcher to throw to the bases. Not only is there a possibility that the runner may steal the base successfully, but there is also the possibility of an overthrow at the base.

Second and third bases should never be overrun.

Every batted ball should be run through the first base at top speed. Fielders make errors.

If there are two outs and a fly ball is hit, base runners should advance immediately without holding the bases to see where the ball is going.

If there are less than two outs and a fly ball is hit, base runners should go only as far toward the next base as will enable them to return safely to the base if the fly is caught. A base runner on third, however, may want to hold until the ball has been caught, in the hopes of running home ahead of the throw from the outfield.

The batter should try to get ahead of the pitcher by having more balls called than strikes. If the count is three balls and no strikes, the batter should let the next pitch go by unless it is in the "groove" which the batter prefers. With the count three balls and two strikes, the batter must get set to hit. The pitcher will no doubt attempt to pitch a strike.

Team strategy varies with the position of runners on bases. The batter should establish a plan and try to carry it through. Some situations demanding clear judgment by the batter and the base runner may be as follows:

1. Runner on first base, score close, one out.

The batter should let the first pitch go by and the runner might attempt to steal to avoid a double play.

The batter should try to hit behind the runner to the right field.

CHAPTER 7. SOFTBALL

This is a good spot for the hit-and-run play.

2. Runners on first and second bases, two outs.

The batter should pick out a good pitch and try for a hit.

3. Runners on second and third bases, one out.

Try for a hit rather than a walk.

Base runners should attempt to steal bases only when it will benefit the team.

1. The best time to steal second is when a weak batter is at bat or against a catcher with a weak throwing arm.

2. The best time to steal third base is after one out has been made. From this position the runner may thus score on an error, a long fly, a ground ball or a squeeze play.

3. The only time an attempt to steal home should be made is with a weak hitter at bat and two outs.

SECTION IV. POSITION PLAY

The various positions of the softball team require special abilities and qualities for skillful play. The player should choose the positions in which she is most interested and for which she is best equipped.

THE INFIELD

THE CATCHER

Catching is one of the most important positions on the team and at the same time one of the most difficult.

REQUIREMENTS

Because of the pressure of the position, good physical build and stamina are essential.

Catching requires not only skillful handling of the ball and a strong throwing arm but alertness in analyzing and controlling every situation. The catcher's position is the best from which to direct the playing of the entire team.

The demands made upon the catcher are numerous, including:

1. The ability to catch every "ball" and "strike."

2. The ability to catch foul tips and pop flies.

3. The ability to throw to every base a quick snap throw, aimed at the side toward which the runner is advancing and low enough so that the baseman can tag the runner without waste motion.

When playing the position of catcher, it is necessary to wear a mask, mitt or glove and a body protector.

The catcher's position behind the bat should be directly behind the plate, close up and under the bat, and in a semi-erect position, body bent forward from the waist, feet parallel. A deep squat position makes it difficult to shoot for high or wide pitches. The catcher's hands and body should be kept still until after the pitch to give the pitcher a target at which to throw.

The catcher's footwork should be such that in reaching for balls to the right or left of the plate she will slide to a point in line with the ball, then drop the right foot back for the throw.

To catch the ball, the catcher should:

1. Be sure to keep the fingers upward for high balls and downwards for low balls.

2. Keep the fingers of the bare hand close together when wearing a mitt on the other hand.

3. If wearing a mitt, catch the ball in the mitt and use the bare hand for a trap.

4. Give with the catch.

5. Pull the hands toward the perfect strike position as the ball is caught.

6. Make a target with the hands for the pitcher.

7. In catching a pop-up, take the ball in front of the body and in the mitt, never overhead if it can be avoided. If the catcher is wearing a mask, she should throw it off before attempting to go after the pop-up.

In making a play at the plate to tag a runner, the catcher should:

1. Move a foot or so toward third base.

2. Place the right foot about 10 or 12 inches from the plate; the left foot a few inches from the base line.

3. Brace herself against a possible collision by a sliding player.

4. Grip the ball firmly in the bare hand and push mitt and ball toward the runner.

The backing-up duties of the catcher involve:

1. Backing-up the first baseman when there is no one on first base and a slow roller is hit toward second base or to the shortstop.

2. Backing up the first baseman when there is a runner on first and a double play is started at second base.

THE PITCHER

Pitching has been estimated to be 70 per cent of defensive baseball.

REQUIREMENTS

Because the pitcher is constantly on duty while the team is in the field, she must have ample strength and emotional stability.

Successful pitching requires control, speed—a good fast ball—and, deception—a good curve ball and change of pace.

CHAPTER 7.   SOFTBALL

The pitcher must be a good fielder. She is particularly responsible for bunts, slow rollers and line drives through the box.

An important defensive duty of the pitcher is covering bases and the plate.

1. On hits toward first base, the pitcher should run with the hit toward first, either to field the ball or to cover the base while the first baseman fields it. Speed is important.

2. She must be ready to cover the plate on a wild pitch or passed ball with runners on base.

3. With a runner on second, she must cover third on hits to the third baseman.

The pitcher's back-up duties are among the most exacting of any of the infielders.

1. The pitcher should back up the plate with runners on base and a hit to right field.

2. With runners on second and third, on a hit to left field, she should back up third base while the first baseman backs up the catcher.

3. With no one on base, she should back up the first baseman.

The pitcher should select from a variety of pitches according to the ability and position of the batter.

1. High to a free-swinging batter, as she is apt to hit a fly ball.

2. Low, if a fly ball or line drive will help the team at bat, as for example when there is a runner on third.

3. Close to a batter who crowds the plate, to drive her back.

4. Wide to a batter sho stands far back from the plate or to one who pulls away as she bats.

5. A fast ball to a batter who stands forward in the box or to a late swinger.

6. A slow ball to a batter who swings fast or to one who stands far back in the box.

THE FIRST BASEMAN

The first baseman should be tall, with the ability to reach to either side of the base for poor throws.

Speed at first base is essential.

The first baseman must have an accurate throwing arm to make plays at any other base.

The position of the first baseman on the diamond varies with the size of the diamond and with the type of play.

1. On the 60-foot diamond, with no one on base she should stand 8 or 10 feet off first base toward second and 10 or 12 feet behind the base line.

2. On the shorter diamonds, she may shorten fielding distances.

3. With a runner on first base, the first baseman will want to play closer to the base in case the runner leads off too much after a pitch and can be picked off by a throw from the catcher.

The first baseman, when receiving a throw for a put-out, must

FIG. 7–42. First baseman reaching for a throw.

be able to get a good stretch toward the fielder. She should keep one foot on the inside corner of the base, while stepping out toward the fielder with the other (Fig. 7–42). Most first basemen prefer to step out onto the foot which corresponds to their gloved hand, *i.e.,* the right foot for a left-handed player.

The first baseman is called upon to catch many bad throws.

1. If the ball is obviously out of reach, she should leave the base and field the ball at once. It will save an extra base.

2. If the ball is high, the baseman should attempt to jump and catch it with both hands. If it is very high, it may be knocked down or caught in one hand, but always use two hands if possible.

3. If the throw is wide to the right of the baseman, the left foot should remain on the bag and the right foot should stretch out as far as possible.

4. If the throw is wide to the left of the baseman, the right foot should remain on the base and a reach be made with the left foot and arms.

The first baseman has definite fielding duties and should work closely with the pitcher so that one covers the base while the other fields. She should try for any ball she may think it possible to field and depend upon the pitcher to cover first base. Bunts and grounders toward first base are her chief responsibilities.

The first baseman is an important cog in relays from the outfield on long hits. If the throw is short or too late she should cut it off and play the ball where it will do the most good.

The Second Baseman

The second baseman must be a speedy fielder and an accurate thrower.

The fielding requirements around second base demand a player who can field to her right or left with equal speed.

It is essential that the second baseman be able to tag a sliding runner without error.

The position of the second baseman on the diamond varies with the size of the diamond and with the type of play.

1. On the 60-foot diamond, her position should be 12 or 15 feet from her base on the first base side.

2. On the shorter diamonds, she shortens her distance from the base accordingly.

3. When there is a runner on second base, the baseman should move over close to the base.

The shortstop and second baseman must work well together, and when the second baseman is fielding a ball the shortstop must replace her on the base.

When waiting for a throw from the catcher to put out a runner who is stealing second base, the baseman should move just inside the base line on the first base side. As the ball is received, the second baseman should use the right foot as a pivot foot, drop the left foot backward and put the ball on the runner.

The second baseman is of prime importance in double plays, either as the fielder or in her position as the baseman.

1. When the second baseman fields the hit, the shortstop should play the base.

2. The throw to the player on the base should be an easy toss if the distance is short, otherwise the ball will be fumbled.

3. The player who covers the base must break for the base as soon as the direction of the hit is determined and be set for the toss when it comes. It is difficult to handle a ball at close range when running.

4. The whip to first base for the second out must be part of the catch. It must be a direct, fast throw.

The second baseman is often involved in a run-down of a player caught off base. If the runner has come from first, the second baseman should chase her back toward that base.

When there are no runners on base, the second baseman can often back up first base or play first base if the first baseman and pitcher have been drawn in to field a bunt.

THE SHORTSTOP

The shortstop is often called the "auxiliary second baseman," and many of the points for playing second base apply to the shortstop.

The shortstop should be the fastest fielder on the team, as most hits go through her position on the left side of the field.

She should be able to throw with the underhand whip as well as a full arm overhand. The underhand whip is necessary as the shortstop is called upon to field many ground balls, and often the ball thrown from a low position will save the split second necessary to make an out.

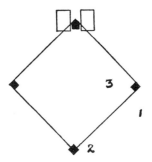

FIG. 7–43. 1, Shortstop backing up third baseman. 2, Shortstop playing second base. 3, Shortstop playing in for a bunt to assist the pitcher.

The position of the shortstop with no runners on base should be as deep as her throwing arm will allow.

Her position on the field varies with the size of the diamond, and on the shorter diamond she should move in closer to the base line.

The shortstop must be adept at moving at top speed to pick up slow rollers. She must never wait for a ball to come to her.

The duties of the shortstop are among the most exacting of any position.

1. The interchange with the second baseman has been discussed.

2. The shortstop is often called upon to cover third base when the baseman fields a bunt or roller.

3. She must back up the third baseman on throws from the outfield.

4. She must back up the pitcher on hits through the box.

5. She must assist on relays from the outfield.

The Third Baseman

A tall player on third base will be an asset, because of the many line drives over third base by right-handed batters.

She must have a good throwing arm, as many of her throws must be across the diamond to first base.

The third baseman should not play as far from her base as the other basemen. Her position is 6 or 8 feet from the base in fair territory, and close to the base line.

Most of the outs at third base are the result of tagging the runner. The baseman should stand close to the base on the inside of the diamond in fair territory. If the throw is bad, the baseman must leave the base and catch the ball, otherwise a run will score.

A good judge of fly balls at third base will be able to catch many foul flies.

The bunt down the third base line is the third baseman's to field, and she must be able to come in fast and field the ball on the run.

The outfield consists of the right fielder, the center fielder and the left fielder. While their territories differ, their qualifications for fielding hits beyond the base lines are similar.

All outfielders must be able to judge and catch fly balls.

Skillful fielding of hard line drives and bounding balls is also essential.

A good throwing arm is a necessity to outfielders.

Outfielders must rove within their territories, playing in for weak hitters and out for strong hitters.

Among the important duties of the outfield is backing up each other and the infield.

The left fielder is responsible for:

Backing up the center fielder.

Backing up hits to the left on the diamond.

Backing up third base on plays to third from the direction of the diamond.

Backing up second base and shortstop on throws from the right side of the diamond.

The center fielder should back up both fielders, infielders on hits through the center of the diamond, and plays from the catcher or pitcher to second base.

The right fielder is responsible for backing up the center fielder, infielders on hits to the right, and plays to first base.

SECTION V. SOFTBALL AND BASEBALL TERMINOLOGY

Assist. Each player who handles the ball, after it leaves the bat, up to the player who makes the put-out, is credited with an assist.

Battery. The pitcher and the catcher.

Batting Average. The number of hits divided by the number of times at bat. The result is expressed in three decimals.

Crowding the Plate. A batter moving close to the plate and refusing to back away with the pitch.

Double Play. Two outs accomplished during a continuous sequence of actions by the defense.

Earned Run. A run scored by a player who has reached base as a result of a hit, walk or a stolen base; in other words, on anything but an error.

Error. A play which allows a base runner to advance by reason of a fumble or a wild throw which fails to make an otherwise certain out. The question of error in the catch of a wild throw or base hit is determined by the scorer, on the basis of whether the fielder had a fair chance to field the ball. A walk, wild pitch, passed ball or a balk are not scored as errors against the pitcher.

Fielder's Choice.   When a fielder elects to try to retire a base runner instead of a batter. If in the judgment of the scorer the batter could not have been retired at first base, the batter is credited with a base hit. If the runner is retired or would have been retired but for an error, the batter is charged with a time at bat but no base hit.

Foul Tip.   A legally batted ball that goes sharply and directly to the catcher's hands and is caught. If not caught it is a foul.

Line Drive.   A ball hit from the bat, low to the infield or outfield.

Pass.   A base on four balls.

Passed Ball.   A legally pitched ball which the catcher fails to hold and control and which has not been touched by the bat.

Put-out.   The player who actually makes the out is credited with the put-out.

Sacks or Bags.   The bases.

Sacrifice.   Advancing a runner with chances that the batter will be put out at first base.

Squeeze Play.   Advancing a runner from third base on a bunt.

Time at Bat.   The batter's term at bat. Bases on walks, sacrifice or interference by the catcher are not scored as times at bat.

Walk.   Gaining first base on four balls.

CHAPTER 7.   SOFTBALL

PENALTY OR GAME SITUATION	WHEN TAKEN	REGULATIONS
Forfeit Game	1. Team fails to appear, or refuses to begin game, or refuses to continue game	Forfeited game in favor of team not at fault. Score is recorded as 7–0 in favor of team not at fault
	2. Team fails to resume play after suspension within 2 minutes of "play"	
	3. Team willfully delays game or violates rules after warning	
	4. If, because of removal of player from game for any cause, there are less than 9 players on either team	
Batter Becomes Base Runner	1. After fair hit	Fair ball is legally batted ball settling on diamond, or first falling on fair territory beyond first and third bases
	2. Catcher drops third strike when first base is unoccupied and less than two outs	Batter out at once after third strike if less than 2 outs and first occupied
	3. After 4 balls called	Entitled to first base without liability of being put out
	4. If catcher interferes with batter striking at pitched ball	
	5. If fair hit strikes umpire or base runner on fair ground	Ball dead and not in play; batter entitled to first base
	6. Person or clothing of batter struck by pitched ball	Batter must make effort to get out of way. Ball dead, runners may not advance unless forced to by batter becoming base runner
Batter Out	1. If any member of her team interferes with player attempting to field a foul fly ball	
	2. Fails to take position at bat within 1 minute	
	3. Hits foul, except foul tip, legally caught before it touched ground	
	4. Bats with either or both feet outside batter's box	
	5. Bunts foul after 2 strikes	Ball dead
	6. Interferes with catcher except if runner stealing is put out	Runners may not advance but may return to base without liability of being put out
	7. Changes from one batter's box to another while pitcher in position to deliver pitch to the batter	
	8. Third strike struck at and missed touches batter's person	
	9. Bats infield fly before 2 outs if first and second or first, second and third bases are occupied	Bunts or line drives are not considered under infield fly rule
	10. After third strike before 2 are out and first base is occupied	Batter may not become base runner after 3 strikes under these conditions even though catcher drops the ball

CHAPTER 7.   SOFTBALL

PENALTY OR GAME SITUATION	WHEN TAKEN	REGULATIONS
Base Runner Out	1. After third strike is dropped; batter must be tagged or thrown out at first under some circumstances	
	2. As batter, hits fair ball legally caught before touching ground	Ball may not be caught in fielder's cap, pocket or other part of uniform
	3. Leaves base before pitch leaves hand of pitcher	
	4. After fair hit or third strike dropped, fielder with ball touches base or runner before runner reaches base	Ball must be retained firmly by fielder. Runner may be touched with hand or glove holding ball
	5. Runs outside 3-foot line from home to first and interferes with fielder taking throw to first	May run outside 3-foot line to avoid fielder attempting to field ball but not to avoid being tagged out
	6. Runs more than 3 feet from any base line to avoid being touched by ball in fielders' hand	Rule applies only when fielder holds ball
	7. Obstructs in any way fielder attempting to field batted ball	
	8. Touched by fielder with ball while ball in play unless runner in contact with base legally entitled to occupy	Ball must not be juggled or dropped; runner safe if base reached before ball held firmly
	9. When forced to leave base by batter becoming base-runner, person or base is touched by fielder with ball before runner reaches next base	
	10. Touched by fair hit ball while on or off base before ball touched by fielder	Runners may not advance unless forced to by batter becoming base runner
	11. Fails to touch base when advancing or returning to base and fielder holds ball on base	An appeal play: No decision by umpire until attention called to it and play made at base. Runs scored by other runners before such outs are counted
	12. Fails to retouch first base at once after overrunning it and touched by fielder with ball	
	13. Fails to retouch base on fair or foul hit ball legally caught and base or person is touched by fielder with ball	Runner may advance as soon as ball is caught
	14. Passes a preceding base runner before such runner has been legally put out	
	15. If coach physically assists runner leaving or returning to third base	Runner not out if no play made on her
	16. If coach runs toward home plate and draws throw to home	Runner nearest third base is out

PENALTY OR GAME SITUATION	WHEN TAKEN	REGULATIONS
Base Runner Entitled to Base Without Liability to Be Put Out	1. While batter, after: Four balls Hit by pitched ball Interference in striking at pitched ball	Batter may take first base, one base for other runners forced to vacate base for batter to take first base
	2. If pitched ball passes catcher and touches backstop or obstruction within 25 feet of home plate	Runners may advance one base. This does not apply to the batter unless it is a third strike and batter is entitled to try for first under other rules
	3. Thrown or pitched ball touches umpire	
	4. Obstruction by fielder unless fielder has ball in hand ready to touch runner	Player obstructed entitled to base, ball in play for other runners
	5. Catcher moves out of position before delivery of ball to aid pitcher to give intentional base on balls	Runners may advance one base
	6. If fielder stops or catches batted or thrown ball with cap, glove or part of uniform while detached from proper place on her person	On batted ball, base runners entitled to 3 bases; on thrown ball, 2 bases; runners may attempt further bases at own risk
	7. On overthrow at first, third or plate, play having started with batted ball and ball touches obstruction or is blocked	Runner being played entitled to one base beyond base of overthrow; other runners entitled to same number
	8. On an illegal pitch the following actions of the pitcher are illegal: Take more than 1 step before delivery of ball to batter Continue wind-up after step Roll or drop ball while in pitching position Make motion to pitch without delivery of ball to batter Pitch when catcher is out of box Hold ball more than 20 seconds Fail to follow through with hand and wrist in line with body Fail to use underhand delivery Take pitching position without possession of ball	Base runners entitled to one base; ball for batter; unless ball is hit into fair territory, in which case ball is in play and no penalty Pitcher entering game may have one minute to warm up not to exceed 5 balls to catcher or fielders

CHAPTER 7. SOFTBALL

PENALTY OR GAME SITUATION	WHEN TAKEN	REGULATIONS
Runner Must Return to Base Without Liability to Be Put Out	1. Foul not caught 2. Illegally batted ball 3. Thrown ball touches coach 4. On dead ball, unless fourth ball forces runner to advance 5. Person or clothing of umpire interferes with catcher's attempt to throw	Ball dead
	6. Batter strikes and misses but ball touches batter's person	Ball dead
	7. Fair hit ball first strikes umpire; runner may advance if forced by batter becoming base runner	

CHAPTER 7. SOFTBALL

8   SPEEDBALL

SECTION I. INTRODUCTION

HISTORY

Speedball developed from a definite need for a fall sport suited to a men's intramural program, a game which did not require highly specialized playing technics, which provided for all-around activity, and which was not expensive to conduct. Speedball answered all of these requirements.

The game, originated by Elmer D. Mitchell, was first played at the University of Michigan in 1921 as part of the men's intramural program. The success of the game was immediate, and the enthusiasm with which it has been adopted by various schools indicates a bright future for the young sport. Speedball today is played in colleges, in recreation leagues, in high schools and in elementary schools; by boys and girls, men and women. California, through its state director of physical education, was the first state to put state-wide promotion behind the game. Other states have since followed. In many places, speedball is being used in inter-county leagues by schools too small to support football.

Girls and women started to play the game about three years after it originated, using men's rules. In 1930, because the game was becoming widespread and because the rules were not suitable for women, a Speedball Committee was appointed by the National Section on Women's Athletics (now DGWS) to make necessary revisions in the rules. Today speedball is a popular high school, junior high school and camp activity for girls.

The speedball field should measure 100 yards by 60 yards, but the size may be reduced for younger girls. The surface should be turf, smooth and well kept.

The ball should be a regulation soccer or speedball. Other equipment is the same as for soccer.

OFFICIALS

As in other field games it is advisable to have two umpires, a scorer and a timer. Each umpire takes one half of the field for the entire game and is responsible for the entire side line on her side of the field (see Fig. 5-1).

Each umpire is responsible for:

1. Enforcing all rules and giving all penalties in her half of the field.

2. Calling all out of bounds along the entire side line and the end line of her half of the field.

3. Calling goals scored in her half of the field.

4. Starting the kickoff in agreement with the other umpire.

5. Recognizing substitutes if she is on the side near the scorer and timer.

6. Taking jump balls in her longitudinal division of the field.

Umpires should keep off the field of play as much as possible, although there are times when it becomes necessary to go on to the field.

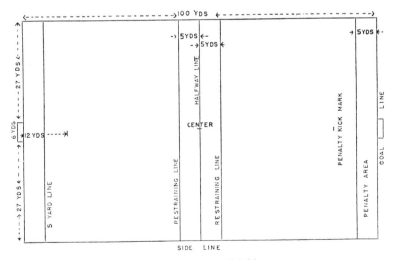

FIG. 8-1. Speedball field.

CHAPTER 8. SPEEDBALL

Arm signals, as in hockey, should be used wherever and whenever possible. The umpires should refrain from awarding any penalty if, in their so doing, the offending team would gain advantage by stopping play for the penalty.

THE GAME

Speedball is a combination of basketball and soccer. A ground ball must be played as in soccer until it has been kicked up and becomes a fly ball. A fly ball may be played either with the hands as in basketball or dropped to the ground and played as in soccer.

A player may dribble at will with her feet but may not bounce the ball. The ball becomes a ground ball when a bounce is attempted and must be played with the feet. A player may guard an opponent in possession of an aerial ball as guarding is permitted in basketball. A player may not run while carrying the ball.

The goalkeeper has no special privileges. She must play a ground ball on the ground but may, as other players, use her hands on a fly ball.

The playing time of 32 minutes is divided into four quarters.

In general the *rules* combine the main points of basketball and soccer with several exceptions. There is no offside in speedball. The very nature of the game eliminates the possibility of such a rule. There are four different methods of scoring:

1. A field goal, 2 points, is scored when a ground ball is played into the cage, as in soccer.

2. A touchdown, 2 points, is a completed forward pass from a player in the field outside the nearer 5-yard line to a member of the same team back of the goal line.

3. A drop kick, 3 points, is scored when the ball is drop-kicked over the goal bar by a player on the field of play outside the nearer 5-yard line.

4. A penalty kick, 1 point, is scored when a penalty kick goes into the goal cage.

SAFEGUARDS IN TEACHING SPEEDBALL

COMMON TYPES OF INJURIES

All injuries which are apt to occur in the game of soccer.
Sprained fingers from incorrect handling of the ball.

SUGGESTIONS TO THE TEACHER FOR HELPING TO PREVENT INJURIES

Those listed under soccer.
Special training in catching and in adjusting speed of pass to proximity of receiver.

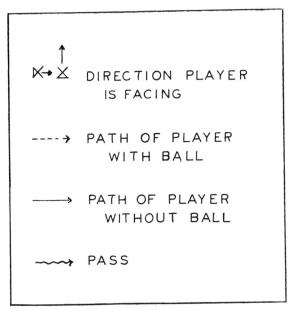

FIG. 8-2. Key to speedball diagrams.

SECTION II. INDIVIDUAL SKILLS AND TACTICS

All soccer skills and all basketball skills, with the exceptions of the bounce to self or the dribble, can be used in speedball. Since these are all described elsewhere, this section will deal only with those skills peculiar to speedball.

LIFTING THE BALL TO SELF (KICKUP)

WITH BOTH FEET

BODY MECHANICS

Starting Position. The ball should be between the player's feet. The weight should be on the outside of the feet.

The inner part of the feet should be in contact with the ball.

The knees should be slightly bent.

The arms should be free at the sides.

The eyes should be on the ball.

The trunk should be bent slightly forward.

Application of Force. The player should jump into the air, equally from both feet.

FIG. 8–3. Kickup with both feet.

The knees should be bent outward, the feet pulling the ball up toward the player.

Contact with the ball should be maintained until the ball is off the ground. The ball should then be quickly released.

The trunk should bend well forward.

The hands should reach for the ball as it is released.

Follow Through. The player should land lightly, knees bent and feet apart.

USE

Used to pick up a stationary ball when there is no immediate possibility of being tackled.

COACHING SUGGESTIONS

Pull the knees up quickly just after jumping.

If the ball tends to slip out forward, turn the toes upward.

Reach well forward and downward for the ball.

Get good foot contact with the ball before jumping.

Pressure against the ball should be equal on both sides.

WITH ONE FOOT ON A STATIONARY BALL

BODY MECHANICS (Right Foot)

Starting Position. The ball should be just in front of the player. The right foot should be placed on top of the ball so that the sole of the foot is in contact with it.

The right knee should be bent.

The weight should be on the left foot.

CHAPTER 8. SPEEDBALL

FIG. 8–4.   Kickup with one foot.

The eyes should be on the ball.

The arms should be free at the sides.

Application of Force.   The ball should be pulled toward the player with the right foot.

As the ball starts rolling, the toe of the right foot should be placed under it.

The right knee should bend upward and outward so that the ball is lifted off the ground.

The player should bend forward to receive the ball off her toe.

Follow Through.   The right leg should follow through upward a short distance after the ball leaves the toe.

USE

Used to pick up a stationary ball. This is a safer way than the lift with both feet if an opponent is near, because the player can recover more quickly to play the ball some other way if the pick-up fails.

COACHING SUGGESTIONS

Get speed on the ball as it is pulled back.

Get the toe well under the ball before starting to lift it.

Give a quick lift of the foot to bring the ball up into the air.

Keep the eyes on the ball until it is caught.

The ball actually comes off the inner part of the top of the instep, rather than directly off the toe.

WITH ONE FOOT ON A MOVING BALL

BODY MECHANICS (Right Foot)

Starting Position.   The body should be in line with the oncoming ball.

The feet should be in a slight forward stride position, knees easy.

FIG. 8–5. Kickup from a pass.

The arms should be free at the side.

The eyes should be on the ball.

The weight should be on the left foot, the right foot slightly advanced.

Application of Force. The toe should be placed under the ball.

The right knee should bend upward and outward so that the ball is lifted off the ground. (It is also permissible simply to allow the ball to roll up the leg without giving any impetus to it.)

Follow Through. The player should bend forward to receive the ball.

USE

Used to pick up a ball moving toward the player.

COACHING SUGGESTIONS

Get the ball onto the foot before starting to lift it.

Be sure the body is directly in line with the ball.

Turn the toe up slightly as the ball is lifted, in order to prevent the ball from rolling off forward.

The foot must actually leave the ground to make this a legal pick-up, or the ball must leave the foot or leg before being caught.

These methods of lifting the ball to self are the only legal ways for a player to convert a ground ball into a fly ball for herself. In the last two methods, the umpire should make certain that the player has actually given impetus to the ball and that the foot comes off the ground.

CHAPTER 8.   SPEEDBALL

With both feet, with one foot on moving ball, with one foot on stationary ball.

1. Demonstrate and explain.
2. Pick up a moving ball with one foot.
3. Pick up a stationary ball with both feet.
4. Pick up a stationary ball with one foot.
5. Body block a ball and pick it up.

SQUAD PRACTICE

Double Line Formation (see Fig. 2–9). With ten players to a line and lines 15 feet apart, roll the ball back and forth, picking it up with one foot.

Shuttle Formation (see Fig. 2–6). 1. Eight to ten players make a squad. Columns are 25 feet apart. X^1 throws the ball with a two-handed overhead pass to X^2. X^2 traps or blocks the ball, picks it up with both feet and throws it back to X^3. X^1 and X^2 go to the end of their columns. *Variation:* Use as a relay race.

2. Ten players to a team, columns 25 feet apart with a line drawn midway between them (see Fig. 2–7). X^1 dribbles the ball to the line and kicks it to X^2. X^2 uses any legal method of pick-up, throws the ball to X^3 with a two-handed overhead pass. X^3 repeats what was done by X^1. Players go to the end of their own column.

Circle Formation (see Fig. 2–15). This is a pick-up relay, ten players to a circle, squad leader in the center, players 5 feet apart. Squad leader has the ball and on signal rolls it to X^1. X^1 picks it up and throws it back with any type of pass or any special pass called for. Squad leader rolls to X^2 and so on around the circle.

LIFTING THE BALL TO A TEAMMATE

BODY MECHANICS (Right Foot)

Starting Position. The ball should be about one foot in front of the player and slightly to the right.

The right toe should be placed under the ball.

The right knee should be slightly bent.

The weight should be on the left foot.

The arms should be free at the sides.

The eyes should be on the target.

Application of Force. The right foot should be lifted into the air with the ball.

The left knee should bend slightly.

The trunk should be inclined forward.

The right knee should straighten.

CHAPTER 8.   SPEEDBALL

FIG. 8–6. Lift to another player.

CHAPTER 8. SPEEDBALL

tion of the lift.

USE

Used to lift the ball for another player to catch.

COACHING SUGGESTIONS

The toe must be under the ball before the lift is started. Don't kick at the ball.

This lift does not send the ball very far.

Height can be regulated by the amount of follow through. For a high ball, follow through higher.

The ball can also be lifted by using the inside of the foot, especially on a moving ball. This is a difficult skill to master and should not be attempted by beginners. The ball should be kicked with the inside of the foot as in soccer, but the foot should bend sharply so that the sole of the foot faces the direction of the pass. The ball actually rolls off the front part of the inside of the foot. It is very much like a flick in hockey insofar as the movement of the ball is concerned.

TEACHING PROGRESSION

1. Demonstrate and explain.
2. Lift the ball to a stationary player.
3. Lift the ball to a moving player.
4. Lift a moving ball to a stationary player.
5. Lift a moving ball to a moving player.
6. Lift the ball with the inside of the foot.

SQUAD PRACTICE

Double Line Formation (see Fig. 2–9).   Lines face about 15 feet apart. Lift the ball back and forth across the space.

Shuttle Formation (see Fig. 2–7).   Ten players to a squad, columns 15 feet apart. X^1 lifts the ball to X^2. X^2 catches it and rolls or kicks it back to X^3 who traps it and lifts it to X^4. Players go to the end of opposite column.

Double Column Formation (see Fig. 2–8).   First player in each column is 30 yards from the goal. Columns 20 feet apart. X^1 and X^2 start forward on signal, dribbling and passing the ball back and forth. As they approach the goal, one player lifts the ball to her partner who drop kicks for goal. Player who kicks recovers the ball. Players return to end of columns.

Column Formation (Fig. 8–7).   Columns of five players face the center of an imaginary circle. X^1 starts with the ball on the ground, lifts it to X^2, who catches it and passes it to X^3. X^3 throws to X^4, who catches

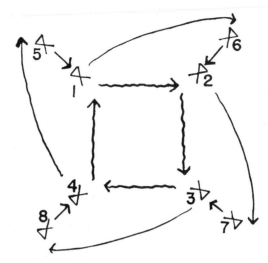

FIG. 8–7. Lifting ball to a teammate, squad practice, column formation.

the ball and rolls it to X^5. X^5 starts the rotation over again after trapping the ball. Players rotate positions in the direction in which the ball travels, going to the end of the next column.

DROP KICK

BODY MECHANICS (Right Foot)

Starting Position. The ball should be held in front of the player about waist height.

The hands should be on opposite sides of the ball, fingers spread.

The elbows should be bent and in close to the body.

The feet should be in a slight forward stride position, the left foot forward.

The eyes should be on the ball.

Application of Force. The ball should be dropped to the ground and the player should take the weight onto the left foot.

The right leg should swing through, the knee slightly bent and the toe pointed toward the ground.

The top of the instep should contact the ball just as it rises from the ground. (Similar to a half volley in tennis.)

The left knee should be bent.

The trunk should bend slightly backward.

The eyes should follow the ball.

Follow Through. The right leg should follow through in an upward direction.

The player should rise on the left toe.

The arms should be free at the sides for balance.

The trunk should incline forward for balance.

CHAPTER 8.   SPEEDBALL

Used as a method of scoring points.

May be used to put the ball in play after it has gone over the goal line without score.

May be used as a pass.

May be used by goalkeeper as a clearing kick.

COACHING SUGGESTIONS

Take the ball just as it rises from the ground. Beginners tend to wait until the ball has bounced high before kicking it.

Get a full leg swing, not just a swing from the knee.

Timing is very important. DROP – STEP, KICK!

Girls seldom attempt to score using this method, perhaps because many of them are unfamiliar with the skill.

For individuals who have particular difficulty in timing, the ball should be dropped from a position well out in front and close to the ground. This calls for a shortened leg swing, involving mostly knee action.

TEACHING PROGRESSION

1. Demonstrate and explain.
2. Drop kick for distance.
3. Drop kick for accuracy.
4. Dribble, trap, pick up and drop kick.
5. Pick up moving ball and drop kick.

SQUAD PRACTICE

Column Formation (Fig. 8–8). 1. One column of eight players lines up behind the goal line. Another column of eight players lines up 15 feet from the goal and in front of it. The column in front of the goal should have three or four balls. X^1 in that column drop kicks for goal and goes to the end of the other column. X^5 in the second column recovers the ball and dribbles it back. X^2 then drop kicks and X^6 recovers. Rotation continues in this way.

2. One column lines up 15 feet in front of the goal and facing it (Fig. 8–9). Second column lines up at right angles to the first and facing it. Eight players are in each column and one or two players behind the goal to recover balls. X^5 lifts the ball to X^1, who drop kicks for goal. Each goes to the end of the opposite column. X^6 lifts to X^2 and the rotation continues. *Variation:* Player with the ball starts to dribble and then lifts.

Single Column Formation (see Fig. 2–1). Players line up in columns of 6 behind the goal line, one player stationed opposite each column to retrieve the ball. Give one ball to each column. Players drop kick for distance, one at a time. All X^1s drop kick and then stand on the spot

CHAPTER 8.   SPEEDBALL

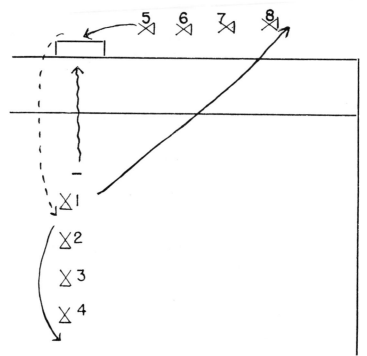

FIG. 8–8. Drop kick, squad practice, column formation.

where the ball first touched the ground. X²s follow and so on, each player standing where her ball first touched. If a player kicks beyond the spot where another player from her column is standing, that player retires. Change the retriever frequently.

DEFENSE TACTICS (INDIVIDUAL)

Individual defense tactics in speedball involve the tactics of fielding, tackling and tackling back, as described in the chapter on soccer, and guarding an opponent with and without the ball, as described in the chapter on basketball.

GENERAL COACHING SUGGESTIONS FOR INDIVIDUAL DEFENSE TACTICS

All players should know defense tactics.
Play the ball, not the opponent!
Use the tackle that is correct for your position in relation to the opponent.

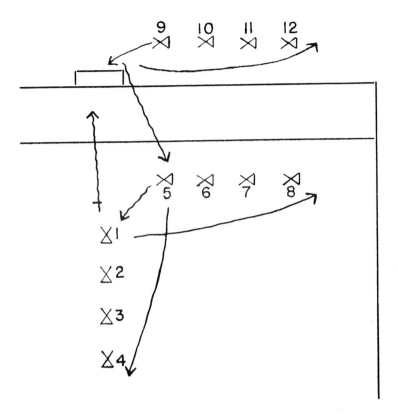

FIG. 8-9. Drop kick, squad practice, another column formation.

Avoid blocking when guarding an opponent without the ball.
Tackle back as soon as you lose the ball.

OFFENSE TACTICS (INDIVIDUAL)

Individual offense tactics involve passing, drawing, centering and dodging, as described in the chapter on soccer; losing an opponent, getting into scoring position and passing, as described in the chapter on basketball.

GENERAL COACHING SUGGESTIONS FOR INDIVIDUAL OFFENSE TACTICS

Pass quickly in the aerial game to avoid traveling with the ball.
Center in order to score a field goal or a drop kick.
Don't move in the same direction in which you pass.
If possible, draw an opponent before passing.
Use various types of tactics, don't stick to one.

A speedball team consists of 11 players lined up as in soccer. The duties of the players are so nearly the same as those in soccer in a like position that a separate discussion of them is not necessary. The five forwards are, in the main, attack players, the halfbacks both attack and defense players, as are the two fullbacks, while the goalkeeper serves purely in a defense capacity.

DEFENSE TEAM TACTICS

The defense team tactics in general involve those employed in both basketball and soccer. Basketball defense tactics are used when an aerial game is being played, and soccer defense tactics when a ground game is played.

Defense team tactics include marking, covering, interchanging, and covering spaces, as in soccer, and the various defense methods— player-to-player, pick-up, zone, shifting zone and combinations—as described in the basketball section.

Defense players must be keenly alive to the possibilities of both

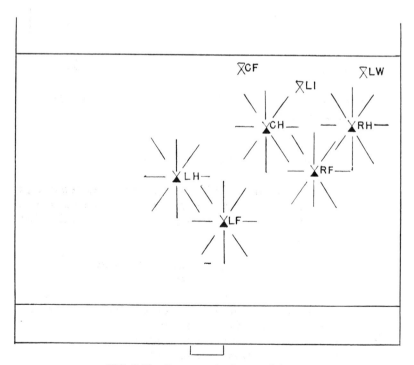

FIG. 8–10. Concentration in zone defense.

the aerial game and the ground game. If an aerial attack is in progress, **327** each of the five defense players should either guard her opposing forward or shift the zone of defense to the opponents nearest the ball. Three halfbacks are helpless against five forwards, so the fullbacks must come in on this type of play. Since intercepting is the strongest defense against the aerial game, close guarding is essential.

If a ground game is in progress, the tactics of marking, covering and interchanging constitute the strongest method of defense.

It is the constant shifting from one type of defense to another which makes the position of back so difficult and so strenuous. As a result of the various types of defense essential in speedball, it is extremely important that the forward line players share the work of defending.

GENERAL POINTS ON DEFENSE

Play the ball, not the opponent.
Keep the ball out of the scoring area.
Work with other defense players. It's not just your job, nor is it theirs alone, to keep a score from being made.
Learn to anticipate the attack of your opponent.
Be ready to shift to attack.
If the opponents play a good aerial game, keep the ball on the ground and vice versa.
Be quick to shift from aerial defense to ground defense and from ground defense to aerial defense.
Study your opponents to see what types of defense are most effective against the type of game they play.

ATTACK TEAM TACTICS

The ball may be advanced by long or short passes on the ground or in the air, or by dribbling on the ground. Once the ball is in the air as a fly ball, many players feel that it should be kept there until accidentally grounded. Grounding the ball on purpose often opens up unexpected possibilities.

The forwards may advance toward the goal in any formation desired since there is no offside rule. Shifting diagonals constitutes the most commonly used method. This means that there may be a V formation of advance, changing to a single long diagonal across the field, and similar changes.

It is sometimes difficult to keep the forwards well spread out. The tendency to crowd toward the player in possession of the ball is disastrous because it makes it easy for the opponents to break up the attack. The backs, close behind the forward line, are very usable for a backward pass to be followed by a pass to a very different part of the field. Occasionally a halfback can slip over the goal line for a touchdown pass.

In the aerial game, especially, the backs are a very definite part of the attack.

If the ball has progressed down one side of the field by aerial passes, a sudden shift to the center for a ground ball and a field goal or drop kick attempt will often catch the defense unprepared. When one type of attack has been started it is not necessary to continue in that method. Team work and head work open up many possibilities which blind play overlooks.

The ground attack resembles soccer in practically all points except that there is no need for forwards to watch for offside. The other main difference is that the ground game may suddenly shift to an aerial game, calling for different attack tactics.

GENERAL POINTS ON ATTACK

Keep the ball moving toward goal.

The halfbacks should be an integral part of the attack.

Centering the ball is not necessary unless a field goal or a drop kick is to be attempted. A touchdown may be scored across any part of the goal line except that in the cage.

A ground game is preferable in a high wind.

Only the concerted action of the whole team makes it possible to score.

The attack must be quick to shift to defense when the ball goes to the other team.

Don't use the same method of attack throughout the game. Varying the attack confuses the opponents.

Look for weaknesses in the defense and plan the attack accordingly.

Shifting from ground to aerial or vice versa before attempting to score is apt to disconcert the defense.

Suggested combinations of ground and aerial scoring methods:

1. Advance the ball down the side line on the ground. When within scoring range lift to teammate, pass to center of field and either ground the ball for a field goal or attempt a drop kick.

2. Advance the ball down the center of the field as for a field goal, lift to teammate, pass toward side line for an attempted touchdown.

3. Advance the ball in aerial attack down the side line, pass toward center, attempt drop kick.

SECTION IV. FORMATION PLAYS

THE THROW-IN

A throw-in is awarded when the ball is played over the side line off one or more members of the same team or when a player with the

with any type of pass by a player on the team which did not cause it
to go out of bounds. From the throw-in the ball may be played either as
an aerial or a ground ball.

THE ATTACKING TEAM

The forwards should be up ahead of the thrower, toward the goal
they are attacking, and at least two of them, the wing and the inner,
should be close to the side line. There is no regulation as to the distance
they must stand from the thrower. The forwards should make spaces
through which a pass can be directed.

The halfback and the fullback on that side of the field should be out
near the side line, ready for a backward pass. They should also be prepared to shift to defense should the opponents intercept the throw.

The player taking the throw-in, generally the halfback, should
come onto the field of play immediately after the throw has been taken.
She may not replay her own ball.

THE DEFENDING TEAM

The forwards on the defending team should, if possible, place
themselves between the thrower and the attacking forwards in an
attempt to intercept the pass. This is an important tactic which many
forwards overlook. By plays of this type, forwards are able to strengthen
the defense of their team.

The halfback and fullback on the side of the field where the throw
is being taken should mark their opponents closely, standing between
them and the goal they are defending. The center halfback should mark
loosely, and the other fullback and halfback should be in covering
positions.

No member of the defending team may be within 5 yards of the
thrower. If the attacking forwards take advantage of this regulation it
is difficult for the defending forwards to adequately block spaces. Defense against the throw-in is difficult because of this regulation. The
defending team has little chance at intercepting a pass to an opponent
standing close to the thrower, and the most satisfactory play is to cover
closely any possible receiver of the pass after the throw-in.

THE TOSS-UP (AERIAL OR GROUND BALL)

The toss-up is awarded for a tie ball, after a double foul, after time
out, if no other penalty has been awarded, and if the ball goes out of
bounds off opponents. The ball is tossed up by the umpire between the
two opponents who held it in tie, or between the two center forwards
at the start of the quarters. Each player faces her opponent's goal. The
ball may be tapped at the height of the toss or as it descends, but not on

the way up. No other player may be within 5 yards of the ball at the time of the toss-up.

There is no defending or attacking team. Members of both teams should attempt to place themselves in the most advantageous position for receiving the ball. All players will find it more satisfactory to play the toss-up from an offensive point of view rather than from a defensive one, unless there is no doubt as to which of the jumpers will get the tip. In a case of that sort members of the opposite team should play defensively.

THE KICKOFF

The object of the kickoff in speedball is for the kicking team to retain possession of the ball. On the kickoff, the ball may be lifted to become an aerial ball. The kickoff is a place kick from the center of the field used at the beginning of the game, at half time, at quarter time and after each score. The kick must be forward and the ball must travel the length of its circumference.

THE ATTACKING TEAM

The team taking the kickoff must be within its own half of the field, and no player may cross the center line until the ball is kicked. The possible plays on the kickoff are similar to those in soccer, namely to either inner or to either wing. The ball may be lifted at the kickoff. If this type of play is used, the ball can be lifted diagonally forward to either inner. The inners must be prepared for this.

As soon as the ball has been kicked, *all* attacking forwards should cross the center line. The halfbacks and fullbacks should move forward in the direction of the kick, and the attack is underway.

THE DEFENDING TEAM

All members of the defending team must be behind the restraining line in their half of the field. No player may cross the line until the ball has been kicked.

The forward line players should cross over as soon as the ball is kicked in an attempt to intercept the pass or to break up the attack. If the opponents get through these forwards, the halfbacks and fullbacks should be ready for them. It is a mistake for the defending forwards to follow the attacking forwards down the field. All they succeed in doing is disconcerting their own defense players. They may, however, follow back of the forward line to intercept a backward pass to the halfbacks. No more than three forwards should attempt this, generally the forwards playing near the ball. The other forwards should hang back.

The halfbacks and fullbacks on the defending team should imme-

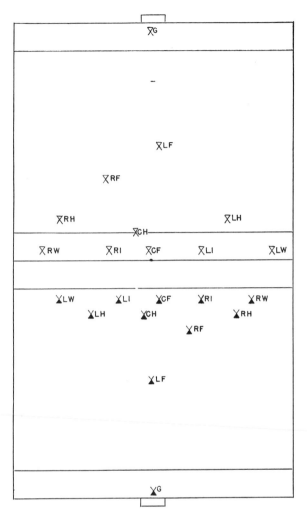

FIG. 8–11. Line-up for kickoff in speedball.

diately shift to concentrate their defense on the side of the field where the ball is being played. Those in the vicinity of the ball should mark closely, the others mark loosely and cover.

OUT OF BOUNDS OVER THE GOAL LINE

BALL PUT IN PLAY BY THE TEAM DEFENDING THE GOAL

The ball is put in play by the team defending the goal when played over the goal line without score by a member of the attacking team in any of the following ways; by a punt, by a place kick, by a drop kick or by a throw-in, taken on the goal line at the point where the ball crossed the line. The ball may be played either as a ground ball or an aerial ball.

THE ATTACKING TEAM

The forwards of the team in possession of the ball out of bounds should place themselves in readiness to receive the ball. If they play well down the field, the ball should be punted to them over the heads of the defending forwards. This is the best type of play to start the forwards on an attack with either a ground game or an aerial game.

THE DEFENDING TEAM

The forwards of the defending team should place themselves between the out-of-bounds player and the forwards of the attacking team, standing quite close to the latter. They should be prepared to intercept the throw or kick. No player of the defending team may be closer than 5 yards to the ball.

The halfbacks of the defending team should mark their opponents. The fullback on the side of the field where the ball is being put into play should mark her opponent, and the other fullback should be in a covering position. All defense players should be nearer the goal they are defending than are their opponents.

BALL PUT IN PLAY BY THE TEAM ATTACKING THE GOAL

The ball is put in play by the attacking team when the defending team plays it over its own goal line. It may be played by a punt, a drop kick, a place kick or a throw-in from a spot on the goal line opposite to where the ball went out. The ball may be played either as a ground ball or an aerial ball.

THE ATTACKING TEAM

The attacking team should be prepared to score on this play. Some of the possible plays are:

1. Lifted place kick to be converted into a touchdown.
2. Short punt or place kick to be converted into a field goal.
3. Throw-in to be converted into a touchdown, drop kick or a field goal.

The out-of-bounds player should take her cue as to the type of play to use from the position of her forwards and from the position of the defending team. The forwards must make spaces through which the ball can be played, otherwise there will be no advantage gained from the penalty. An excellent scoring opportunity occurs here, for it is possible to return the ball to the player sending it in from out of bounds and score a touchdown.

CHAPTER 8. SPEEDBALL

The halfbacks of the attacking team should play close behind the forwards, because in this type of play they are often used for scoring. This is especially true in case of a touchdown or a drop kick.

THE DEFENDING TEAM

No member of the defending team may be within 5 yards of the player taking the out-of-bounds ball. The halfbacks and fullbacks should closely mark their respective opponents. This marking must be very carefully done in order to prevent scoring.

The forwards of the defending team should be nearer their own goal than the attacking forwards, ready for a pass out from the defense players.

THE PENALTY KICK

A penalty kick is a drop kick from the penalty kick mark and is awarded in the following cases:
1. A foul by the defending team within its own penalty area.
2. A foul by the defending team back of its own goal line.
3. Any type of team foul.

During the course of the penalty kick, all players except the kicker must be 5 yards from the ball.

THE ATTACKING TEAM

All members of the attacking team must be outside of the penalty area and no closer than 5 yards to the ball. There is no required line-up. After the ball has been played, the forwards should rush toward the goal in an attempt to score on a follow-up play. The halfbacks should back up closely.

THE DEFENDING TEAM

The teammates of the goalkeeper may be on the goal line, except between the goal posts, or on the field of play outside of the penalty area.

The strongest defense against the penalty kick calls for the full-backs and halfbacks behind the goal line and the forwards on the field of play. Each defense player should place herself opposite her particular opponent on the opposing forward line. When the kick is taken, the defense players should come out quickly to mark their opponents. There is a decided tendency to bunch in front of the goal, which leaves the attacking forwards free to make use of the touchdown or drop kick method of scoring.

CHAPTER 8.   SPEEDBALL

A free kick is awarded for a foul committed anywhere on the field except by a member of the defending team within her own penalty area or back of her own goal line. It is a place kick from the spot on the field where the violation occurred. No opponent may be within 5 yards of the ball.

THE ATTACKING TEAM

The general tactics of the attacking team are the same as for a throw-in. The possibility of receiving a lifted ball should not be over-looked in the case of a free kick.

THE DEFENDING TEAM

Here, too, the tactics are similar to those used in guarding against the throw-in.

SECTION V. POSITION PLAY

Play in speedball is essentially so similar to that in soccer, inso-far as position play is concerned, that it seems unnecessary to discuss it in detail.

The forward line, the right wing, the right inner, the center forward, the left inner and the left wing bear the brunt of the attack. Each of these players needs to be skilled in the various technics of the game. It is essential that they be able to convert a ground ball into a fly ball or their attack is weakened.

The halfback line plays much more of an attacking game than in soccer. They participate more frequently in the actual scoring of points. The halfbacks are often used for touchdown scores or for drop kick scores. As in the other field games, they are the hardest-worked players on the field.

The fullbacks, too, are used more in the attack in speedball. Not infrequently a fullback is found participating in the aerial attack. They must always be ready for a backward pass from a forward who cannot get a forward pass through.

The goalkeeper is the last defense player. She is responsible only for the goal cage and scores made across the goal line at other points are not her responsibility. Occasionally the goalkeeper feels concern about the entire goal line. This must be prevented, because she cannot concentrate her attention on one spot and do a good piece of work there while thinking about other possible scores. The goalkeeper has no special privileges in speedball, hence she must be constantly on the alert as to whether the ball may or may not be played with the hands.

Because of the type of play involved in the game of speedball most
players, with the exception of the goalkeeper, cover more territory, both up and down the field and across the field than they do in hockey or soccer.

SUMMARY OF SPEEDBALL RULES

WHEN TAKEN	REGULATIONS	WHAT HAPPENS IF REGULATIONS ARE NOT FULFILLED
Free Kick		
1. Awarded for foul committed any place on the field except by a member of the defending team inside her penalty area or back of goal line Attempting drop kick or touch-down from penalty area Blocking Charging Delaying the game Double juggle Handling ground ball Kicking, tripping, pushing Holding ball Unnecessary roughness Failure to report Snatching, tagging Traveling Overguarding	a. Place kick from spot where foul occurred b. Opponents 5 yds. away c. Ball must travel distance of circumference d. Kicker may not replay the ball	Repeat Repeat, if advantage gained Free kick opponents Free kick opponents
Throw-in		
1. Out of bounds over side line off one or more players of same team 2. Player with ball steps out of bounds	a. Ball thrown in at point where it crossed side line b. Thrower may not replay the ball c. Opponents 5 yds. away	Repeat Throw-in opponents Repeat, if advantage gained
Out of Bounds over Goal Line		
1. When ball goes over goal line off one or more players of the same team	a. May be punted, drop-kicked, place kicked or thrown in from spot where ball went out of bounds b. Opponents 5 yds. away c. No replay d. Must go at least the distance of the circumference of ball e. Must not touch line or field prior to punt or drop kick	Repeat Repeat, if advantage gained Out-of-bounds opponents Out-of-bounds opponents Out-of-bounds opponents

WHEN TAKEN	REGULATIONS	WHAT HAPPENS IF REGULATIONS ARE NOT FULFILLED
	Penalty Kick	
	a. Drop kick from penalty kick mark	Free kick opponents on penalty kick mark if other kick used
1. Foul by defending team inside own penalty area or behind own goal line	b. Defending goalkeeper stands behind her own goal line	Repeat
2. Any team foul Illegal substitution More than 3 time-outs More than 11 players on field	c. Teammates of kicker on field of play outside of penalty area	Free kick opponents on penalty kick mark
	d. Teammates of goalkeeper behind goal line or on field of play outside penalty area	Repeat
	e. Players 5 yds. from ball and outside penalty area	Repeat
	f. Kicker may not replay ball	Free kick opponents
	g. An attempt for goal must be made	Free kick opponents
	h. Ball must bounce behind penalty kick mark	Free kick opponents
	Kickoff	
1. At beginning of game	a. Place kick from center of field	Repeat
	b. Ball must go forward at least its own circumference across halfway line	Free kick opponents
2. At beginning of each quarter	c. Kicker may not replay ball	Free kick opponents
3. After a score	d. No opponent may cross the restraining line until ball is kicked	Free kick opponents
	e. No teammate may cross the center line until ball is kicked	Free kick opponents
	Toss-up	
1. In case of tie ball between opponents (either aerial or ground ball)	a. Players tap ball after it reaches highest point	Free kick opponents
	b. Neither player may catch ball	Free kick opponents
2. After a double foul	c. Must be tapped by one or both players	Repeat
3. Out of bounds over side line or goal line off opponents	d. Players stand in imaginary 6-ft radius circle, with back toward own goal until ball is tapped	Repeat
	e. Other player 5 yds. away	Repeat, if advantage gained
	f. No more than 2 taps permitted within circle	Free kick opponents
	g. No toss up closer than 5 yds. to boundary line	Repeat

CHAPTER 8. SPEEDBALL

VOLLEYBALL 9

SECTION I. INTRODUCTION

HISTORY

Volleyball, the most adaptable of the team sports, was originated by Mr. William G. Morgan at the Holyoke, Massachusetts, Young Men's Christian Association in 1895. The game now played by men and women, by experts and beginners, by children and adults, in elementary schools and colleges, in gymnasiums and on playgrounds, began as a deliberate experiment, contrary to most sports which have some tie with ancient pastimes. Mr. Morgan's objective was the creation of a skilled activity requiring more players and less space and exertion than basketball.

The original equipment consisted first of a rope (later an elevated tennis net) stretched across the gymnasium and an inflated basketball bladder. The need for a special ball, which Mr. Morgan designed, became immediately apparent. A rule permitting a player to advance with the ball by bouncing it was discarded early in favor of the fundamental requirement after which the game was then named: the ball had to be hit in flight, or volleyed, without striking the playing surface.

With the impetus given the game through Y.M.C.A. endorsement and promotion, the growth in popularity was rapid. The greatest advance came during World War I, when it was used extensively in recreation programs for members of the armed forces.

Women began to play a modified version of volleyball immediately after it was originated. The first official rules for women were published in 1924. Variations from the men's game persisted until the early 1960s. In that period, the official rules for women were changed to eliminate any substantial differences from the game for men.

Official rules for women are now published every two years in the *Volleyball Guide,* prepared by the Division for Girls and Women's Sports of the American Association for Health, Physical Education and

Recreation, a department of the National Education Association, Washington, D.C. The *Guide* includes modified rules for young and inexperienced players as well as the official rules.

EQUIPMENT AND ITS CARE

Volleyball equipment requires little care beyond checking the net to make sure it is tightly stretched and keeping regulation balls blown to a specified pressure.

The Court. The court should be 60 by 30 feet with at least 20 feet clearance overhead. A center line 2 inches in width should divide the court. The net should be tightly stretched at the four corners between uprights or walls which are entirely outside the court. The top should be level and measure 7 feet 4¼ inches from top center to the playing surface.

Behind each end line is a serving area which is a continuation of the side lines to a depth of 6 feet. Where space is limited or players are young or inexperienced, the serving area may be within the court (Fig. 9–1).

The Ball. The ball may be either rubber or a rubber bladder covered by a leather case. The leather-covered ball should weigh 7 to 9 ounces and carry 7 to 8 pounds pressure. The circumference is 26 to 27 inches. The rubber ball should carry not less than 5 or more than 8 pounds pressure.

At least one ball should be provided for each squad of six players.

OFFICIALS

The officials for a match are: a referee, an umpire, two scorers, two timekeepers and two linesmen.

The Referee. The official in charge of the game is the referee. She should:

1. Station herself at one end of the net for a clear view of the entire court.

2. Blow the whistle for time in and time out.

3. Decide and indicate a point scored or side out.

4. Impose all penalties.

5. Recognize substitutes and, in general, conduct the game.

The Umpire. As assistant to the referee, the umpire should:

1. Station herself on the opposite side of the court from the referee.

2. Call violations and fouls on her side of the court and any not seen by the referee.

Scorers. The scorers' table is on the same side of the court as the referee. They should:

1. Record the official score.

2. Check to see that proper serving orders are maintained.

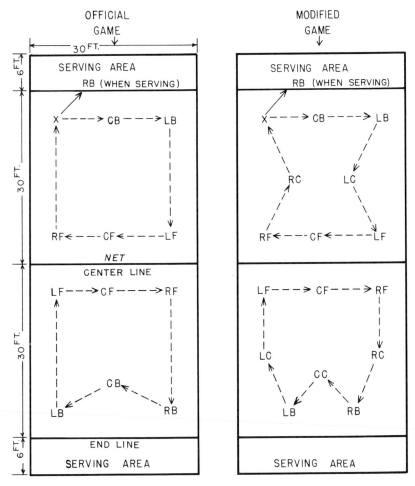

FIG. 9-1. Court dimensions, positions of players, and direction of rotation.

3. Inform the referee when a game has been completed on the basis of the score.

Timekeepers. One stopwatch is used for playing time, another for time out. The official timekeeper should:

1. Start watch when server contacts the ball and stop it whenever the ball is dead.

2. Stop watch when referee whistles for time out.

3. Sound whistle at expiration of playing time and time out.

4. Inform referee when 8 minutes of playing time have elapsed in the first two games of a match and after 4 minutes of playing time in a third game.

Linesmen. Linesmen are stationed at opposite corners of the court,

CHAPTER 9. VOLLEYBALL

out of the way of play but in line with server. Each should have one end line and one side line in clear view. Linesmen should:

1. Signal *good* or *out* when the ball strikes near one of these lines.

2. Assist scorers in seeing that players follow the serving and rotation orders.

3. Watch particularly for foot faults by server.

THE GAME

The object of the game is to serve or return the ball over the net into the opponents' court in such a way that the opponents fail to return it legally.

Team. Each team consists of six players in positions designated as left forward (LF), center forward (CF), right forward (RF), left back (LB), center back (CB), and right back (RB).

Modified rules for young or inexperienced players recommend eight players to a team, adding a left center (LC) and a right center (RC).

Position of Players. Before each serve, players take their positions on the court in their own areas as illustrated in Figure 9–1. The team having the ball for service is the *serving team.* The opposing team is the *receiving team.*

The server is the right back of the serving team. When she serves, she must be inside her team's serving area, feet behind the end line. After the server has struck the ball, she and all other players may cover any section of their own playing court. A player may leave the court to play the ball.

Putting the Ball in Play. The ball is put in play by a *legal serve*

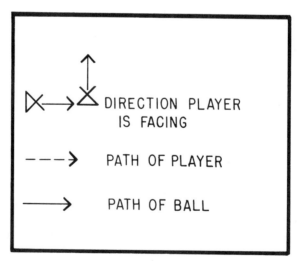

FIG. 9–2. Key to volleyball diagrams.

when the right back of the serving team, standing in her team's serving area, hits the ball over the net into the opponents' court.

1. The ball is served:

a. At the start of the game by the team whose captain won the choice of serve.

b. At the beginning of the second half by the team not having the serve at start of game.

c. After a point is scored (serving is by team scoring, the serving team).

d. After side out (service shifts to opposing team).

2. The ball may be hit with hand, fist or forearm and either underhand or overhand.

3. A *foot fault* is called if the server steps on or over the end line before the ball is hit while in the act of serving.

Term of service. The same server continues to serve until the referee calls side out.

Playing the ball. The ball must be passed or returned before it strikes the surface of the court.

1. The ball may be hit by no more than three players on a team before it is returned to the opponents' court.

2. The ball may be hit with the hands, fists or forearms only.

3. Each player may hit the ball only once in succession.

4. The ball must be given immediate impetus on contact. Holding, pushing, lifting or throwing the ball are illegal hits.

Scoring. Only the serving side scores.

One point is scored by the serving team when the opposing team fails to return the ball legally.

Side out is called when the serving team fails to serve or return the ball legally. The opposing team gains a term of service, but no point is scored.

Rotation. After side out has been called, all players on the team about to begin a term of service shift one position clockwise as indicated in Figure 9–1. Each player in turn must serve and play each position.

Serving order. Players come into the right back position to serve in the pattern of rotation shown in Figure 9–1. All six players must be included in the serving order. Each player has a term of service each time the serving order is repeated.

Game. One game is completed when 8 minutes of *actual playing time* have elapsed or a team scores 15 points. The winning team must lead by 2 points.

1. If a team is not 2 points ahead when 15 points have been scored or after 8 minutes of actual playing time, play continues until a team is 2 points ahead.

2. *Actual playing time* is the period which elapses from the server's initial contact with the ball on each serve until it is dead. The ball is dead at any time it is temporarily not in play.

Match. An official match is completed when a team wins two of a possible three games.

CHAPTER 9. VOLLEYBALL

Because the ball is struck with the hands, there is always danger of injury to the fingers. Well-taught players assume hand positions with slightly bent fingers to eliminate this hazard. Jumping to spike or to reach the ball under other circumstances involves the risk of sprains in landing. Careful conditioning of players and avoidance of fatigue will do much to prevent such injuries. As in all team sports, players who must wear glasses should be provided with glasses guards.

SECTION II. INDIVIDUAL SKILLS AND TACTICS

THE PASS

The pass is the most important, the most frequent and the most neglected tactic in volleyball. For every serve and spike, there are many passes. A team's attack can be no more effective than its passing. Therefore, practice given to passing should receive considerable time and effort.

THE OVERHAND PASS
(FOR BALLS ABOVE THE CHEST)

BODY MECHANICS

Starting Position. The palms should face forward and upward, thumbs toward each other.

The fingers should be spread and flexed, wrists bent back.

The elbows should be out from the body and flexed.

The knees should be slightly flexed, the body tilted backward from the waist.

The body is usually in better balance with the left foot forward, if the player is right-handed.

The player should be directly under the ball as it is hit.

Application of Force. The hands should tilt backward to meet the angle of the flight of the ball.

The ball is hit by a quick flexion of the wrists and extension of the elbows.

The palms turn inward as the ball is hit.

If necessary, a jump may be made as the hands make contact with the ball to add greater force.

Extension of the knees and ankles and forward flexion of the trunk will contribute to the force of the stroke.

Follow Through. The arms and the entire body should follow through in the direction the ball is to go.

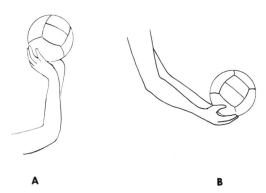

A   **B**

FIG. 9–3. Position of the hands for passing. A, Ball above chest, fingers upward and behind ball. B, Ball below chest, fingers and thumb under ball.

THE UNDERHAND PASS
(FOR BALLS BELOW THE CHEST)

BODY MECHANICS

Starting Position. The palms should face up with the thumbs out.

The fingers should be spread, finger tips flexed, and little fingers an inch or so apart.

The wrists should be bent back, the elbows flexed slightly and free from the side.

The feet should be in easy stride position for good balance.

Application of Force. The hands should be well under the ball to give space for a good lift and backswing.

The wrists should be flexed with a snap just as the ball strikes the finger tips. The ball should not strike the palm.

The forearms should stiffen.

The knees and hips should be extended, putting the added force of the body behind the stroke.

Follow Through. The arms should swing forward and upward in the direction the ball is to go.

THE DIG PASS

A more advanced method of passing balls hit downward by an opponent is the dig pass. It is particularly valuable against the spike.

BODY MECHANICS

Starting Position. The fingers should be clenched and the palms upward.

The wrists and forearms should be rigid and placed in a low position.

The legs and waist should assume a crouch position, one foot in

FIG. 9–4. Underhand pass.

front of the other. This position should be maintained throughout the stroke, as there is not enough time to permit the extension of the knees and hips.

Application of Force. The upward motion begins at the shoulder. As the ball is contacted, the forearms move upward from the elbow.

The wrists remain rigid.

Follow Through. The arms should swing forward and upward in the direction the ball is to go.

COACHING SUGGESTIONS

The ball should be batted with the fleshy part of the finger tips (except for the dig). Balls batted with the palms and the heels of the hand are hard to control.

Both hands should be employed whenever possible in order to provide better control.

The angle of the hands at the time the ball is hit will determine the direction the ball takes. If the hands are too vertical, the ball will often be netted; if the hands are horizontal, the ball will rise vertically or go backward overhead.

The hands should be kept parallel; otherwise the ball will not be accurately directed.

Fingers must be kept flexed to prevent the ball from going back overhead and to prevent injury to the fingers.

A fast ball must be hit with more force than that with which it is traveling if it is to be hit across the net with one stroke. A jump will increase the force.

CHAPTER 9. VOLLEYBALL

Beginners must be coached to get the body behind the stroke.

The eyes must be kept on the ball at all times.

Correct body position must be rapidly and accurately determined as soon as the ball has been sent toward the receiver.

The speed and spin of the ball must be reduced by the passer to allow a teammate to handle it.

The ball should be directed upward and toward a teammate to give her time to get under the ball. The ball should travel in an arc rather than in a straight line.

The ball should be passed with a definite objective, usually toward the player in the most advantageous position for the next pass or return.

TEACHING PROGRESSION

1. Explain and demonstrate the positions for the underhand and overhand passes.

2. Throw and catch a few balls, emphasizing the importance of slightly flexed fingers and the thumb in contacting the ball.

3. Exchange passes with a teammate at short distances.

4. Increase the speed and distance of the pass.

5. Return passes sent from right or left, overhead or low.

6. Introduce the dig pass.

SQUAD PRACTICE

Relay Formation with Leader (see Fig. 2–2). The leader tosses the ball to player 1, player 1 hits it back to the leader and goes to the end of the line. Continue through the squad.

Use same formation as a relay with established restraining line.

Shuttle Formation. Half the squad is on either side of the net (Fig. 9–5).

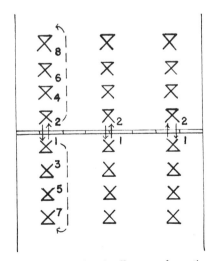

FIG. 9–5. Overhand volley, squad practice.

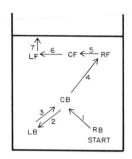

FIG. 9–6. Passing contest.

X¹ sends the ball to X² and goes immediately to the end of the column. X² returns the ball to X³ and goes to the end of the column, and so on. The ball should be kept in play, with each player dropping back as soon as her turn is completed. They move close to the net to make the play.

Use the same formation as a relay.

Use as an elimination contest to determine which team can keep the ball in the air longer. When a player fails to get the ball across the net her team is eliminated.

Two Squads in Line Formation across the Net from Each Other. Return the ball across the net and down the line. Each player should return the ball in her regular turn.

Team Formation—Passing Contest (Fig. 9–6). Start the ball with the RB. The object of the game is to see which team can first pass the ball in the order indicated, each player using one hit. If an error is made, the ball must start again with the RB. Watch for holding. LF must send the ball over the net.

Team Formation—Placement Practice. Start the ball by throwing it across the net. The ball is kept in play as in a regular game, but each player must change the direction of the ball as she plays it. If the ball goes out of bounds, start again with a toss. Passing the ball before returning it across the net should be stressed.

"Teacher and Class" Formation (see Fig. 2–2). Have each player return the ball back to the leader, keeping the ball in continuous motion through the entire squad. For competition, keep a record of the number of successive passes in each squad.

Double Lines, 6 or 8 Feet Apart (see Fig. 2–10). X¹ passes the ball to X³, X³ to X² and so on. When the ball gets to X⁸, she passes to X⁷, X⁷ to X⁶ and so on.

Use as a relay. Rules must be enforced. All teams must be the same distance apart. A poor pass must be retrieved by the passer and started again from her position.

Passing Game (Fig. 9–7). Stretch a rope across the court 7¼ feet above the floor to divide the half court. Draw three circles 5 feet in diameter about 3 feet from the net. Squads line up in relay formation beyond

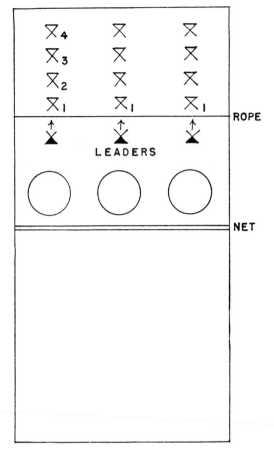

FIG. 9-7. Spot passing.

the rope with leaders on the opposite side. The leader passes the ball to each player, who attempts to hit it over the rope and into the circle. One point is scored for each successful hit into the circle. Continue for a designated number of times for each player.

Inter-squad Competition. Determine which squad can keep the ball in the air the longest. No player may play the ball more than once in succession. Eliminate squads for holding. Have the squad leaders check for violations of rules.

Team Formation in Front of the Net. Start the ball by having the right back toss the ball and pass it to the left forward, the left forward to the right forward, and the right forward then hits the ball across the net.

Various paths may be used, starting the ball with one of the backs and moving it forward.

The Dig Pass. Place the squad leader above the other players, on a chair or bench. The leader throws the ball downward to the other mem-

CHAPTER 9.   VOLLEYBALL

bers of her squad, who have formed a semicircle around her. Sharp quick passes from a steep angle will improve the ability of the players to retrieve spikes and other hard-hit balls below the chest.

RECOVERING THE BALL FROM THE NET

The rules provide that a ball which has been hit into the net may be returned if it is recovered before it strikes the floor. The net must be stretched tightly if the ball is to be recovered successfully. A netted ball will rebound only a few inches from the net and drop directly downward or it will follow the net straight downward.

BODY MECHANICS

Starting Position. The player must move quickly toward the net and get the hands well under the ball, palms upward.

A forward lunge with the hips well flexed or a drop to a squat position is usually necessary to get under the ball.

The arms should reach well away from the body.

The side should be toward the net if possible.

Application of Force. The ball should be returned upward and sideward to another forward or backward over the shoulder, as it is almost impossible to return the ball directly across the net from this position.

The force is largely wrist flexion with an upward and backward swing from the shoulders.

The knees should extend and lift the body with the upward swing.

Follow Through. The fingers should point toward the body while the follow through of the arms is high and backward.

COACHING SUGGESTIONS

Instant action is essential. Net players should never be more than 4 or 5 feet from the net unless necessary to save a poorly hit pass. Balls normally hit over the head of forwards should by handled first by backs.

The ball should be lifted high and backward to give a teammate time to get under it. It will be difficult for other players to gauge the direction of the recovery. A high pass will give them opportunity to play it.

The recovery player must get close to the floor under the net, but she must avoid stepping on the center line or striking the net.

TEACHING PROGRESSION

1. Explain and demonstrate the path the ball is likely to take as it hits the net and drops.

2. Have the players toss the ball into the net from several feet away

CHAPTER 9.   VOLLEYBALL

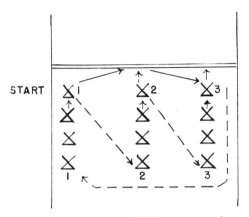

FIG. 9–8. Recovering ball from net, squad practice.

and try to catch it before it strikes the floor to observe the direction the ball will take.

3. Hit the ball into the net and recover it.

4. Adjust to a fast ball thrown or hit into the net by another player.

SQUAD PRACTICE

Relay Formation in Front of the Net, 6 to 8 in a Squad. Draw a line 2 feet in front of the net.

X^1 in each squad *tosses* the ball into the net, moves forward to catch it before it touches the floor. X^1 passes to X^2 and goes to the end of the line and so on.

Line up the teams behind the 2-foot line and use as a relay. The ball must be thrown from behind the line. After it is recovered, it may be thrown to the second player.

Have player hit the ball into the net, recover it and try to pass it back to the player directly behind her.

Relay Formation—3 Squads (Fig. 9–8). X^1 hits the ball into the net, X^2 recovers and passes the ball to X^3. X^3 passes it over the net. X^1 goes to the end of column 2, X^2 to the end of column 3 and X^3 to the end of column 1.

SERVES

The serve is a basic skill which every player must master. It is essential that each player have at least one type of serve that she can direct and control.

There are three general types of serves: underhand, overhand and sidearm.

Hand positions for serves are illustrated in Figure 9–9.

CHAPTER 9.   VOLLEYBALL

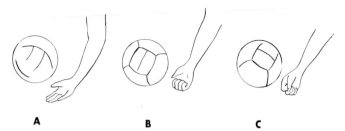

FIG. 9–9. Hand positions for serve. A, Open hand. B, Knuckles and heel of hand. C, Fist, thumb side up. The position in C offers least control of the ball.

THE UNDERHAND SERVE

BODY MECHANICS (Fig. 9–10)

Starting Position. The ball rests in the palm of the left hand, fingers pointing to the right, the thumb toward the net. The ball should be off the right side of the body.

The left foot should be forward 10 or 12 inches, the shoulders squarely facing the net.

The left knee should be slightly flexed, the right knee relaxed, with the weight on the right foot.

The right hand should be relaxed at the side, fingers flexed, elbow slightly bent.

Application of Force. The right hand swings backward and upward in the backswing, elbow still slightly flexed.

The trunk should rotate toward the right to give length and height to the backswing.

The left arm may remain poised in the starting position or be drawn back slightly.

FIG. 9–10. Underhand serve.

The forward swing is forward and upward in line with the body, with most of the force coming from the shoulder.

The ball should be struck on the underside while it rests on the left hand.

The right arm stiffens as contact with the ball is made.

A final wrist snap should be given as the ball is hit.

The speed of the serve is increased by:

1. Increasing the speed of the arm swing.
2. Rotation of the trunk.
3. Full arm swing from the shoulder.
4. Extension of the ankle, knee and hip.
5. Transference of weight to the forward foot.

Follow Through. The arm must swing upward to give the ball enough height to clear the net, but it should move in the direction the ball is to go.

The fingers should be extended if the open hand is used.

USES

This is the easiest serve to master and should be used by beginners.

Serves for placement are more easily controlled with the underhand serve than with the other serves.

COACHING SUGGESTIONS

The ball may be struck with:

1. The palm.
2. The fist, knuckles and heel of the hand making the contact with the ball.
3. The heel of the hand, with fingers curved and spread.
4. The fist, with the thumb and first finger side up. (This serve is the least effective because control of direction of the ball is difficult.)

The palm is preferred by some and the heel of the hand by others. The fingers can guide the ball in either of these positions.

The fist with knuckles and heel of the hand striking the ball will provide the most force, thus the speediest serve. Accuracy will be more difficult for beginners to attain. However, this serve is the one that more expert players should master.

Beginners must be watched to see that they do not hit the ball with the wrist. Bruises will result.

A skillful serve is placed accurately. To improve accuracy:

1. Flatten the arc of the swing by transference of weight.
2. Keep the shoulders in line with the net.
3. Swing the arm parallel with the body.
4. Swing the arm and follow through in the direction the ball is to go.

To increase the speed of the serve:

1. Lengthen the backswing by stepping backward.

2. Stiffen the arm.

3. Increase the speed of the arm swing.

4. Get the body weight into the serve.

TEACHING PROGRESSION

1. Explain and demonstrate the serve.

2. Review hand positions to determine which one each beginner can start with to get the required distance.

3. Start with a serve of a short distance, emphasizing the body position and directing the ball.

4. Serve across the net.

5. Increase the speed of the serve.

6. Serve to designated area.

SQUAD PRACTICE

Team Formation in One Half of Court, a Second Squad in Line Formation at the Opposite End Line (Fig. 9–11). X^1 serves across the net. If the first serve is out, she takes a second serve. X^1 goes to the end of her line and X^2 moves up to serve. Continue until all have had several serves. The team across the net from the serve disposes of the ball by returning it back to the serving side, using the best possible passing tactics. After

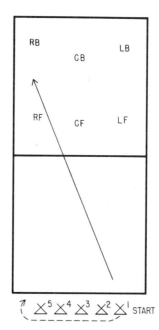

FIG. 9–11. Underhand serve, squad practice.

CHAPTER 9. VOLLEYBALL

each ball has been returned to the serving side, a new serve is made. Rotate teams. Keep a record of each team's percentage of accuracy on the serve and their accuracy in returning the serve.

Serve Placement, Squad Competition (Fig. 9–12). Two, four or six squads may compete on one court. Divide each court into four zones. Assign a scorekeeper to each squad. Squads line up behind end lines as indicated in figure. The first player in each squad serves. Points are recorded by the scorekeeper as follows: 1 point for serves into zone next to net, 2 points for second zone, and so on, up to the fourth zone

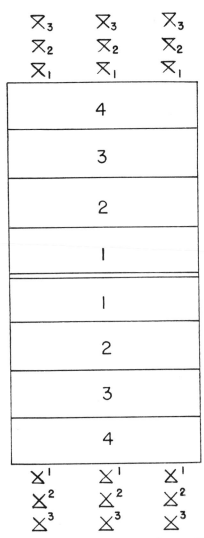

FIG. 9–12. Serve placement, squad competition.

354   at the end line. *Two points are deducted if the serve is out of bounds or otherwise illegal.* After each player serves, she goes to the end of the line. The game may continue for an indefinite number of serves. Serves must be made in turn and only one player from each squad should serve at a time.

Serve Placement. Mark off a 6-foot square in each corner of the half court.

Each player serves two balls at an indicated corner, then goes to the end of the line.

Competition may be arranged by assigning a value to each square and keeping a record of each team's achievement. Give 1 point for each serve landing in bounds and 4 points for a serve in a marked square.

THE OVERHAND SERVE

BODY MECHANICS (Fig. 9–13)

Starting Position. The ball is held easily in both hands in front of the body and slightly to the right.

The left foot should be advanced 10 or 12 inches.

The left toe should be pointing toward the net, the right foot parallel with the end line behind it.

The shoulders should be square with the net.

The knees should be slightly flexed.

Application of Force. The ball should be tossed about 3 feet above the right shoulder.

FIG. 9–13. Overhand serve.

CHAPTER 9. VOLLEYBALL

The right arm should be raised so that the elbow is just above the shoulder.

The trunk rotates slightly to the right and the weight is transferred to the rear foot.

The right arm should swing at the ball with an overhand throwing motion, meeting the ball with the hand at about head height.

The fist gives more power than other hand positions, but direction is more difficult to master.

The fingers of the serving hand should be slightly curved if the ball is hit with the heel of the hand and fingers.

The force of the stroke depends upon:

1. The speed of the hand when the ball is hit.
2. Extension of the elbow.
3. Flexion of the wrist forward as contact with the ball is made.
4. Rotation of the trunk.
5. Transference of the weight from the rear foot to the forward foot.

Follow Through. The hand should follow the direction of the ball as far as possible, then swing downward across the body.

The fingers should extend in the direction of the ball if the open hand is used.

USES

The overhand serve, with its more direct trajectory than the underhand, can be a vital part of a team's offensive rather than simply a means of putting the ball in play into the opponents' court.

Because the serve is difficult to control, its consistent use probably will be limited to more advanced players.

COACHING SUGGESTIONS

The server should stand behind the end line near the center of the court to allow for a margin of error to the right or left in the direction of the ball.

The player must keep her eyes on the ball to hit it squarely.

The entire body should be behind the serve.

The ball must not be thrown ahead of the body or it will be netted.

SQUAD PRACTICE

Competitive Serve. Teams line up on opposite sides of the court behind the end lines. The object of this game is to determine the number of serves required for every player to accomplish a legal serve.

The first player on each team serves. If the serve is good, the player drops out of line; if it is out, she goes to the end of the line and moves up in turn for her second trial, and so on. The scorer should merely record the number of serves needed to accomplish the objectives of the contest. Lowest score wins the game.

CHAPTER 9.   VOLLEYBALL

The position of the body and the technics of the side-arm serve are similar to the underhand serve except that the ball is hit with a swing that is horizontal with the floor. The ball can be hit very hard with this serve, but is difficult to control. For that reason few players can use it effectively. If a player is proficient in this type of serve, she should be allowed to use it, but the majority will find the underhand or over-hand serves better adapted to their capabilities.

I<small>NCREASING THE</small> E<small>FFECTIVENESS OF THE</small> S<small>ERVE</small>

P<small>UTTING</small> S<small>PIN ON THE</small> S<small>ERVES</small>

The underhand and overhand serves may be varied by the application of spins to the ball with the following results:

1. The ball will be more difficult for the defense to handle for a pass.

2. The course of the ball will change in flight and be more confusing to the receiving team.

Spin is applied by the fingers, causing the ball to rotate on its vertical or horizontal axis. Figure 9–14 shows some of the spins which the ball may take.

The effects of the spins are as follows:

1. Top spin: drop.

2. Back spin: rise preceding a sharp drop.

3. Lateral spin: curves in the direction in which the nose of the ball rotates as the ball is hit.

In causing the ball to rotate, the technics of the serve are varied only in the manner in which the hand strikes the ball.

TOP SPIN

Top spin is applied as follows:

In the underhand serve, the fingers are drawn slightly toward the body under the ball.

In the overhand, the ball is hit a little above the center while the fingers are over the top of the ball as the arm swings forward and up-

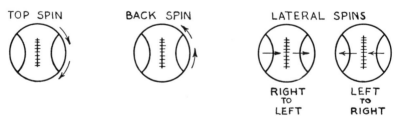

FIG. 9–14. Application of spin to increase effectiveness of serve.

CHAPTER 9. VOLLEYBALL

OUTCURVE
RIGHT TO LEFT

FIG. 9-15. Outcurve.

ward. The lacings should be upward and forward when the ball is tossed for the overhand serve.

BACK SPIN

Back spin is practically impossible to achieve with the underhand serve, but a skillful player can cause the ball to rotate backward with the overhand serve.

The ball is hit at the back with a forward and downward swing. The lacings or valve should be down.

This serve is very difficult to execute and is not practical for beginners.

LATERAL SPIN

Outcurve. The technics are the same as for the underhand serve except in the way the ball is hit (Fig. 9-15).

The ball is held in the left hand with the lacings or valve to the right and slightly forward. The fingers hit the ball on the right side with inward rotation of the forearm. The thumb leads.

The effect of this spin is a direct course with a sudden curve to the left (the opponents' right court) near the end of the flight.

The same spin may be produced with an overhand serve by hitting the ball on the right side with the fingers, little finger leading.

Incurve. The body positions are the same as for the underhand serve.

The ball is held in the left hand with the lacings or valve to the left and slightly forward. As the ball is hit, the forearm rotates outward and the ball is hit on the left side, little finger ahead (Fig. 9-16).

If the overhand serve is used, the thumb leads when the fingers strike the ball on the left side.

The effect of this spin will cause the ball to curve to the right (the opponents' left court).

CHAPTER 9. VOLLEYBALL

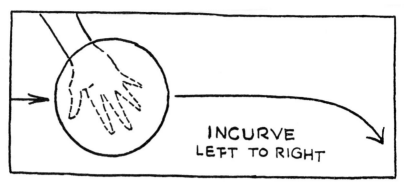

FIG. 9–16. Incurve.

PLACEMENT OF SERVES

The first consideration in serving is to place the ball where the opponents will have the greatest difficulty in handling it.

The server should observe the positions of the opponents and try to choose a spot which seems open.

In general, the best places for the serve are to the far corners.

Areas near the side lines may also be selected, particularly those opposite the center of opponents' court (Fig. 9–17).

When the ball is hit to the far corner of the court, it means that the opponents will have to pass the ball several times before the ball will be in a position for effective attack.

For the majority of players, the underhand serve is best adapted to placements.

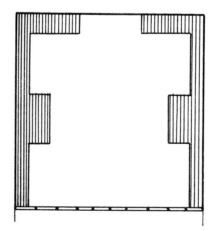

FIG. 9–17. Placement areas for serve.

CHAPTER 9. VOLLEYBALL

FIG. 9–18. Set-up for the spike.

SET-UP FOR THE SPIKE

The set-up is a pass which places the ball high in position for a teammate to spike at the net (Fig. 9–18). This is a fundamental pass and usually the second in the sequence of three hits permitted a team.

BODY MECHANICS

Starting Position. The wrists should be bent backward, with the palms upward.

The elbows should be parallel with the body and in an easy position from the sides.

If the ball is taken low, the little fingers are toward each other. If the ball is taken high, the thumbs are toward each other. The ball will be more easily directed if it is taken rather high.

The knees should be somewhat flexed, the body relaxed.

The set-up player should stand with her right side to the net and to the right of the spiker when possible, if the spiker is right-handed.

Application of Force. Most of the force comes from bending the wrists, but the arms should swing upward with the ball.

The ball should be lifted at least 10 to 12 feet above the top of the net and about 6 to 12 inches from it.

The pass should travel parallel to the net.

Follow Through. The direction of the follow through should be upward and toward the spiker.

CHAPTER 9. VOLLEYBALL

The set-up is the essential pass preliminary to any spike. All passing should be directed toward a set-up and a spike if possible.

COACHING SUGGESTIONS

Two hands are necessary for an accurate set-up.

Control of the ball for a set-up is essential. The spiker, to kill the ball, needs a set-up that is dropping from at least 10 feet and in front of her. The set-up player must be close to the net to avoid an angle pass to the spiker.

The initial pass to the set-up forward will usually be a long pass from a back. The first pass, or the pass to the set-up forward, should be in a high arch to give her time to get under the ball. Every player should be proficient in the long pass to the set-up player.

TEACHING PROGRESSION

1. Explain and demonstrate the set-up.
2. Toss the ball several times to establish the height the ball should travel and the distance from the net.
3. Start the ball with a toss and set it up.
4. Receive a pass, then set up the ball.

SQUAD PRACTICE

Relay Formation with Leader in Front of the Net. Leader stands to the side as coach and in position the spiker would assume.

Have each player toss the ball to the leader several times at the proper height and distance from the net.

Toss a high, easy ball to the set-up player to hit to the leader. Rotate the leader and other squad members.

Set-up Practice (Fig. 9–19). X^1 starts the ball by throwing it to X^2. X^2 sets it up for X^3. X^3 returns the ball across the net. X^3 goes to the end of column I, X^2 to the end of column III and X^1 to the end of column II. If players have mastered the fundamental of spiking, X^3 may spike.

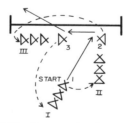

FIG. 9–19. Set-up and spiking practice.

CHAPTER 9. VOLLEYBALL

FIG. 9–20. The spike.

THE SPIKE

The spike is a hard hit or smash that brings the ball directly downward across the net (Fig. 9–20).

BODY MECHANICS

Starting Position. The player stands facing the set-up player.
The body should be relaxed, arms back, knees flexed.
The weight should be forward, ready for the leap.
Application of Force. The ball should be struck at the highest possible point the player can jump and reach.
The hand comes over the top of the ball so that its flight is downward.
With the ball placed a foot or more in front of the spiker, a step and leap into the ball may be made. The take-off for the jump should be on the left foot.
The right elbow should be just higher than the shoulder as the ball is hit in about the same position as in the overhand throw.

CHAPTER 9. VOLLEYBALL

The arm should stiffen as the ball is met at the beginning of the downward swing.

A quick flexion of the wrist not only directs the ball downward but also adds force to the stroke.

The body should turn in mid-air, bringing both shoulders in line with the net as the ball is hit.

Follow Through. The arm should swing forward and downward in the direction the ball is to go.

The spiker should land facing the net.

USE

If the spike is mastered, it is the most effective weapon of the forwards' attack. The center forward is in the best position to receive a pass from any position and for spiking in either direction.

COACHING SUGGESTIONS

An effective spike can be made only if the forward is well off the floor.

The wrist must flex as the ball is hit, otherwise the ball will go out of bounds.

The spiker must be careful in striking the ball that the hand or arm does not swing into the net.

Unless the set-up is perfectly placed, the spiker will have to make adjustments of distance and direction preceding her jump. Her waiting position should be alert to meet such a situation.

TEACHING PROGRESSION

1. It is essential to a spike that the player be able to get off her feet in a good jump. Practice in jumping is a necessary preliminary. A good jumping practice is step, step, jump. For a right-hand spike it would be right, left and up, reaching with the right hand.
2. Explain and demonstrate the spike.
3. Toss the ball for self, jump and spike it.
4. Receive a pass and spike.
5. Place the spike to definite areas.

SQUAD PRACTICE

Line up beside the net and have players jump to determine the height above the net which they can reach.

Relay Formation in Front of the Net. 1. Each player tosses the ball for herself, jumps and spikes it.

2. Put a player to the right of the relay line to toss balls for the squad to spike.

Triangle Formation (Fig. 9–21). X^1 returns the ball to X^2 across the

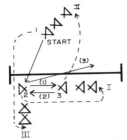

FIG. 9–21. Spiking, squad practice.

net. X² sets up the ball for X³. X³ spikes it. X³ goes to the end of line II, X² goes to the end of line I, X¹ to the end of line III.

FOOTWORK

One of the criticisms of volleyball is that it lacks activity. The difficulty is in the player rather than the game. A player who stands flatfooted and waits for the ball to come to her will never be a good volleyball player.

A player must be active within her own position, shifting with the play of the ball. If necessary, a player should leave her position, to assist a teammate, but she must return immediately to her own area.

Mastery of the jump is essential to volleyball. Spiking, reaching an overhead ball, the block, adding speed to the ball and other volleyball activities require the ability to get off the floor.

The weight should be kept under control at all times with short slides, steps and quick running starts.

Timing of footwork is likewise important. A jump that is too late or too soon is useless effort. The biggest factor in timing is the coordination between hands and eyes. The eyes must follow the ball at all times to insure the best contact between the ball and the hands.

INDIVIDUAL TACTICS

Volleyball requires that every player be skilled in defensive and offensive tactics. Specialization will be mainly in the spike because of the advantages of height. Otherwise, excellence is demanded of every player during the defense or offense.

DEFENSE

RECEIVING THE BALL

The body should be in readiness for action, with the feet in good balance, either side stride or forward stride. The defensive player should face the opponent with the ball.

The arms should be drawn slightly backward, elbows nearly straight, knees flexed, the weight on the toes. With the arms in this position, it is possible to scoop the hands under a low ball or to swing upward into a chest-high or overhead ball.

If the opposing forwards have the ball, the hands should be in front of the chest, thumbs inward, elbows flexed. The fingers should be flexed.

The eyes must be on the ball at all times.

The weight should be shifted quickly to get the body in line with the ball.

The player should be in line with the ball as soon as it is hit.

If the ball is coming to the right of the player and there is not time to get in line with the body, the player should lunge forward on her right foot and lift the ball to a teammate.

If the ball is to her left, the player should lunge on the left foot and get under the ball.

If the ball will be well overhead, and the player must run back for it, she should turn her back to the ball and lunge as far as possible to reach for it. This does not apply to forwards. In general, forwards should allow balls out of reach over their heads to be played by the backs.

The defenders must be ready to crouch low to receive a spike if a block is not feasible.

BLOCK

The block is a defense against the spike. One, two or three players may be involved in a blocking attempt. A multiple block is more effective than one by a player alone (Fig. 9-22).

The blocker stands close to the net and jumps with the spiker.

The arms are thrust directly forward and the ball strikes tensed, straight fingers.

The hands should be parallel, fingers spread and pointing back overhead. The ball then will roll back for other players on the team to handle for a better return than a rebound. Beginners should curve the fingers and let the ball rebound into the opponents' court.

The arms must not swing forward as the body is coming down or a net foul will result.

The most difficult part of the block is the timing. The eyes must follow the ball closely or the blocker will leave her position unprotected.

OFFENSE

Individual offensive tactics are mainly passes in the 1-2-3 maneuver, the kill with a spike, and the long, hard serve to the far corners of the opponents' court. Because it is not always possible to achieve a perfect set-up, the offensive players must be versatile enough to make an offensive return that is not a spike. In fact, an offensive stroke, instead of a set-up pass, may be used as a variation of the 1-2-3 offense as a team strategy.

CHAPTER 9. VOLLEYBALL

FIG. 9-22. Blocking.

THE OFFENSIVE RETURN

The offensive return is not as difficult for beginners as the spike. It should be part of the preparation of every player to be used when the ball is too far from the net for a spike. The return should be directed to a corner of the opponents' court or an uncovered spot.

The offensive return is performed best when the ball is dropping from a height of 4 or 5 feet above the net and in front of the player. A jump may or may not be used. The jump makes it possible to play the ball at a greater height and direct it with little or no arch into the opponents' court.

The left side should be to the net, the arms back, the body tilted forward from the waist and the knees flexed.

The weight should be forward.

The timing of the stroke requires adjustment to the moving ball and a high enough jump so that the ball will not be netted.

The ball should be hit as close to the top as possible with one or both hands. With one hand it is possible to get more height in the jump.

The ball is hit with curved fingers or the fist.

With the hit, the body turns sharply to the left and the player should land facing the net.

The arm should be pulled in quickly to the body, the shoulders dropped and, finally, the wrist snapped to complete the stroke.

In placing the return, the player should try to find a space between two players. Its effectiveness is lost if the ball is hit directly to an opponent, unless the opponent is a weak player.

A change of pace in the stroke often takes the defense unaware. If the player fakes to play the ball hard, then tips it gently to an open space, the results may be as effective as a hard hit. At no time should the return be a high loop to permit defenders to get under it.

The player must not wait until the ball has dropped too low before hitting it. Passers should be coached to set up the ball high at all times. If a pass is too far from the net for a spike, but well above the net, the offensive return can be placed to the disadvantage of the defenders almost as effectively as the spike.

THE OFFENSIVE SERVE

The serve is technically the method of putting the ball into play, but it should be considered as part of the offense. If the serve is a soft, easy one, it puts the ball in play but it gives the opponents an advantage. A hard-hit, well-placed serve can be an offensive stroke that will make it impossible for the receiving side to pass the ball into position for an offensive return or spike. The overhand serve to the corners of the opponents' court is a good offensive serve. The various curves on the served ball also give the receiving team difficulty in returning the ball.

SECTION III. TEAM TACTICS

The real challenge in volleyball is in playing as a team. Too often players concentrate on returning the ball on the first or second hit, whether or not conditions are favorable for the offense.

Another tendency of beginners is to crowd around the spot where the ball will be received. A vacant position, particularly in the forward line, may prevent a successful sequence of passes.

When it becomes necessary for a player to leave her position to aid a teammate, she should complete the play and return immediately to her own area. No hard and fast rule can be laid down as to when to leave a position, but players must learn to anticipate the play and adjust accordingly.

If a player is in difficulty, her nearest teammate should help handle the ball and her position should in turn be covered by her nearest teammate. Players must back each other up without crowding.

A ball which obviously will fall between two players should be played by the player who can take it on her right side. She should, however, call for the ball by saying either "my ball" or "I have it" to avoid mishandling of the play by both.

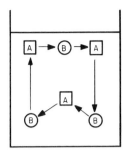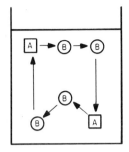

FIG. 9–23. Players in A position are the teams' best spikers. Players in B positions are the best set-up passers. Assignments hold only when rotated into forward line.

OFFENSE

A team which is unable to score points will never be a winning team, therefore it is essential to develop a strong team attack.

PLACING OF PLAYERS

Theoretically, every player should be a capable offensive player. Tall players have an advantage in spiking. In the team offensive, shorter players may be specialists in passing and the offensive return. A team that coordinates its passing to end in a spike can outplay one that ignores team patterns.

When the spiking power is limited to two or three players, their place in the order of rotation should be carefully planned. Every other player or every third one should have a strong return hit.

Alternating attack players or placing them in every third position will mean that a good attack player is always at the net.

Figure 9–23 illustrates the positions of the best attack players at the start of a game. It should be emphasized that these players may spike only when they have rotated into a forward position. Backs may not spike at the net. They may move into the forward line to "save" a ball that has been mishandled, but a spike at the net by a back is illegal.

Good set-up players should be to the right of the most skilled spikers.

TEAM PLAY

The general aim of the offense should be to pass the ball in succession to end in a spike by the best attack forward in the front line at that time. Because of the rotation pattern, the best spiker may be in the right, center or left forward position. A good set-up player should always be beside her. If the spiker is right-handed, a set-up pass from the right side usually will be her preference.

Figure 9–24 shows the 1–2–3 sequence of long pass, set-up pass and spike when the best spiker is in the center forward position. Set-up player and spiker must be close to the net.

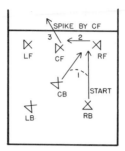

FIG. 9-24. Pass from center or right back to right forward to set-up for spiking.

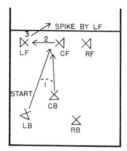

FIG. 9-25. Pass from center back or left back to center forward to set-up for spiking.

When the best spiker is in the left forward position, the initial long pass should go to the center forward to set up for the spike (Fig. 9-25).

DEFENSE

AGAINST THE SPIKE

The most effective method of defending against the spike is known as the multiple block. If possible, all three players in the front line jump together and side by side, the middle defender playing opposite the spiker. The six hands form a wall against the spiked ball.

The three back-court players change position during this play to cover part of the area left vacant by the blockers. The center back must be particularly alert to move within 4 or 5 feet of the middle blocker in order to defend against balls which may slip past the defenders or bounce off their hands directly behind them.

Spike from the Opponents' Right Forward (Fig. 9-26). The three-player block is the most difficult of the defenses. The single block is rarely effective. When a team is either beginning to learn a team blocking defense or limited in players with blocking height or ability, a two-player block should be attempted. Figure 9-26 shows the formation for a two-player block against a spike by the opponents' right forward. The

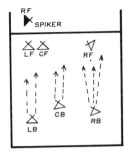

FIG. 9-26. Defense against spike from opponents' right forward.

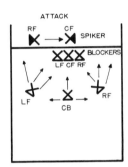

FIG. 9-27. Defense against spike by opponents' center forward.

three back-line players must move in to recover a ball missed or tipped back by the forwards. Backs should rely on a dig pass.

Spike from the Opponents' Center Forward (Fig. 9-27). The multiple block brings the three forwards to the center of the court and close to the net. All of the court beyond that small area must be covered by the backs. The backs must move forward at the beginning of the set-up pass.

AGAINST THE OFFENSIVE SERVE AND RETURN

The offensive serve or return may be expected to be aimed at the corners of the back court of the defenders. The defenders will find that the double wedge makes a useful formation. The center forward and center back play ahead of the players to the right and left in their respective lines (Fig. 9-28).

The center forward may attempt a block from the point of the wedge formation. The opposing spiker may send the ball to her right or left. The spiker then will have to be more accurate and the defenders' positions will be stronger.

When the offense is coming from either the right or left, close to the net, the wedges swing to the appropriate side. The center forward is the point of the wedge opposite the offensive player. The side forwards drop back (Fig. 9-29).

The double wedges may be set up so the points are to the end lines.

CHAPTER 9. VOLLEYBALL

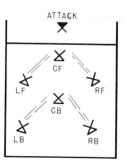

FIG. 9–28. Double wedge defense against a center attack.

This means that the center forward and center back drop back and the side forwards and backs play farther back than the side players in their respective lines. These wedges are strongest against a spike that is not defended by a block. On an offensive return or serve, wedges with the points closer to the net than their respective sides offer the better protection of the far corners.

GENERAL COACHING SUGGESTIONS FOR TEAM DEFENSE

The backs must not crowd in too close to the forwards or there will be too much undefended back-court area.

Players in the forward positions must handle only those balls which are obviously within their reach. They must not jump to play balls high overhead. An effective initial pass cannot be started from high overhead.

Some players will find it possible to defend against the spike by kneeling on one knee, hands in front of face. This position should not be too set as the player will be unable to cover her area completely.

If the offensive forward is back from the net, the defensive positions should be back from the net.

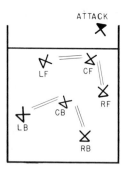

FIG. 9–29. Double wedge against a side attack.

CHAPTER 9. VOLLEYBALL

Each player is responsible for approximately one-sixth of her team's court.

POSITIONS DURING THE SERVE

SERVING TEAM

The left forward moves a little to the left of her area, left side to the net and about 3 feet from the net.

The center forward stands to the left of her area, left side to the net, and about 3 feet from it.

The backs stand facing the net; the left back 8 or 10 feet from the end line, the center back 4 to 6 feet from the end line. The right back should follow her serve to a position parallel with the left back.

RECEIVING TEAM

The receivers take up positions which will bring them facing the ball as it is served. A double wedge may be set at once. Positions will vary somewhat according to the spot where the server is standing in her serving area.

The left and right backs turn so that they are facing the ball. The center back is more in line with the server and faces the net squarely. The left and right backs move toward the outside of their sections and about 6 feet from the end line.

The center back stands near the middle of her court.

The right and left forwards turn slightly so that they face the ball. The center forward faces the net. The serve almost certainly will be a long ball. On the serve, forwards may drop back in their areas.

The center forward is 3 or 4 feet from the net. The right and left forwards are 6 or 8 feet from the net and toward the outside of their sections.

MODIFICATIONS OF THE OFFICIAL
VOLLEYBALL RULES
(FOR LESS SKILLED OR YOUNG PLAYERS)

The official rules are followed with a few exceptions. The major differences in the rules are:

The net may be at a height of 6 feet 6 inches for elementary school and at 7 feet for the average high school girl.

Teams are composed of 8 players as indicated in Figure 9–1. A right and left center are added.

Rotation, nonrotation, or a combination of both for part of each game may be played.

In the nonrotation game, the original right back is a roving player during a term of service for her team. She takes the position on the court of the player whose turn it is to serve. At the conclusion of the term of service, these two players resume their original places.

Every player must serve in turn. In the rotation game, the serving order that must be followed is shown in Figure 9–1. In the nonrotation game, any order in turn is legal but, once established, must be followed throughout a game. Every player has a regular place in order.

The serve may be assisted by one hit by one other player on the serving team. This is optional.

A serve that strikes the top of the net and legally enters the opponents' court is a *let* serve. All *let* serves, assisted or otherwise, are repeated.

The hit has a different interpretation from that in the official rules. The ball may be hit by only three persons on a team before it is returned across the net. A hit is interpreted as one hit or two hits in succession by the same person. In other words, a player may set up the ball for herself, then pass. Her team is charged with one hit only on such a play.

The essential skills of volleyball are the same in the official and non-official games. The double hit in the modified game permits better passing and should be used until players become skilled enough to pass on the first hit. If the double hit is used, the first should be considered as a set-up to oneself and some of the elements of the set-up pass developed.

Rather than spending time on teaching an assisted serve, it would be better to move the serving area 6 feet within the court and try for a regular serve from the shorter distance.

PENALTY OR METHOD OF PUTTING BALL IN PLAY	WHEN TAKEN	REGULATIONS
	GENERAL PROCEDURES	
Choice of service or court	At start of game referee tosses coin: winner may choose either first service or court	
Change of court or service order	At end of first and second games and middle of third game, teams alternate courts	Order of service may change at end of first and second but not during third game
Time-out		
1. Referee	Time out may be called when ball is not in play, only by referee	Ball is in play until referee blows whistle
2. Substitution	Time out shall not exceed 15 seconds	
3. Rest	Time out shall not exceed 1 minute	Each team is allowed two time-outs per game; a third time-out for rest may be taken at cost of point or side-out for delaying game
4. Injury	Time out shall not exceed 5 minutes	
Double foul	Opposing teams commit fouls during same play	Repeat play
	Defaulted Game	
At start of game	*Illegal* 1. Fail to have 6 players at any time 2. Refuse to play after instructions by referee to begin	*Explanation* Score of defaulted game is 1–0

Point or Side-out

(Point if receiving team is offender, side-out if serving team is offender)

Play of ball on either serve or pass	*Illegal* 1. Hit ball with any part of body other than hands or forearms	*Explanation*
	2. Hit ball outside boundaries of opponents' court or outside net markers	
	3. Throw, push or kick ball	Ball must be clearly batted
	4. Hit ball into obstruction above court	

CHAPTER 9.   VOLLEYBALL

PENALTY OR METHOD OF PUTTING BALL IN PLAY	WHEN TAKEN	REGULATIONS
Serve	*Illegal* 1. Fail to hit ball over net 2. Commit foot fault 3. Serve out of order	*Explanation* Ball must clear net without touching it Server must be behind end line until ball is hit Original serving order must be maintained throughout game; substitute must enter serving order in position of player replaced
Pass or return over net	*Illegal* 1. Fail to hit ball before it strikes playing surface in bounds 2. Contact ball more than once in succession 3. Fail to return ball in three hits	*Explanation* Ball may be handled by players A, B, C or players A, B, A Simultaneous contact of ball by players of same team counts as one hit; simultaneous contact of ball by players of opposing team is not counted as a hit for either team
Net play	*Illegal* 1. Touch net with any part of body 2. Step on center line or into opponent's court 3. Touch ball on opponent's side of the net	*Explanation* Follow through over net is permitted if no contact is made with net Ball may be played when any portion of it crosses top of net
Position play	*Illegal* 1. Fail to be in position when ball is served 2. Interchange positions persistently during play 3. Spike by back-line player at net	*Explanation* Player may leave her area only after ball is hit on serve Player may leave boundaries of court to play ball if necessary
Substitution	*Illegal* 1. Substitution when ball is in play by team not serving 2. Enter game for third time	
Delay of game	*Illegal* 1. Consume excess time before serving, in rotating, or in recovering ball 2. Take over 15 seconds for substitution after each team has had two substitutions	
Misconduct	*Illegal* 1. Derogatory remarks by player or coach to or about officials or opponents 2. Attempt by coach or player to coach deliberately from side lines	

SELECTED LIST OF SOURCE MATERIALS
FOR TEAM SPORTS

BASKETBALL

Anderson, Forrest. *Basketball Techniques Illustrated.* New York: Ronald Press Co., 1952.

Bell, Mary M. *Women's Basketball.* Dubuque: Wm. C. Brown Co., 1964.

Broer, Marion. *Efficiency in Human Movement.* Philadelphia: W. B. Saunders Co., 1960., pp. 267-274.

Division for Girls and Women's Sports. *Basketball Guide.* Washington, D.C. (Published annually.)

Teague, Bertha. *Basketball for Girls.* New York: Ronald Press Co., 1962.

HOCKEY

Broer, Marion. *Efficiency of Human Movement.* Philadelphia: W. B. Saunders Co., 1960, pp. 309-313.

Division for Girls and Women's Sports. *Field Hockey and Lacrosse Guide.* Washington, D.C. (Revised biennially.)

_____. *Selected Field Hockey–Lacrosse Articles, NSWA & NSGWS Guides, 1930-1954.* Washington, D.C. (Revised biennally.)

Lees, Josephine T., and Shellenberger, Betty. *Field Hockey for Players, Coaches, and Umpires.* New York: Ronald Press Co., 1957.

Patterson, Ann, Ed. *Team Sports for Girls.* New York: Ronald Press Co., 1958, pp. 91-145.

SOCCER

American Association for Health, Physical Education, and Recreation. *How We Do It Game Book.* Revised edition. Washington, D.C., 1963.

_____. *Physical Education for High School Students.* Washington, D.C., 1963.

Division for Girls and Women's Sports. *Soccer–Speedball Guide.* Washington, D.C. (Published biennially.)

Salt, E. B., Fox, G. I., and Stevens, B. K. *Teaching Physical Education in the Elementary Schools.* Second edition. New York: Ronald Press Co., 1960, pp. 228-241.

Sevy, Ruth, Ed. *Selected Soccer and Speedball Articles.* Washington, D.C.: Division for Girls and Women's Sports, 1963.

SOFTBALL

Division for Girls and Women's Sports. *Softball Guide.* Washington, D.C. (Revised biennially.)

Kerr, Marion, Ed. *Selected Softball Articles.* Washington, D.C.: Division for Girls and Women's Sports, 1962.

Mitchell, Viola, *Softball for Girls.* Revised edition. New York: Ronald Press Co., 1952.

SPEEDBALL

Armbruster, David A., and others. *Basic Skills in Sports for Men and Women.* Third edition. *Speedball*: pp. 182-191. St. Louis, Mo.: C. V. Mosby Co., 1963.

376   Division for Girls and Women's Sports. *Soccer–Speedball Guide.* Washington, D.C. (Published biennially.)

———. *Selected Soccer and Speedball Articles,* 1935-1964. Washington, D.C.

VOLLEYBALL

Division for Girls and Women's Sports. *Volleyball Guide.* Washington, D.C. (Published biennially.)

Laveaga, Robert E. *Volleyball.* Second edition. New York: Ronald Press Co., 1960.

Lockhart, Aileene, Editor. *Selected Volleyball Articles.* Washington, D.C., Division for Girls and Women's Sports. Revised 1959.

Welch, G. E. *How to Play and Teach Volleyball.* New York: Association Press, 1960.

INDEX

INDEX